Conversations on African Philosophy of Mind, Consciousness and Artificial Intelligence

Aribiah David Attoe • Samuel T. Segun
Victor Nweke • Umezurike John Ezugwu
Jonathan Okeke Chimakonam
Editors

Conversations on African Philosophy of Mind, Consciousness and Artificial Intelligence

Springer

Editors
Aribiah David Attoe
Centre for Leadership Ethics
University of Fort Hare
Alice, South Africa

Victor Nweke
University of Koblenz and Landau
Campus Koblenz, Germany

Jonathan Okeke Chimakonam
Department of Philosophy
University of Pretoria
Pretoria, South Africa

Samuel T. Segun
School for Data Science and Computational Thinking
Stellenbosch University
Stellenbosch, South Africa

Umezurike John Ezugwu
Nigeria Maritime University Okerenkoko
Delta State, Nigeria

ISBN 978-3-031-36162-3 ISBN 978-3-031-36163-0 (eBook)
https://doi.org/10.1007/978-3-031-36163-0

This Springer imprint is published by the registered company Springer Nature Switzerland AG
The registered company address is: Gewerbestrasse 11, 6330 Cham, Switzerland

This book is dedicated to the Late Prof. Kwame Gyekye.

Contents

Chapter 1
Introduction

Aribiah David Attoe, Samuel T. Segun, Victor Nweke, Umezurike John Ezugwu, and Jonathan Okeke Chimakonam

Abstract Philosophy of mind as a branch of philosophy has been growing. With a vast array of literature stemming from Plato to Descartes, down to Daniel Dennett and Paul and Patricia Churchland, there is no doubt that a lot has been said in that area regarding the mind-body problem, consciousness, the role of the human brain, etc. More so, with the advancement in neuroscience, newer and more interesting discussions linking neuroscience to philosophy of mind is inevitable. Equally as interesting, is the philosophical work that is done in relation to the development of Artificial Intelligence in terms of robotics, artificial intelligence systems, technology-based human enhancements, etc. In all these, the African perspective has been largely underexplored and the salient perspectives of modern and contemporary African philosophers are rarely engaged. What we do in this chapter is to present an

A. D. Attoe (✉)
Centre for Leadership Ethics, University of Fort Hare, Alice, South Africa

Conversational School of Philosophy (CSP), Calabar, Nigeria

S. T. Segun
School for Data Science and Computational Thinking, Stellenbosch University, Stellenbosch, South Africa

V. Nweke
Conversational School of Philosophy (CSP), Calabar, Nigeria

Institute of Cultural Studies, University of Koblenz and Landau, Campus Koblenz, Germany

U. J. Ezugwu
Conversational School of Philosophy (CSP), Calabar, Nigeria

General Studies Unit, Nigeria Maritime University, Okerenkoko, Nigeria

J. O. Chimakonam
Conversational School of Philosophy (CSP), Calabar, Nigeria

Department of Philosophy, University of Pretoria, Pretoria, South Africa
e-mail: jonathan.okeke@up.ac.za

A. D. Attoe et al. (eds.), *Conversations on African Philosophy of Mind, Consciousness and Artificial Intelligence*,
https://doi.org/10.1007/978-3-031-36163-0_1

overview of the general concerns of this book. This concern is two-fold – the first part tackles issues related to consciousness, identity, and the mind-body problem, and the second part generally deals with issues related to Artificial intelligence and human enhancement.

Keywords Artificial intelligence · Consciousness · Human enhancements · Mind · Robot

The desire to know, to question, and to extend the frontiers of human knowledge as well as the capacity of human persons often reflects the deep curiosity in human beings about things in the world, how they work, and in what ways we can manipulate them. However, nothing is more curious than our minds and our consciousness. It is baffling to some, that something so intimate and personal – something that (and quite rightly so) belongs to us – can at the same time be so elusive and mysterious (ironically) to its own probing. Perhaps this little paradox ought not to baffle us too much. We often own and drive cars without necessarily knowing, in as much detail as the auto-mechanical engineer would know, how a car is put together and what makes it work. That lack of knowledge does not preclude us from learning (hopefully from a driving school) how to move a car and navigate roads with it.

As human beings began to look away from the stars to focus their gaze on themselves and those around them, it became seemingly apparent, that the human subject was not just ordinary flesh and bones. The reason for this thinking is not far-fetched at all. When an individual, thought, judged, perceived, willed, etc., those actions and the accompanying experience were not tangible material things like the hands and feet the individual could easily touch and feel. It seemed like conscious experience was intangible and immaterial – unlike the body. Coupled with the fact that consciousness expressed itself in terms of a "self" or "ego", it then became apparent that whatever intangible stuff expressed our thoughts, controlled our body, and represented itself as us could only be beyond the purview of space-time (separate from our bodies in some way but yet within, and in control, of it) and could only be the purest manifestation of the human being. And so, ideas such as *sunsum, ori,* mind, spirit, soul, and qualia, all emerged as candidates to represent this other worldly stuff. However, the question that continually nagged this sort of thinking was the question about how this immaterial stuff could successfully interact with the material body as they were radically different – one material and the other immaterial. Various explanations began to spring up to solve this problem. Theories like the vitalism of the anonymous traditional African philosophers of the Congo, the quasi-physicalism of the anonymous traditional African philosophers of Akan and Yoruba communities, Descartes' failed interactionism, Malebranche's occasionalism, Leibniz's pre-established harmony, Thomas Huxley's epiphenomenalism, down to David Chalmers' protophenomenalism,[1] and Samuel Segun's equiphenomenalism, have all emerged to provide an explanatory model that incorporates the immaterial nature of the self and conscious experience (Gyekye, 1978; Chimakonam et al., 2019). Try as they might, though, the earlier question of how an immaterial mind and a material body interact, or how the former emerges from the other, has yet to be successfully dealt with.

The development of science and technology in the last few centuries has allowed scholars of mind to rethink the nature of the mind and has also allowed them to probe deeper into the human body in their search for mind. Neuroscience, especially, has provided us with a treasure trove of information about the human body – especially the brain and the nervous system – that has encouraged philosophers of mind to have a rethink about the nature of the mind, and whether such a thing exists at all (Churchland, 1981, 2002; Dennett, 1991). Understanding the nature of perception and response to stimuli, via the working of the brain, neurons, neuronal impulses, etc., has led to the belief that perhaps the functions attributed to the mind are indeed the function of body states. Particularly of interest to scientists and philosophers alike are the personality and cognitive changes in individuals with brain damage, as well as the effect of drugs on consciousness. How is it possible that the damage to a particular part of the brain could elicit the loss of memory – memory being a supposedly immaterial component of consciousness? How is it that certain "mushrooms" could so affect an immaterial mind that its very content is distorted? Perhaps the better explanation is that we have been looking at a non-existent place for non-existent reified things. Maybe a shift in focus is needed, and this is where the hard problem of consciousness emerges. For by shifting focus to the brain and other related body parts, the question still remains: how do we account for subjective experience, for qualia, within this body-only materialist framework. All these questions have been the concern of modern and contemporary philosophers, who have all sought to unravel the mind-body dilemma in many ways. What is immediately noticeable, however, is the fact that the salient perspectives of modern African philosophers like Kwasi Wiredu, Kwame Gyekye, and Jonathan Chimakonam are rarely engaged. Furthermore, newer perspectives on consciousness and the mind-body problem from the African place are mostly tied to the views of anonymous traditional African thinkers.

Beyond recognizing consciousness and the problems associated with that notion, the gaze toward the human being has also revealed the various inadequacies inherent in the human being, and has fuelled the desire to overcome those inadequacies and/or limitations. Throughout history, this desire to break free from what limits us has led to the development of new technologies and technological revolutions. Presently, we are immersed in the fourth industrial revolution, which has been powered by the invention of powerful supercomputers, the internet, social media, smartphones, artificial intelligent systems, robots of all kinds, algorithms, etc. This epoch has also

[1] It must be noted that Chalmers' "protophenomenalism" is a different theory from Aribiah Attoe's "proto-phenomenalism".

revealed the power of technology when manipulated toward certain ends, which may be savoury or unsavoury. For instance, while machine learning and algorithms may help predict weather conditions, thus helping farmers know when to plant, it is also wireless technology that allows for the detached killing of perceived enemies by drone strikes. It is also carefully constructed social media apps that have led many lost friends to connect and many innocent persons to encounter sexual predators, homicidal maniacs and fake news. The fourth industrial revolution is technology driven, and not philosophy driven, but it is apparent that philosophy ought to be an important component of this revolution. It is the philosopher's job to rein in the seemingly unfettered advance of the fourth industrial revolution. It is the philosopher's job to ask the hard and important question; how do we insert ethics into artificial intelligence systems? What does the fourth industrial revolution mean for the future of the human race? In what ways does the fourth industrial revolution remove the limits placed on the human being by the human body and what does it mean to be transhuman in this world? While the questions above are important questions, it is curious to also note that the salient contributions of African philosophers are only beginning to emerge. It is also surprising that not many African philosophers have fully made their foray into philosophical questions concerning the epistemology and ethics of AI.

This book seeks to bridge these gaps by inviting scholars to directly engage with these barely explored topics. Indeed, we believe that this book is, to our knowledge, the first of its kind, as it seeks to broaden the global conversation to unravel African perspectives on the issues of mind, artificial intelligence, and other issues related to it. Not only is it unique for African scholars, but it also exposes other philosophical traditions to the African point of view with regard to the philosophy of mind, AI, and others. This project is in keeping with the ongoing efforts to build the African philosophy literature in different areas not only for research but also for classroom discussions both within and outside Africa.

This book is divided into two sections. The first part tackles issues related to consciousness, identity, and the mind-body problem. In the second chapter, James Tartaglia presents arguments that seek to locate Kwame Gyekye's discussion of Akan thought about mind in contemporary idealism. In chapter three, Oladele Balogun discusses what is described as "central state materialism" within the context of the Yoruba perspective. Balogun ultimately faults the desire by some to reduce the materialism contained in the Yoruba view to central state materialism.

Ada Agada, in the fourth chapter, argues for a recourse to panpsychism (specifically, what he calls "proto-panpsychism") as the proper approach that incorporates consciousness within the framework of African ontology, which allows for both material and non-material entities. In the fifth chapter, Clarton Fambisai examines the "ability hypothesis" in the context of Kwasi Wiredu's explanation of the Akan concept of mind. Fambisai goes to great lengths to show that when the ability hypothesis is considered within the context of the Akan concept of mind, the thesis provides novel support for what is known as the "knowledge argument".

The sixth chapter, by Enyimba Maduka, offers a critical examination of Chimakonam's theory of identity – "Sense-phenomenalism". Maduka, specifically contends with Chimakonam's idea that personal identity, and by extension knowledge of the self, is only possible through interactions with other people in the world. The last chapter in this first part of the book, written by John Giddy, draws from ideas in African thought, like vitalism, to show that some African ideas about consciousness and mind do not constitute a dualism.

In the second part of this book, chapters generally deal with issues related to the fourth industrial revolution. Ojochogwu Abdul, for instance, seeks to examine transhumanism from an Afro-futuristic perspective. While Aribiah Attoe and Amara Chimakonam attempt an answer to the question of life's meaning from an African perspective, suggesting that the communal normative function theory provides the most plausible grounding for a traditional African account of what would make a trans human existence meaningful. Thaddeus Metz, in the tenth chapter, draws from African norms, a critique of utilitarianism as a possible foundation for the ethics of artificial intelligence. In the next chapter, Diana Ofana tackles the thorny issue regarding the personhood of Artificial Intelligence Systems (AI/AIS). She reveals that within the African context, AI cannot (and ought not to) attain personhood. Chris Wareham, in a contrary view to Diana's, argues strongly that although *prima facie* robots could not be persons, the African account of personhood could still accommodate Artificial intelligence systems such as AI.

Mary Carman and Benjamin Rosman, on their part, tackle the thorny issue of deciphering how AI systems can make judgments that take into account the differing values across cultures. To do this, they adopt what they call the "principle of explicability" as one that, at least, accounts for African interests and also ensures a just and fair machine learning system.

References

Chimakonam, J., Uti, E., Segun, S., & Attoe, A. (2019). *New conversations on the problems of identity, consciousness and mind*. Springer Nature.

Churchland, P. (1981). Eliminative materialism and the propositional attitudes. *Journal of Philosophy, 68*(2), 67–90.

Churchland, P. (2002). *Brain-wise*. The MIT Press.

Dennett, D. (1991). *Consciousness explained*. Back Bay Books.

Gyekye, K. (1978). Akan concept of a person. *International Philosophy Quarterly, 18*(3), 277–287.

Part I
Conversations on Mind, Body and Consciousness

Chapter 2
Gyekye and Contemporary Idealism

James Tartaglia

Abstract I begin with a defence of both Gyekye's universalist and African metaphilosophies. In light of these metaphilosophies, I discuss the contemporary Western hegemony of materialist philosophy of mind and its origins in Gilbert Ryle's *The Concept of Mind* (1949), showing that the existence and nature of the traditional Akan philosophy, as elaborated by Gyekye, casts serious doubt on some influential founding motivations for materialism. I then argue that traditional Akan philosophy is best aligned with contemporary idealism. Gyekye's endorsement of dualism is shown to have not been intended as ontologically fundamental, while panpsychism is rejected on the basis of the resistance it offers to the Akan commitment to transcendence. Contemporary idealism, however, is able to accommodate all the main components of traditional Akan philosophy, making both experiential primacy and transcendence central to a metaphysical understanding of reality. *Sunsum* (spirit) and *ōkra* (soul) are understood in terms of the distinction between the phenomenal and horizonal conceptions of experience, with consciousness always requiring a distinction between the phenomenal world within an experiential horizon, and the independent being that transcends the horizon.

Keywords Philosophy of mind · Personal identity · Kwame Gyekye · Metaphilosophy · Metaphysical idealism

2.1 Gyekye's Metaphilosophy

Kwame Gyekye (1939–2019) was a Ghanaian philosopher with a programmatic vision for the development of African philosophy, which he set out in his main work, *An Essay on African Philosophical Thought: The Akan Conceptual Scheme*

J. Tartaglia (✉)
Department of Philosophy, Keele University, Keele, UK
e-mail: j.tartaglia@keele.ac.uk

A. D. Attoe et al. (eds.), *Conversations on African Philosophy of Mind, Consciousness and Artificial Intelligence*,
https://doi.org/10.1007/978-3-031-36163-0_2

(Gyekye, 1987). As far as Gyekye's general metaphilosophy is concerned, his view on the nature of philosophy, it is perfectly simple and no different from my own, namely, that philosophy is a universal discipline which deals with a distinctive subject matter consisting of related topics of natural human interest (ibid.: xiv–xv, 9–10). We all come to self-awareness in a reality that exists for no apparent reason, possessed of minds and bodies, and living a temporal life that requires us to make choices, some moral, some political, and around that basic constellation of facts, philosophical inquiry was bound to spring up, as indeed it has, all around the world. This is only worth saying because it has been denied so often. Some have doubted whether philosophy ever emerged in Africa, but as Gyekye shows, these doubts depend on dubious criteria for what counts as philosophy, as well as misunderstanding of what traditional African views have amounted to. African philosophy is not unique in having attracted deniers. Richard Rorty doubted whether philosophy ever emerged in India (Tartaglia, 2014). Perhaps the underlying reasons for this kind of suspicion, at a time when awareness of non-Western philosophical traditions was spreading in the West, are that some wanted to think of philosophy as a distinctively European achievement, while others remained under the dismal shadow of the nineteenth century positivist view that philosophy is a more or less random collection of issues which have yet to yield to scientific investigation, or else do not deserve to be taken seriously because they are dubious. (More accurately, I think, those of a positivistic mind-set consider the issues dubious *because* they cannot be approached scientifically.) In any case, Gyekye is surely right that it is 'given to humanity to philosophize' (Gyekye, 1987: 9) and the facts bear him out. Growing awareness of non-Western philosophical traditions, and the resulting denial, was only possible because the concerns of those traditions were recognisably philosophical.

Gyekye's universalist metaphilosophy ought to be uncontroversial, then, but his African metaphilosophy is original, programmatic, and visionary. As Gyekye sees it, African philosophy needs to draw upon the sayings, anecdotes, and stories that were passed down as an oral tradition within African cultures, in order to provide the foundations for a distinctive new discourse. Traditional African philosophy, as embodied in these oral traditions, should be the basis for building a new one. Gyekye's method for getting clear about what this traditional philosophy consisted in, at least among the Akan, was to travel around villages to ask questions; and as soon as the philosophical character of his interests was clear, he tells us, he would invariably be directed to the local expert in such matters. The philosophy within these sayings passed the test of time, Gyekye thinks, because they survived centuries of philosophical debate within a preliterate society.[1] We do not know the names of the people who originated them, as we know it was Heraclitus who said 'we step and do not step into the same rivers', but to be accepted as a philosopher in Akan society, a young man would surely not be able to start making philosophical

[1] Gyekye uses the term 'preliterate' throughout the book; initially, in the preface, to make the point that although traditional Akan philosophy was not written down, it was still, in his view, the product of the individual intellects of individual philosophers, and hence should not be characterised as an 'ethnophilosophy' (ibid.: xix).

pronouncements and have them automatically taken seriously. They would have to prove their worth, just as a philosopher today must. They would meet with scepticism, have to engage in debate, explain their meaning, and for their sayings to be repeated centuries after their death, they must have earned considerable consensus. There is every reason to take this traditional philosophy seriously, then, as Gyekye sees it, and to use it as the basis of a new and distinctively African philosophy.

This situation presents a great opportunity and Gyekye showed the way to seize it. That there is no written canon of African philosophical literature stretching back over the centuries is not the disadvantage it might at first seem, because it allows traditional African philosophy to provide inspiration without excessive constraint. A framework can be better than a composition, however great that composition might be, for inspiring new ideas. Since Indian and Chinese philosophy possess canons of classic philosophical literature, largely from the ancient world, a great deal of what you hear about these philosophies today consists in commentaries on ancient philosophers and attempts to apply their views to contemporary debates – the relevance of the Buddhist doctrine of 'no-self' to discoveries in neuroscience, the relevance of Confucius to contemporary debates in political philosophy, etc. Seminal figures who died thousands of years ago loom large because the identity and recognisability of these philosophies depend on them. The shadows cast by the founding figures of Western philosophy, by contrast, are usually less restrictive; past philosophers do still have contemporary disciples, but the mainstream positions have acquired an independent life. David Armstrong, for example, defended a Platonic theory of universals, but nobody could mistake him for a historian of philosophy offering a new interpretation of Plato, or for trying to show Plato's continued relevance, or that Plato was 'right all along'. Armstrong was an Australian philosopher contributing to a contemporary debate by offering a theory Plato would no doubt have rejected, once he had struggled to make sense of it.

Gyekye says that, 'if a philosophy produced by a modern African has no basis in the culture and experience of African peoples, then it cannot appropriately claim to be an African philosophy' (ibid.: 33), and that African philosophy 'needs to be the results of the reflective exertions of an African thinker, aimed at giving analytical attention to the intellectual foundations of African culture and experience. That is all' (ibid.: 211). I think he was right about that. Schopenhauer incorporated Indian philosophy into his metaphysical system, but it would be odd to say he contributed to Indian philosophy – rather, he made a contribution to German (or European, or Western) philosophy which incorporated ideas from Indian philosophy. Similarly, an African philosopher can make a contribution to the debates in the major philosophy journals today, but unless it draws on a distinctively African philosophy – an African solution to a universal philosophical problem – it is not African philosophy, in Gyekye's view; and he chides African philosophers for being in too much of a 'hurry' to do exactly this (ibid.: 212). The eighteenth century Ghanaian philosopher, Anton Wilhelm Amo, produced German, not African philosophy, says Gyekye (ibid.: 34).

At the end of his book, Gyekye notes that, 'It is never too late in human history to start from where one should start' (ibid.: 212). Imagine what the Greek philosophers of Plato's generation might have done, equipped only with the fragments of the pre-Socratics we now have (with the names of the authors redacted), but surrounded by non-Greek philosophical traditions to learn from. African philosophers today will find themselves in a similar situation by attending to Gyekye's metaphilosophy – a situation of massive potential. The result of traditional African musical forms starting to develop in North America and the Caribbean in the late nineteenth century was that twentieth century music was transformed the world over. The same kind of positive transformation might yet be enacted by African philosophy in the twenty-first century. Gyekye showed the way to make it happen.

Now in order to enact this programme, the first step is to elucidate the traditional foundations, which is what Gyekye spends the bulk of the book doing. In the process of bringing out an Akan perspective on the nature of mind, freedom, causality, ethics, etc., it is sometimes difficult to discern Gyekye's voice: does he agree with the views he is presenting? This is not a problem in his writings generally; if you look to his later essay on the relationship between religion and science (Gyekye, 2009), for instance, his view is quite clear, namely, that religion and science are not in conflict, it being a dogma of Western philosophy that they are. His own position also comes across unambiguously in the metaphilosophy that frames *An Essay on African Philosophical Thought*. The reason his voice is less defined when recounting the Akan views is explained by this metaphilosophy. He is laying the foundations for a new African philosophy, not building one of his own; although he does acknowledge that 'the interpreter's own insight' is bound to be involved to some extent (Gyekye, 1987: 11). His aim is to analyse and elucidate Akan views so that it becomes possible to determine which 'should be salvaged and which should be jettisoned' (ibid.: 41). As such, it is enough for his purposes to bring out and sharpen up some distinctive and interesting positions and themes, without explicitly committing himself on any of them.

Nevertheless, I doubt any reader of the book could fail to sense that Gyekye is highly sympathetic to the Akan views; on one occasion, when he discusses ESP (ibid.: 201–3), rather too sympathetic. I very much doubt there is need for more scientific investigation into telepathy in case it turns out to be genuine, as Gyekye says, not least because the idea of it is philosophically dubious – the only thoughts I can have are my own, so 'reading' somebody else's thoughts could only amount to thinking that my own have the same content, which raises the question of what could justify my believing this. But even here, a 'salvage' rather than 'jettison' might be possible, if something scientifically and philosophically credible can be said which relates to this notion in an extenuated fashion, in accordance with the suggestion above that the traditional views might be most fruitfully viewed as a framework of inspiration. For example, when jazz musicians improvise, their interactions are sometimes said to be 'almost telepathic'; I would stress the 'almost', but not rule out there being something philosophically interesting to say here. Still, as sympathetic as Gyekye is to the Akan views, he is never uncritical. To take just one example, he rejects the suggestion that the Problem of Evil does not arise for Akan philosophy, as it does for Christian philosophy, despite this having been seen as to the credit of former; the problem just arises in a different form, he argues (ibid.: 123–8).

Gyekye never claims to provide a definitive account of *the* Akan philosophy, only a 'reconstruction' based on 'the philosophical ideas held by *some* individual Akan thinkers' (ibid.: 54–5). This might seem to clash with the suggestion that these ideas are representative of *African Philosophical Thought*, as per the title of the book, so he devotes his final chapter to meeting this objection, arguing that there is an underlying unity to the philosophy of traditional cultures throughout Africa, on the basis of various considerations, some historical. Whether this be accepted or not, the views he elucidates certainly present *one* concrete interpretation of *one* traditional African philosophy. Given the forward-looking nature of his project, I doubt he would want to see it held up by interminable disputes about what Akan, much less African traditional philosophy, really amounts to; he was understandably sceptical that such questions could ever be answered. Differing interpretations are always possible, but debating them for their own sake is a task for the history of philosophy.

Gyekye certainly succeeded in bringing out distinctive and interesting themes from traditional Akan philosophy. One particularly promising idea is that of a humanistic philosophy free from antipathy to religion (ibid.: 143–6); Western humanism has, from its origins, been driven by such antipathy, and this has not served it well. Perhaps Akan philosophy can inspire a fresh and more socially useful take on this idea. The topic I shall be pursuing, however, is Gyekye's philosophy of mind, or soul. The main reason for my interest is that it is resolutely anti-materialistic, as indeed is traditional African philosophy generally, according to Gyekye. I think, and have argued at length, that materialist philosophy of mind is a failed experiment, one which has dragged on for nearly 70 years now – too long (Tartaglia, 2020, esp. Chapters 2 and 3). There are signs this era is drawing to a close, and this presents an opportunity for African philosophy, devised along Gyekyean lines, to enter the mix within our collective efforts to build something better.

2.2 Soulless Materialism

The failed experiment with materialism began with Gilbert Ryle's *The Concept of Mind*. Despite its formative influence, Ryle rejects materialism in that book, and, contrary to the popular image of Ryle as the main representative of behaviourism in philosophy, he rejects behaviourism too; the latter is hard to dispute when Ryle ends the book with a section entitled 'Behaviourism', which begins with his prediction that the book 'will undoubtedly, and harmlessly be stigmatised as "behaviourist"' (Ryle, 1949: 300), before proceeding to explain why it should not be so stigmatised.[2] It is perhaps unsurprising that such misunderstandings have sprung up, because the book has not aged well. It is long, circuitous, and packed full of exam-

[2] This point is emphasised in Julia Tanney's introduction to the new edition I cite from, as well as in her online *Stanford Encyclopedia of Philosophy* article on Ryle.

ples of fine-grained distinctions to be observed within ordinary discourse about people's minds and mental habits, which are rarely interesting to consider in and of themselves, and even more rarely lead anywhere that clarifies Ryle's overall position.[3] The main thing today's readers are likely to notice is Ryle's scorn for Cartesian dualism, repeated *ad nauseam*, on the grounds that it advocates 'occult', 'queer', or 'ghostly' entities.

The negative message of the book is that the concept of mind does not commit us to the existence of an inner life of consciousness pitted against an external world of physical objects, and that this belief results from a specifically philosophical error. The positive message is much more elusive, but does eventually show its face in the chapter on imagination, I think. Up until this point, Ryle has repeatedly denied that the mind is an inner experiential arena, but without showing any tendency to deny that we can think silently, have tunes running 'through our heads', conjure up visual images, etc. – which is a puzzling combination. But in this chapter he says,

> a person picturing his nursery is, in a certain way, like that person seeing his nursery, but the similarity does not consist in his really looking at a real likeness of his nursery, but in his really seeming to see his nursery itself, when he is not really seeing it. (ibid.: 225)

So if you have a tune running through your head, to take another of his examples, there is no tune and no act of listening, there only seems to be. In other words, since Ryle is clear that seeming to hear the tune is not having a conscious experience of a certain type; it is making a false judgement that you are hearing the tune. This is the account of experiential seeming held by Ryle's student, Daniel Dennett (1991: 364), probably the most influential philosopher of the materialist era, and it is generally regarded as a form of eliminativism. Having a tune run through your head which nobody else can hear is a real episode, for Ryle, but not an episode of conscious experience. It is an episode of making a false judgement, akin to judging that $2 + 2 = 5$. With the idea of judgement stripped of any connection to consciousness, a robot could do this.

Ryle maintains that experience does not take place in 'my own private theatre' (Ryle, 1949: 44; see also 137, 140, 149, 154, 187, 200, 222, 291) and is continually hostile to Descartes, while Dennett's best-known idea is that consciousness should not be thought of as a 'Cartesian Theater' (Dennett, 1991); so it is Ryle's idea really, as well as his terminology. Ryle's suspicion of consciousness was rooted in the Ordinary Language Philosophy movement, which saw all philosophical problems as arising from abuses of language by philosophers, with the remedy (not solution – there is nothing to solve) being to pay more attention to how we ordinarily talk, so that the artificial and falsifying language that professional philosophers devised can be forgotten. Perhaps, then, Dennett simply inherited this suspicion and found it

[3] Ernest Gellner, in his 1959 attack on linguistic philosophy, *Words and Things* (the word 'attack' is in the subtitle), observed that, 'Evasiveness is implicit in the ideas and in the practice of Linguistic Philosophy' (Gellner, 1959: 50). Ryle, as editor of the journal *Mind*, refused to allow Gellner's book to be reviewed on the grounds that it was malicious; as indeed it was (Czeglédy, 2003: 13).

confirmed by what he learned from cognitive science and neuroscience, since these sciences provide the basis of his own criticisms of the 'Cartesian Theater'. And perhaps Ryle is best understood as an eliminativist too, albeit not a materialist one, since materialism is a metaphysical position, and he thinks all such positions are ailments to be cured by closer attention to ordinary language. That would certainly subvert the usual history: eliminativism is generally regarded as an excessive and implausible development within 1960s materialism, which took place after Ryle's 'behaviourism' had already been abandoned in favour of reductive materialism.

The association between believing in ghosts and Cartesian dualism was probably the greatest influence Ryle's book had, and is to be found in all the pioneers of twentieth century materialism. It led to a forgetting of the history of philosophy, in which Cartesian dualism was always controversial, even within Descartes' lifetime, and in which it was amended alongside other alternatives to materialism. It disguised the lack of any argumentative basis for materialism, by tempting its advocates to set up a false dichotomy: the only alternatives are materialism or Cartesian dualism, nobody in their right mind believes in ghosts, so materialism is the only credible option (see Tartaglia, 2020: Chapter 3). Once this dichotomy began to exert its influence, the long history of strong political connotations to materialism, beginning in ancient Greece, was easily overlooked, and replaced by an exclusive focus on the metaphysic. To English-language philosophy, materialism started to seem like nothing more than a bastion of sanity to protect us from belief in ghosts, as well as an expression of respect for modern science owed by any educated person – rather than as the intellectual foundations of an ancient crusade against organised religion which was, at that time, being enacted on a vast scale in the communist world.

The Identity Theory of Mind, according to which mental states are brain states, was pioneered by two English philosophers in the 1950s, Ullin Place and Jack Smart, who were initially attracted to behaviourism by Ryle, but went on to reject it. The first appearance of that theory was in the context of a 1954 paper by Place, criticising Ryle's analysis of the concept of 'heed' (Place, 1954). Place and Smart were concerned that a behaviourist analysis of a sensation – a severe pain understood as just screaming and the flailing of arms, perhaps, or just a disposition to this behaviour – would miss out the current reality, the actual feeling being responded to. Place and Smart thought this reality must be something physical, and the best physical candidates, they thought, were brain states.

Ryle warned against this kind of reaction (Ryle, 1949: 12; see also 63–8, 300–303). His target was *any* kind of reification of sensations, thoughts and other mental episodes, as well as of the mind itself; this was the cardinal sin of Cartesian dualism, and to try to find physical replacements, as Place and Smart did, was to repeat that mistake. In responding to his criticism of the Cartesian 'ghost in the machine', his followers missed the fact that he was just as critical of the 'machine' as of the 'ghost'. If he was an eliminativist, as suggested above, then this attitude makes sense: there is nothing to account for except the nature of our false judgements. Ryle says that minds and bodies exist 'in two different senses' (ibid.: 12), and although he never adequately clarifies this, I think he meant that while physical processes 'exist' in the sense that they can be the objects of true or false judgements, mental processes 'exist' in the sense that we make false judgements about seeing or hearing things we are not really seeing or hearing; the distinction, for Ryle, is to be found, and understood exclusively, within the logic of ordinary language. Any kind of mechanistic understanding of mind, then, would make the mistake of reification, since mechanical explanations require 'things' to connect, whether they be immaterial, material, or behavioural patterns. Twentieth century materialism did not heed Ryle's advice. The language of mental 'states' became firmly entrenched, and when materialists moved from the reductionism of the Identity Theorists to non-reductive accounts, most notably functionalism, a brain state was still required to 'realise' the functional/mental states – philosophically, because something concrete and thing-like was needed to make the experience happen, and practically, to enact the mechanistic theories in machines that mimic our intelligent behaviour.

In this context, it is very interesting to consider Akan philosophy of mind. The language the Akan philosophise in is materialistic, unlike English and other related European languages, and yet Akan philosophy of mind is anti-materialistic. So, for example, if you say, in English, 'I am tall' or 'I am ugly', then the 'I' can be substituted for 'my body': 'my body is tall', 'my body is ugly' – awkward, but basically what we mean. When we refer to types of conscious awareness, however, the situation is different. If you say 'I am happy' or 'I am hopeful', you are not saying 'my body is happy' or 'my body is hopeful' – to the extent that we can make sense of these statements, it is only through familiarity with materialism; it is not what we instinctively mean, but loyalty to that theory might make you think it must be what we mean in the final analysis.

When you switch to Akan, however, the etymological meaning of 'I am happy' is 'my eyes are brightened', and for 'I am hopeful', it is 'my eyes are on it' (Gyekye, 1987: 166). Of course, we do not ordinarily attend to the etymology of our words, so when an Akan says 'M'ani agye', they do not mean 'my eyes are brightened', but rather 'I am happy'. The latter is the correct translation; if, while gazing into a mirror, an Akan person were to witness their eyes suddenly becoming brighter as the result of an unwanted medical intervention, then they would presumably say something quite different to report the result. But the point is that Akan, as opposed to English, erects no barrier to substituting 'my body' for 'I' in mentalistic statements like 'I am happy', because the 'I' is already making reference to a part of the body, the eyes. Consequently, the Akan language offered no encouragement to Akan philosophers to conceive their minds as distinct from their bodies, quite the contrary, and so any temptation to think that opposition to materialism is encouraged by, or even largely explained by, the quirks of European languages is immediately rendered dubious. The Akan philosophised with the language they had, which is naturally conducive to materialism, but they rejected materialism. Others have philosophised with languages resistant to materialism, and by and large, despite the institutional hegemony of materialism in Anglophone academia since the 1960s, they have rejected it also (Tartaglia, 2020: Chapter 2). This suggests that belief in immaterial minds is not the result of being misled by language, of not attending carefully enough to its logic, but rather the result of giving a plausible description of the basic existential situation human beings occupy, then reasoning on its basis.

Ryle thought that dualism is the result of a specifically philosophical mistake, one that was made by European philosophers. He makes some sketchy speculations about the historical roots of this mistake, saying that, 'Descartes was reformulating already prevalent theological doctrines of the soul in the new syntax of Galileo' (Ryle, 1949: 13) and that the resulting conception of consciousness was 'in part a transformed application of the Protestant notion of conscience' (ibid.: 141). Rorty, who applauded Ryle for initiating a tradition that taught us how *not* to take consciousness seriously (Rorty, 1982), told a more detailed story along these lines in *Philosophy and the Mirror of Nature* (Rorty, 1979: Chapter 1), as part of his attempt to deconstruct the mind-body problem. Very roughly: it all began when Plato conceived the human intellect as transcendent to the physical world, able to 'see' the forms which grant knowledge of universal truth, since Plato considered this the crucial ability which raises humans above the level of animals; then Descartes united conscious experience to Plato's transcendent intellect to salvage the secondary qualities excluded from the world by Galileo's mechanistic science – with the unification justified on the grounds that both intellectual truths and sensations can be indubitable.[4]

Given that the Akan came up with an immaterialist conception of mind in isolation from European intellectual history, the best that can be said for the above stories is that they might contain some truths about the particular route European philosophers took to arrive at the same place. The intellectual pressures Ryle and Rorty thought were decisive, however, seem very unlikely to have been anything of the kind, in light of the existence of an Akan equivalent. Of course Descartes and Plato were influenced by their intellectual environments and histories. The traditional Akan philosophers would have been influenced by intellectual pressures of which we are ignorant. Plato, Descartes, and the nameless Akan philosophers, however, could all grasp universal truths whether their eyes were open or closed, and when they closed their eyes, they could hardly have failed to notice that the visual experiences previously informing them of objects in their immediate vicinity were no longer doing that, but rather presenting a dark and inconstant pattern that others were not aware of. It is no miracle that they arrived in the same place, because they were reasoning on the basis of the same facts (Gyekye, 1987: 186).

The mere fact of the existence and anti-materialist nature of Akan philosophy of mind provides an immediate antidote to the fanciful but influential notion that dualism, and perhaps even believing that we are conscious, is explained by intellectual errors in our history. This is just one strand in the wider trend of hostility to consciousness in the materialist era, and indeed, to anything else the metaphysic cannot accommodate. Philosophy has been set on a warpath against the natural ways of seeing things, with this naturalness coming to be seen as a sure sign of naivety,

[4] Ryle was not the first to think this way; Rorty's historical deconstruction was mainly influenced by Dewey (1930).

religious longing, superstition, scientific ignorance, being in the grip of a historical error, insufficient attention to the logic of language, etc. The automatic assumption became that anything awkward for materialism must be an illusion; and as accusations of illusion were cast all over our lives, few stopped to wonder if the problem might not actually be this ancient metaphysical theory, which, in its current incarnation, provides the intellectual foundations for an artificial intelligence revolution set to transform our world in a yet to be determined manner. It would be nice to instead have a philosophy which resonates with our experience, as a prelude to enriching it with new insight, rather than one that clashes with it at every turn. Then philosophy might become more publicly visible, and the intellectual foundations for meaningfully debating our future might be developed.

2.3 Traditional Akan Philosophy and Contemporary Idealism

'Soul' is the original English translation for the Greek word *psychē*, but we have come to favour 'mind' instead, for historical reasons that are fairly inconsequential; originally, because 'soul' seemed too physical, which is rather ironic with hindsight (Tartaglia, 2020: Chapter 7). These days, I think 'soul' is preferable, because it distances us from the materialists' (and their opponents') talk of 'mental states'. The language of 'states' is problematic in this area. If I talk about the current state of the economy, my statement is ontologically empty – nobody would suppose that this state is something with its own nature, irrespective of human classificatory practices, akin to a tree, planet, or sensation. It is just a loose way of talking about an unspecifiable number of things; mainly, these days, people interacting with each other on computers. States need to be ontologically filled-in, which suits the materialist project of filling them in with grey matter, but not the project of trying to experientially account for our identities. Think of a person's mind as a series of mental states and you are immediately distanced from the idea of the mind as a substantial unity. But 'soul' retains this connotation, and has the added bonus that it is more natural to think of a person as essentially a soul than a mind, since the latter, in everyday discourse, suggests pure intellect.

Now Gyekye tells us that the Akan have a tripartite conception of a person, consisting of soul, spirit, and body, which he thinks is best reduced to a combination of a body and a bipartite soul (Gyekye, 1987: 98). Spirit and soul are not really distinct, he argues, because spirit is simply the active part of the soul. So a person is a unity of body and soul, which is a kind of dualism, albeit not necessarily a fundamental metaphysical one. When we reach the fundamental level, then given the wider ontological commitments of Akan philosophy which Gyekye tells us about, it seems to me that a further reduction is required, thereby allowing us to simply say that a person is a soul. Then, we are able to understand the Akan philosophy as offering an idealist account of personhood.

There are two problems with attributing a metaphysically dualist conception of personhood to traditional Akan philosophy. The first is that this philosophy is committed to 'disembodied survival' (ibid.: 100). In that case, if a person is a combination of body and soul, and only the soul survives death, then the person does not survive death – only their soul does. But if *you* can survive the demise of your body, this means *you* were never essentially a person in the first place. If you were, you would need your body to carry on existing. A part of you will continue to exist, but since the same could be said of your body, in that it will continue to exist as a corpse, a commitment to disembodied survival requires that the continued existence of your soul is the crucial factor in your survival, and hence that having a body was never essential to you in the first place.

So, to combine a metaphysically dualist conception of a person with disembodied survival, you have to deny that we are essentially people. This can easily be avoided by saying that a person is essentially a soul and only contingently has a body. When Locke distinguished a 'person' from a human being, and thereby initiated the personal identity debate in Western philosophy, he was also motivated by considerations of life after death (Tartaglia, 2020: 144). He was trying to find criteria for continued survival that were accessible to us, given the limitations of human understanding that are the focus of his philosophy, and since he thought we cannot know substances, such as souls, he thought the best we could do was to make judgements on the basis of psychological continuity – retention of memory, etc. What he wanted to be able to track, but thought of as constitutionally hidden from us, was the continuation of our essential natures, required for us to carry on existing rather than cease to exist. Subsequent debates have retained this motivation, despite gravitating to the currently popular negationist psychological continuity position – which I consider absurd – according to which, for example, if ten computers can accurately mimic my personality after my death, then I will survive as ten people.[5] The other focus of interest in personal identity, apart from survival, is in the normative aspects of personhood. This interest is also present in Locke, who saw the main value of his epistemically modest conception of personhood in jurisprudence; to ensure that people were not punished for crimes they could not remember, for instance. Normative applications of personhood are not emphasised in Gyekye's discussion of Akan moral theory, however, which he argues is 'not religiously grounded' (Gyekye, 1987: 143), but rather focused on the welfare of communities, and which requires the moral development of *sunsum* (*spirit*) (ibid.: 152). So given that the issue of survival is integral to the Akan notion of a person, and metaphysical dualism has no clear role to play in supporting the normative uses of personhood in Akan moral philosophy, it seems unnecessarily problematic to hold that a person dies with their body, with only the soul surviving – since that just raises the question of whether *you* survive.

---

[5] These kinds of position originate with Parfit (1984) and are often aligned with Buddhist views; Parfit himself made this connection.

The second problem is that Akan philosophy is one in which, 'ontological primacy, in my view,' says Gyekye, 'is given to the invisible'; where 'invisible' is glossed as 'immaterial, unperceivable, spiritual' (ibid.: 166). If that is right, then we can immediately conclude that Akan philosophy is either metaphysically idealist or panpsychist. If souls and their experiences have ontological primacy, then they have the independent existence which everything else relies upon, just as materialists believe that the particles and forces discovered by contemporary physics (or a future one) possess the independent existence. This would make natural sense of an Akan saying Gyekye discusses: 'Could God die, I will die' (ibid.: 100). Since our souls are considered an 'indwelling spark of God', and God (Onyame) is a spiritual being which is 'the ultimate ground of being' (ibid.: 69), God's death would entail my own.

It is not clear that Gyekye would disagree with this further reduction – from body and soul, to just soul – despite his never making it. When he attributes 'interactionist psychophysical dualism' to traditional Akan philosophy, saying he considers it a 'realistic doctrine' (ibid.: 103), it certainly looks as if he is advocating dualism as usually understood, namely, as a fundamental ontological division between distinct but interacting substances. But viewed in the context of the book, that cannot be right. Gyekye repeatedly says that Akan ontology is pluralistic, but also makes claims of ontological primacy, sometimes within close proximity, and this is because he thinks, 'African ontology is neither wholly pluralistic nor wholly monistic, but possesses attributes of both' (ibid.: 197). He says that Akan ontology is 'hierarchical' (ibid.: 69); as, indeed, most ontologies are. So all he can mean by 'pluralism', I think, is that in addition to fundamental, independent existence, which for the Akan is 'essentially spiritualistic' (ibid.: 197), there are other types of entities to be credited with non-independent existence; rather as a moderate, non-eliminativist materialist might say that experience is real, but has a dependent, or supervenient, existence, one which depends upon brain states. Gyekye's endorsement of dualism should be considered in the same light, then. He has ontological hierarchy in mind, such that an ontologically non-fundamental body interacts with an ontologically fundamental soul – otherwise, the claims about ontological primacy would make no sense. Such distinctions of level have precedent; Armstrong's commitment to mind-brain identity theory, for instance, was meant to be considered at a non-fundamental level, since at the fundamental level he was a Platonic realist (Armstrong, 1980).[6]

It seems clear that Gyekye is describing either an idealist or a panpsychist metaphysic, then. Gyekye opts for panpsychism. He rejects idealism on the grounds that idealists hold that 'what is real is only spirit', materialists hold that 'what is real is only matter', but Akan ontology holds that reality 'possesses attributes of both' (Gyekye, 1987: 197). I do not think this reasoning bears much scrutiny. Gyekye seems to be equating idealism with one exceptionally controversial form of it, namely, Berkeley's eighteenth century empirical idealism, which did indeed deny

[6]Ada Agada also points out that Gyekye's dualism should not be considered an 'ontological distinction' (Agada, 2017: 31).

the reality of matter.[7] But an idealist need only argue that matter exists in a less fundamental manner than mind, in accordance with a hierarchical ontology, such as that of the Akan. Gyekye provides no reason to rule out idealism in general, then.

The context in which he endorses panpychism is provided by his rejection of the idea that Akan philosophy is pantheistic, on the grounds that God is held to transcend his creation in Akan philosophy, rather than encompass or pervade it. He then goes on to say that, a 'more appropriate description of the Akan system might be panpsychism: Everything is or contains *sunsum* (spirit)' (ibid.: 75). Since he also tells us that Akan philosophy holds that spirit can exist apart from the soul, as the 'activating principle' of natural objects (ibid.: 98), and that 'spirit' is used to describe both God and other purely spiritual beings, as well as 'mystical powers' that 'constitute the inner essences or intrinsic properties of natural objects' (ibid.: 73), that does seem to be right – those are stereotypically panpsychist commitments.

But this attribution depends on Gyekye having his facts right, of course – which, given his modest and realistic ambition, only requires that it is based on some views held within traditional Akan philosophy. Kwasi Wiredu doubted even this, saying that, 'Among the Akans a piece of dead wood, for example, is regarded as notoriously dead and is the humorous paradigm of absolute lifelessness' (Wiredu, 1998: 31). In defence of Gyekye, Ada Agada suggests that Wiredu's resistance results from thinking of panpsychism as a form of superstition; but, as he points out, panpsychism has undergone a major renaissance in recent philosophy, through the likes of David Chalmers, Galen Strawson, and Philip Goff. Agada, who thinks that belief in spirit pervading the physical world is deeply rooted in traditional African philosophy, advocates panpsychism as the best means to reconcile spiritual monism with the transcendence of God – he thinks it creates affinity between the material world and the God said to transcend it, allowing transcendence and immanence to be reconciled through the idea that God is the 'transcendent principle whose effects are yet distributed throughout the universe' (Agada, 2017: 33). This leads him to disagree with Gyekye's dismissal of pantheism, and move more towards Wiredu's view of a God unified with the material world, on the grounds that a 'complete rejection of pantheism renders the reconciliation of immanence and transcendence impossible' (ibid.: 33).

It seems to me, however, that idealism provides a more natural, theoretically coherent, and independently credible way to combine a commitment to both experiential (or spiritual) primacy and transcendence. Panpsychism is a naturally immanentist philosophy with no obvious use for transcendence, and if you look to the most influential traditional metaphysic with panpsychist implications, namely, Spinoza's, you do not find it; just as you do not find it in the contemporary theories. The standard contemporary motivation for panpsychism is to account for the existence of conscious experience: experience exists as the intrinsic nature of physical reality, thereby explaining human consciousness as self-awareness of our intrinsic

[7] Gyekye also seems to be equating materialism with eliminative materialism in this passage; but not elsewhere in the book.

natures, and also explaining why the materialist picture misses out experience, namely, because physics only extrinsically characterises the world (Goff, 2019). There is no need for transcendence to accomplish either of these explanatory tasks. Panpsychism and transcendence can be combined, but it starts to look as if the latter has simply been tacked-on because traditional Akan philosophy is committed to it – and that is not to do the best we can to develop that philosophy, as per Gyekye's project. Agada does provide independent motivation, but it is immediately problematic: if God is transcendent, then how could we ever know that his nature has an affinity with the physical world? And how could an effect in the physical world have a transcendent cause? Panpsychism and transcendence do not mix well, I would suggest.

For the contemporary idealist, however, transcendence is absolutely integral to understanding experience, and experience is ontologically primary. To understand this account, in broadest outline, we first need to distinguish between the phenomenal and horizonal conceptions of consciousness.[8] The phenomenal conception is the familiar one employed by dualists, materialists, and panpsychists, according to which experience is something you are aware of – it is a phenomenon, like a pain or tickle, something which subjectively appears to you. It is *that* feeling or visual experience, etc. The horizonal conception, on the other hand, is of the unified field of an individual's consciousness, within which there are appearances of both sensations, like pains and tickles, and physical objects, like trees and rocks. The horizon is not one of these appearances, nor all of them put together, but rather the field in which appearance happens. We are never aware of the horizon, and yet the unified experience we have of other things, like sensations and physical objects, presupposes its existence. It is what appearance occurs *within*, for each and every one of us – the individual, unified opening onto reality which a piece of dead wood lacks.

Where there is a horizon, there must be transcendence; experience requires transcendence. To see this, consider what Gyekye tells us about the Akan view of dreaming: 'in dreaming it is the *sunsum* [spirit], not the *ōkra*, that leaves the body. The departure of the *ōkra* (soul) from the body means the death of the person, whereas the *sunsum* can leave the body, as in dreaming, without causing the death of the person.' (Gyekye, 1987: 97) Experience cannot literally leave the body because it is not spatial, so it was never inside the body in the first place – this needs to be interpreted, then. What happens in dreaming, on the idealist model, is that experiences – considered phenomenally, as appearances you are aware of – no longer inform you about the physical world, but rather close you off from that world; in that sense, then, they 'leave the body'. The physical world is transcendent to the conscious horizon of the dreamer. Even if you were to dream about your sleeping body, seeing it in perfect detail, perhaps, it would not actually be your body but rather an illusory dream-body, because your actual body transcends the dream. But although *sunsum* can leave the body, in this sense, nevertheless your

[8] I adopt this terminology from J.J. Valberg (2007), although the distinction itself is firmly rooted in the history of philosophy. For a fuller exposition and defence of the idealism I am outlining here, see Tartaglia, 2020: Chapter 4.

horizon – which I take to be the idea behind *ōkra* – cannot permanently leave the body without death resulting. Again, it is never literally in the body, but in ordinary waking life it situates your body at the centre of reality. Your body is at the phenomenological centre of your horizon, as the thing to which sensations and physical objects appear. So *ōkra* cannot 'leave the body' in the sense that it cannot cease to present your body as being at the centre of reality.

Within the idealist model, independent reality is always deferred to a context that transcends the horizon of consciousness. Consciousness encloses us within a phenomenal reality, from the perspective of which reality is always transcendent – as is seen in the case of dreaming, where whatever reality there is to the illusory experience being had within the dreamer's horizon must be found in a context that transcends that horizon. The ontologically fundamental, independent nature cannot be found within the horizon of waking life either, however, which is to say that it cannot be found within the horizon which contains the physical world. This is attested to by the failure of materialism to account for experience, and the constant pressure its advocates feel to deny its existence. On the idealist model, independent existence transcends the horizon of waking life, just as physical existence transcends the horizon of a dream. This would explain many things that have puzzled philosophers from all traditions, not least why our ordinary pattern of causal explanation is obviously inapplicable to explaining the existence of the whole of reality – to explaining why there is something rather than nothing. The reason is that the independent reality we are trying to account for is transcendent, and hence transcends the horizons in which our standard patterns of explanation apply.

Idealism preserves and explains all the main commitments of traditional Akan philosophy. It gives central place to both *sunsum* and *ōkra*, understood, respectively, as experience conceived phenomenally and horizonally. It requires transcendent existence as a condition of there being any experience at all; and once a transcendent context is accepted, the possibility is open for the Akan God to reside there. The transcendent reality is the independent nature of experience, so the ontological primacy of experience is affirmed, but the physical world also appears within horizons of consciousness, and idealism provides no reason to deny anything science tells us about it, so long as this is not interpreted in accordance with the metaphysics of materialism. Experience and the physical world do appear to interact, in accordance with Gyekye's dualism, but this is not to be interpreted ontologically since these are types of appearance within a horizon transcended by independent reality. *Sunsum* is indeed the active part of the soul, in the sense that free decisions and actions are phenomena within a horizon. The Akan belief in disembodied survival is accommodated, since the soul could survive the death of the body if there is a horizon of experience which transcends the horizon of the physical world; I do not think there is, personally, but the idealist metaphysic accommodates people with and without faith. The only element of the Akan philosophy I cannot see a way to preserve is the idea that *sunsum* can exist without *ōkra* in inanimate objects, which sounds paradigmatically panpsychist; but Gykeye does not dwell on this, Wiredu strongly disputed it, so perhaps, as Gyekeye might put it, we can 'jettison' that bit.

Could this kind of idealist picture really be what traditional Akan philosophy was driving at? Well, if Gyekye was right that philosophers of all times and traditions reflect on 'a common ground of shared human experiences' (ibid.: 9), as he surely was, and if idealism provides a good philosophical account of that common ground, as I think it does, then I cannot see why not.

References

Agada, A. (2017). The apparent conflict of transcendentalism and immanentism in Kwame Gyekye and Kwasi Wiredu's interpretation of the Akan concept of God. *Filosofia Theoretica: Journal of African Philosophy, Culture and Religions, 6*, 23–38.

Armstrong, D. M. (1980). Naturalism, materialism, and first philosophy. In D. M. Armstrong (Ed.), *The nature of mind* (pp. 149–165). University of Queensland Press.

Czeglédy, A. P. (2003). The word and things of Ernest Gellner. *Social Evolution and History, 2*, 6–33.

Dennett, D. C. (1991). *Consciousness explained*. Little, Brown and Company.

Dewey, J. (1930). *The quest for certainty*. George Allen and Unwin.

Gellner, E. (1959/2005). *Words and things: An examination of, and an attack on, linguistic philosophy*. Routledge.

Goff, P. (2019). *Galileo's error: Foundations for a new science of consciousness*. Rider Press.

Gyekye, K. (1987/1995) (revised edition). *An essay on African philosophical thought: The Akan conceptual scheme*. Temple University Press.

Gyekye, K. (2009). Relationship between religion and science: An overview. *Legon: Journal of the Humanities, 20*, 1–22.

Parfit, D. (1984). *Reasons and persons*. Oxford University Press.

Place, U. T. (1954). The concept of heed. *British Journal of Psychology, 45*, 243–255.

Rorty, R. (1979). *Philosophy and the mirror of nature*. Princeton University Press.

Rorty, R. (1982). Contemporary philosophy of mind. *Synthese, 53*, 323–348.

Ryle, G. (1949/2009). *The concept of mind*. Routledge.

Tartaglia, J. (2014). Rorty's thesis of the cultural specificity of philosophy. *Philosophy East and West: A Quarterly of Comparative Philosophy, 65*, 1016–1036.

Tartaglia, J. (2020). *Philosophy in a technological world: Gods and Titans*. Bloomsbury.

Valberg, J. J. (2007). *Dream, death, and the self*. Princeton University Press.

Wiredu, K. (1998). Toward decolonizing African philosophy and religion. *African Studies Quarterly, 1*, 17–46.

Chapter 3
A Central State Materialistic Interpretation of the Yoruba Concept of Person: A Critique

Oladele Abiodun Balogun

Abstract In recent times, there have been a series of unresisted temptations to argue that the Yoruba concept of the human person fits very well into the framework of central state materialism, which states that mental events are identifiable with physical events occurring in the brain and central nervous system. This is because ***ara*** (human body), which is purely physical, can be taken to perform both material and immaterial functions. The chapter argues that while this is true; nonetheless, it is totally incorrect to reduce the Yoruba to central state materialists. The chapter states unequivocally that the performance of other vital components of the human person like **emi** (life-giving entity), **ori** (the bearer of human destiny), and ***ese*** (symbol of physical legs and spiritual efforts), suggests that the Yoruba concept of person, falls within the purview of dualism. It is argued further that the dualism of the Yoruba, which encourages harmonious interaction in the performances of both organs (material and immaterial), is fundamentally different from Cartesian dualism, which operates on the watertight distinction between the functions of the body and mind. The chapter recommends that a proper understanding of the Yoruba concept of a person can serve as a philosophical defence of Yoruba beliefs in spiritual entities, resolution of the traditional mind-body problem, and decolonization of the concept of mind, in contemporary Yoruba thought.

Keywords Central state materialism · Dualism · Traditional Yoruba concept of person

O. A. Balogun (✉)
Department of Religious Studies and Philosophy, Redeemer's University, Ede, Osun State, Nigeria

A. D. Attoe et al. (eds.), *Conversations on African Philosophy of Mind, Consciousness and Artificial Intelligence*,
https://doi.org/10.1007/978-3-031-36163-0_3

3.1 Central State Materialism

Central state materialism as a theory in the philosophy of mind states that each of the mental processes could be described in purely physicochemical terms, that is mental processes are causally dependent on physical processes (Green, 1981). This should not be interpreted to mean that central state materialism is a general term for materialistic/reductionist theories of mind since central state materialism can be differentiated from other forms of materialism and reductionism. While materialism stresses the fact that there are only bodies and matter and that minds or mental processes are really collections of bodies, reductionism argues that consciousness or mental processes can be reduced to brain processes with the emphasis on the focus of central state materialism that mental processes can be explained or identified or interpreted in purely physicochemical terms. Central state materialism, which is also sometimes called central state identity theory, was formulated in the 1950s. Identity theory holds that sensations, states, and processes of the mind are identical to states and processes of the brain. The origin of identity theory can be traced to the work of U.T Place (1956), Herbert Feigl (1967), and J.J.C Smart (1959). The identity theory affirms that mental states are identical to brain states, that is, it is not merely correlated with them, caused by them, realized by them, superadded to them, etc. (Polger, 2009: 2).

What identity theorists like Ullin Place (1956) tried to do, was to avoid the criticisms of behaviourism and Cartesian dualism by postulating that mental states, though internal are nevertheless physical. This was different, on the one hand, from the behaviourist theory that denied that mental states are internal and, on the other hand, different from functionalism, which sees mental states as constituents of their functions.

Ullin Place (1956) argues that particular states of mind are identical with particular states of the brain. For instance, when someone has an ache in the leg, the ache is identical with some neurological processes going on in the person's brain. By this argument, Place (1956), asserted that a conscious mental state is identical to some processes that occur in the brain. For Place, the emphasis is not on the meaning of the word 'pain' but on the phenomenon in the word 'pain'.

According to Polger (2009: 1), central state identity theorists believe that mental activities (states, events, processes, or properties) are identical to types of brain activities (states, events, processes, or properties, respectively). This implies that mental states are actual brain states. The mind for them is just a part of the physical body and the brain is reducible to a neurological state.

A recent theory of central state materialism, however, can be traced to David Armstrong's *A Materialist Theory of Mind.* Armstrong's theory is considered a more exhaustive analysis of the identity theory of Place (1956) and Smart (1959).

Armstrong started his philosophical life as a behaviourist but due to the influence of Smart, later moved to the view that mental states are states of the central nervous system, and more especially the brain. Frank Jackson (2008: 413) notes that Armstrong developed his central state version of the identity theory by arguing first that the concept of a mental state 'M' is the concept of a state that plays a distinctive causal role that connects stimulus, behavioural response, and other mental states.

Furthermore, as stated by Jackson, Armstrong argues that to ask after the identity of a given mental state 'M' is to ask what state plays the distinctive, causally intermediate role assigned by the concept of 'M'. Armstrong goes on to argue that, for each psychological state, it will turn out to be some state or other of the brain that plays the role in question. He concludes, therefore, that, as an empirical matter of fact, mental states are identical with brain states (Jackson, 2008: 414).

3.2 Yoruba Concept of Person

The Yoruba describes the human person as *eniyan*. In the Yoruba concept of person, it is believed that the *eniyan* is designed by *Olodumare* and his divinity, *Orisanla.* In Yoruba Philosophy, the human person is viewed as a whole rather than being comprised of separate parts that are given more than others as is the case in Western Traditional Metaphysics philosophy. In other words, the human person in the Yoruba philosophy is closely tied with the idea of a personality or inner head called **ori** (Balogun, 2007). It is believed that the human person is made up of two aspects—the physical, which comprises of ***ara*** (human body), and the spiritual, consisting of ***emi*** (life-giving entity) and ***ori*** (inner head or bearer of human destiny). This is sometimes described by some scholars as a tripartite conception of the human person with the breakdown into ***Ara*** (human body), ***Emi*** (life giving entity), and ***Ori*** (inner head or bearer of human destiny). Recently, scholars like Kola Abimbola brought in the concept of ***ese*** (inner legs and symbol of human efforts) as the fourth component of human person in Yoruba thought (Abimbola, 1970, 2006; Adegboyega, 1998; Adekoya, 2010; Balogun, 2007).

The Yoruba also conceived the human body (*ara*), which is purely physical to comprise other vital and fundamental organs such as *opolo* (brain), *ifun* (intestine), and *okan* (physical heart). *Opolo* is the part of the human body that is responsible for thought and consciousness. It is a material component located in the human head and it is capable of performing mental and physical activities. According to Gbadegesin (1983: 150), '*opolo* is recognized as the live wire of thought and ratiocinate activities'. Thus, when a Yoruba person says '*opolo re tidaaru*' (it means the person is insane) or '*ko niopolo*' (which literally means he does not have a brain), it signifies a lack of intelligence (or that the person lacks the mental capacity to use his brain properly) or such a person is mentally unstable. And when the Yoruba asserts '*opolo pipe*' (someone with a complete brain), it refers to one who is intelligent and mentally fit.

Another important component of *ara* (human body) is *okan* (physical heart). *Okan* is recognised as the seat of emotion, responsible for the circulation of blood, storing information, and processing emotion. Aside from the physical attributes of circulation of blood, it also performs psychological functions; as such when a Yoruba man or woman wants to encourage or motivate a person, the advice is '*se okan re giri*' (build up your psyche), when a person is in difficult situation or encounters misfortune, the counsel is '*ma baokan je*' (do not be disheartened) and also when a person is referred to by the Yoruba as '*eni to niokan*' (which literally means he has a heart) it connotes that the fellow is brave or courageous.

Okan and *opolo* are said to work hand in hand. Idowu, (1962:78) noted that 'before the information is processed by the body after the sensory information is transformed into *opolo* (brain), it must go through *okan* first for the purpose of memory'. So, as *opolo* processes thought and consciousness, *okan* is important for the recollection and storage of information. All the above examples confirm that, in the traditional Yoruba perspective, *okan*, which is physical has the ability to perform both physical and mental functions because activities like bravery and courage are purely mental.

Ifun (intestine), another component of *ara* (body) a physical entity, is a waste storage facility within the human body and helps to ensure stability. As an organ, *ifun* (intestine) is also responsible for ensuring strength and resilience, which are mental processes. Hence, when the Yoruba asserts '*oni funkan*' (a person with one intestine), it translates to a weak person or someone who is not resilient or gives up easily on any issue.

According to Cleveland Clinic Medical Professional (2020), researchers have ascertained that a lesser-known nervous system in the human gut (also referred to as the 'second brain') interacts with the brain in the head. Together, 'the two brains' (that is the brain in the head and the nervous system in the gut), play a key role in certain diseases and affect the overall health of an individual. Research has shown that the gut-brain axis, the communication network between the two brains, is involved in various physiological processes, including digestion, immunity, and metabolism. Any disruption in this communication can lead to various health issues, such as inflammatory bowel disease and other related diseases.

This is further corroborated by another modern research (Karolinska Institute, 2020) which states that the gut also known as the gastrointestinal tract, which is approximately seven-metre long, has its own functionally distinct neurons. Since this enteric nervous system (ENS) operates autonomously, it is sometimes referred to as the 'second' or 'abdominal' brain which affects the mood, behaviour, and emotions through the gut-brain axis.

Thus, just like saying that a person has an active enteric nervous system (ENS) in medical term, the Yoruba says, *oni kun lile,* which literally means to be strong-willed or strongly determined, the Yoruba is trying to show that *ikun* (gut) perfoms rational activities. *Ifun*, *opolo*, and *okan* are fundamental organs in the human body that form the physicomaterial makeup of the human personality with definitive functions and concurrently perform immaterial functions (Delbert, 2020). Moreover, the gut, which is literally translated either as *ikun* (a general term used to refer to any of the organs contained in the gastrointestinal tractor or abdominal cavity) or *ifun-ounje* (intestinal tract responsible for food digestion).

Hence, a careful analysis of *ara* (human body) with its vital organs shows clearly that these organs perform both material and immaterial functions in a harmonious manner without any form of contradiction. The immaterial aspect of *eniyan* (human person) comprises *Emi* (life-giving entity), *ori* (inner head), and sometimes *ese* (inner leg). After the creation of the human body designed by *Orisanla* (Arc divinity), *emi* (life) is given to the body by *Olodumare* (high deity), which in return activates the lifeless body of the human person. Makinde refers to *emi* as the 'divine breath' of *Olodumare. Emi* is vital to the conception of *eniyan* because it is considered an immortal entity and the life force of the human person.

Emi is the activating element of existence and consciousness. According to Abimbola (1970: 78), *emi* does not perish, rather when a person dies, it returns to *orun* (heaven) and takes its place among the ancestors. This is captured in Makinde's words:

> The Yoruba sees the body as a protector of the soul because the soul lives in the body as a person dwells in a house. But while a house remains a home, although there might be nobody living in it, the body without the soul is dead and destruction of the body is an automatic disappearance of the soul. While the demise of the soul also means death of the body (1984: 192).

It should be pointed out that in Makinde's narrative, the soul and *emi* (a life-giving entity) are used interchangeably, and as such the soul, in the above quotation, actually refers to *emi*, and once *emi* departs from the body, it becomes lifeless. The *emi* is believed to be imperishable due to the fact that it originated from *Olodumare* (God). Hence while *ara* (body), created from the earth decays and perishes, after death, *emi* returns to its creator. Care must be taken not to confuse *emi* with the soul or mind in Western philosophy. This is because e*mi* is a life-activating entity given to the lifeless body by *Olodumare* after *Orisanla* has finished with the molding of *ara*.

Another immaterial aspect of the human personality is *Ori* (inner head). *Ori* is responsible for the activity and worth of man in the material world. *Ori* is the bearer of destiny and the essence, which guides the life and activities of a person (Balogun, 2007: 18). *Ori* for the Yoruba can be acquired in different ways. According to Adegboyega (1998: 34), it can be affixed at creation, which is known as Ayanmo (that which is affixed), or received while kneeling (Akunlegba), or chosen while kneeling (Akunleyan), or that which has been written (Akosile).

Gbadegesin (1999: 36) notes that '*ori* has a dual ch*ara*cter, in that, it refers to the physical head, and also the make-up of the human person'. The Yoruba interpret *ori* as the inner head responsible for human destiny rather than literally meaning physical head. *Ori* is an immaterial entity, an indicator of a person's purpose in life synonymous to the 'chi' (spiritual guide) in Igbo tradition. A person can either receive a good *ori* or bad *ori* depending on the nature of his given or chosen *ori* at the house of the potter known as *Ajala.* According to Abimbola (1970: 163), '*Ajala* is believed to be an incorrigible debtor, a drunkard, and an irresponsible creator', and therefore is by his ch*ara*cter capable of molding good and bad heads (*oris*). This is why some *ori* are good while some are bad because he is believed to have made some carelessly due to his irresponsible nature.

A fourth element added by Kola Abimbola (1970: 85) is *ese* (leg), a physical component of the human person. It is believed that though *ori* is responsible for human destiny; it cannot operate properly without the support of *ese* (leg) in ensuring that human beings get to their destination both physically and spiritually. *Ese* here refers not only to the physical leg responsible for movement but signifies human efforts. Although the human person is predestined based on the choice of the *ori*, a person cannot achieve success or fulfil his destiny without effort and struggle even though he possesses a good *ori*.

Ese, therefore, represents hard work, struggle, and human effort. It involves decisive struggle to achieve desired results and outcome in the material world. Thus, Abimbola believes that *ori* alone does not determine the human personality but usually involves the support of *ese* (leg). This is why the Yoruba believe that whatever your *ori* has destined you to be in life, it is your ese that will take you there. This is explained more succinctly in the words of Abimbola (1970):

> It must be emphasized however, that the Yorùbá concept of the choice of destiny through *ori* also emphasizes the need for hard work to bring to fruition the potentiality for success represented by the choice of a good *ori*. This leads us to believe in *ese* (leg) as an important ingredient of human personality. *Ese* (leg) is regarded by the Yorùbá as a vital part of the human personality, both in a physical and spiritual sense. *Ese*, for the Yorùbá, is the symbol of power, strife and activity. It is therefore an element which enables a man to struggle and function adequately in life so that he may bring to realization whatever has been marked out for him by the choice of *ori*. Like *ori*, *ese* is regarded as an *orisa* (lesser deity) which must be catered for in order to achieve success. Therefore, when a man makes sacrifices to his *ori*, part of the sacrifice is also offered to *ese* (p. 85).

This informs why the Yoruba put emphasis on hard work and good character, so as to ensure that the individual achieves his purpose in life through honesty with a good moral character, known as *iwa*.

The Yoruba concept of a person recognises a harmonious performance of the material and immaterial functions by *ara* (human body) and its vital organs, such as *Okan*, *Opolo,* and *Ifun*, even though they can be said to be physical and can be perceived in concrete terms. By implication, it means that, for the Yoruba Yoruba thinkers, mental activities such as thinking can be attributed to the functioning of physical organs, like *Opolo*, *Ifun,* etc. In addition, it is also obvious from our analysis, that a single organ in the Yoruba concept of person cannot be solely held responsible for the performance of either material or immaterial activities, unlike in, say, cartesian dualism where the mind is solely responsible for the performance of mental activities. The Yoruba do not have such a concept of mind, and this explains why there is no Yoruba equivalent for the concept of mind since no single organ can be pinpointed, in their own analysis, as solely responsible for performing mental activities (Makinde, 1984). Thus, any attempt to equate mind with *okan* (physical heart) as argued by some scholars will not only be conceptually wrong but amount to misinterpretation and distortion of the Yoruba concept of person, which arose as a result of undue influence of Westernization (Abimbola, 1970; Balogun, 2007; Gbadegesin, 1991). The point becomes clearer when one realizes that for traditional Yoruba thinkers, mental activities are not attributed to a single organ or component of a person, likewise, physical functions are not altogether attributed to the physical or material element of a person. In the Yoruba conception of person, the material functions and immaterial functions are jointly performed by both physical and spiritual elements of the human being as exemplified in the case of *ese* (leg), which acts as support in fulfilling human destiny (*ori*); and *opolo* (brain), which functions as the seat of cognitive and logical reasoning as well as emotive projections, and so on.

It is based on this analysis of the Yoruba concept of person that I believe informed the temptations to argue that the Yoruba concept of a person fits into the framework of central state materialism. This is because the material organs/components of the human person carry out immaterial functions. However, this perception is wrong and does not do justice to Yoruba thought; rather we believe that traditional Yoruba thinkers can actually be referred to as dualists. However, the Yoruba dualistic view should not be confused with the Western dualistic theory or the Cartesian dualism.

3.3 Cartesian Dualism

In Cartesian philosophy, a person is distinctly divided into mind and body, a form of dualism that ensures the bifurcation of human person into mind and body and each of these organs does not interfere with the activities of the other (Howard, 2023). In Cartesian dualism, which is associated with Rene Descartes, human body is solely and distinctly responsible for physical processes such as; walking, dancing, clapping, and so on, while mind is also distinctly responsible for mental processes such as thinking and decision making (Descartes, 1996). The bifurcation of the human person into mind and body led to the traditional mind–body problem, a major philosophical problem in Western philosophy which focuses on the relationship between the body, that is purely physical, and the mind, which is purely mental (Ducasse, 1961). In other words, the watertight distinction between mind and body, as exemplified by Descartes, heralded the traditional mind–body problem, which centres on the relationship and the point of interaction between the mind and the body, and this problem is still looking for a solution from philosophers of mind till today (Howard, 2023).

The traditional mind-body problem does not only focus on the composition of a person but tries to unravel the nature of the relationship and the point of intersection between a person that is uniquely physical and non-physical. It raises further questions, such as: Can the mind, which is immaterial, interact with the body, which is purely physical?

Descartes is widely known for his theory of psychophysical interactionism, which stipulates that the mind and body through two different entities, interact at the part of the brain known as the pineal gland (Nellickappilly, 2018). In other words, Cartesian dualism recognises the fact that mind and body are fundamentally different, nonetheless, the two still interact at the point of the pineal gland. The above Cartesian argument has been a subject of controversy amongst Philosophers and Scholars as the pineal gland, as we have come to discover, is merely the body's biological clock, regulating the body's circadian cycle.

3.4 A Critique of Central State Materialism

Various theories have been postulated by Western philosophers of mind in a bid to resolve the mind-body problem. These include theories such as interactionism, monism, dualism, and materialism, but none of these theories has successfully resolved it.

In my previous paper on *The Nature of Human Person in Traditional African Thought*, I argued that the traditional mind–body problem, as exposed in Western philosophy of mind, is non-existent in the Yoruba concept of person. Furthermore, I discussed the various theories put forth by Western philosophers in trying to resolve the problem without any recorded success. I tried to show that the traditional mind–body problem does not exist in traditional Yoruba thought based on the Yoruba conception of the human person, which recognises that mental processes can be performed by the physical organs of the human body.

Hence, the above discourse on the interpretation of human person within the Yoruba thought system could imply a central state materialistic interpretation (Abimbola, 1970, 2006; Adegboyega, 1998; Adekoya, 2010). In other words, the Yoruba concept of person can be given a central state materialistic interpretation (Green, 1981). For instance, a peripheral look at the Yoruba concept of person suggests that mental processes like thinking, bravery, cowardice, resourcefulness, and so on, can be attributed to the physical organs of *ara* (human body), such as '*okan* (heart) '***o'****opolo* (brain), *ifun* (intestines). This kind of orientation is not fundamentally different from the thesis of the central state materialists, which stipulates, in my view that mental processes are either identical with physical processes or can be explained in purely physico-chemical terms (Green, 1981).

Furthermore, the postulation of the Yoruba that all the immaterial constituents of a person such as *emi* (life-giving entity), ' ori(the bearer of destiny), and *ese*(symbol of spiritual efforts), usually manifest in physical terms is another obvious reason. For example, ***'ori'*** is represented by a physical head and ***ese*** is represented by physical legs, all of which are responsible for the performance of mental activities as well, showing that the interpretation depicts a central state materialist or the identical theorists.

However, care must be taken not to regard the traditional Yoruba as a confusionist, because the traditional Yoruba believe that first and foremost, a human person is a purely physical entity backed up by spiritual forces. Hence, they begin explanation of any event or any phenomenon with the natural, which may eventually be backed up with spiritual explanations after the natural points have been exhausted. As a matter of fact, it has been argued by some scholars, that the activities of some spiritual forces like theoretical entities such as spirits and gods, are extensions of natural explanations (Balogun, 2005: 50–63).

To this end, the Yoruba believe that those physical organs are capable of performing those mental activities attributed to them, because of the material nature of human person. This is coupled with the understanding that in traditional Yoruba cosmology, there is a thin division between the physical and the spiritual. Yet it will be conceptually wrong to ignore the aspect of the spiritual forces backing the natural explanation and that is why the Yoruba can never be regarded as a Cartesian dualist but better regarded as what I call a harmonious dualist, since there is always a harmonious interaction between physical and immaterial organs, physical and mental explanations.

Moreover, all the characteristics given to physical entities by the central state materialists such as being able to be located in space, being concrete, having a definite mass as well as being visible, also are the defining characteristics of *ara* (human body), which is a component of person in the Yoruba concept. Where some internal organs of a person like *okan* (the heart), even though physical are not easily visible, it does not mean that it cannot be seen because if the human body is dissected, the *okan* would be exposed and therefore visible, whereas the cartesian pineal gland cannot be seen even when the brain is dissected. This resemblance between the two has given rise to the erroneous thought by several individuals and scholars that the Yoruba fits well into the central state materialist.

This paper argues further that it will be erroneous to reduce the Yoruba to central state materialists as this negates the Yoruba belief in spiritual entities and the view that the soul is capable of temporarily leaving the body and occupying space as seen in the cases of witches and other spiritual entities. Suffice to note that, for the Yoruba, there is no watertight distinction between the body, or the physical and spiritual because ***ara*** (physical body) and ***emi*** (life-giving entity) though exist sep*ara*tely, work harmoniously. The validity of this harmonious interaction between the physical and the spiritual organs of a person in Yoruba thought further confirms that the Yoruba cannot be classified as a central state materialist since in the central state materialist's theory, any form of interaction whether harmonious or inharmonious does not exist.

Furthermore, the Yoruba belief in dualism, which recognises a clear distinction between physical and spiritual entities despite their abilities to interact, provides a strong argument against categorizing the Yoruba as central state materialist. This is particularly evident in the fact that the Yoruba view 'physical' and 'spiritual organs' as separate entities, whereby the spiritual organs possess unique functions that are neither identical to physical organs nor their process.

Likewise, the watertight distinction between physical and spiritual organs as espoused by Descartes, does not hold water since there is no single organ that can be held responsible for mental processes in Yoruba thought. Hence, the Yoruba does not have the equivalence of the word 'mind'. To argue that the Yoruba has the equivalence of 'mind' will only amount to conceptual distortions and imposition of Western ideas on Yoruba worldview. It is on this basis that scholars like Balogun (2019) have argued for conceptual decolonization of mind.

It must be noted that the central state materialists' response to the traditional mind-body problem is fundamentally different from the Yoruba's response to the same problem. While the central state materialists approach the problem by arguing that brain processes are identical or synonymous with bodily processes, which no longer gives room for any form of interaction, the Yoruba attempt to respond to the issue by suggesting a harmonious relationship between the physical and spiritual elements of a person. This necessitates the argument of some scholars that the traditional mind-body problem is a mirage or non-existent in the Yoruba concept of person.

As I end this write-up, a deep reflection on the Yoruba worldview, cultural values, and lifestyles, will definitely suggest that the Yoruba are not likely to be central state materialists. The traditional Yoruba thinkers, for instance, believe in the world of the ancestors, and as such teach some moral doctrines that may make one end up as an ancestor, which ordinarily violates the principles of materialism. The Yoruba society is a polytheistic society with some events attributed to the activities of multiple gods. The success and failure in life's endeavours among the Yoruba are often attributed to the kind of *ori* (inner head), which one has chosen in the primordial rather than their physical activities or efforts. The dualism of the Yoruba is reflected in everything that pertains to them and like a proverbial saying that a bird cannot fly with one wing, the spiritual elements cannot be divorced from the physical. This is not to say to the traditional Yoruba, that the spiritual is a product of the physical. The traditional Yoruba are not property dualists who believe in the existence of one material substance in the world, which is physical, but with two essentially different kinds of properties (physical and mental properties) (Vintiadis, 2013), but they rather believe in both physical and spiritual components of human person with the ability to interact harmoniously, not spirit as a property of the physical. This further explains the Yoruba belief of *emi* (life-giving entity) going to *Orun* ('the after life'), after the termination of human body (*ara*), which is purely physical.

3.5 Conclusion

It is pertinent to end on the note that while it is true that there are elements of central state materialism in the Yoruba concept of person, it will amount to a gross misunderstanding to classify the Yoruba people as exclusively central state materialists. This will overlook the essential role of spiritual entities in their understanding of personhood and their preferred means of explanation. While the chapter does not claim that all issues relating to the Yoruba concept of person have been exhausted, as it gives room for further research and interrogation on the subject of 'person' in Yoruba thought, it has in no doubt refuted the thesis that the Yoruba concept of person fits very well into the framework of central state materialism.

References

Abimbola, W. (1970). The concept of human personality. In *La nation de Personne en Afrique Noire* (Vol. 544, pp. 73–89). Centre National de la Recherche Scientifique.

Abimbola, K. (2006). *Yoruba culture: A philosophical account*. Iroko.

Adegboyega, O. (1998). *Destiny: The unmanifested being (A critical exposition)*. African Odyssey.

Adekoya, D. O. (2010). *The concept of Eniyan in Yorùbá thought system*. An unpublished thesis written 2010, Department of Philosophy, University of Ibadan.

Balogun, O. A. (2005). The role of gods and theoretical entities: An extension of natural explanations in traditional African thought. *WAJOPS: West African Journal of Philosophical Studies, Enugu, 8*, 50–63.

Balogun, O. A. (2007). The concept of Ori and human destiny in traditional Yorùbá thought: A soft-deterministic interpretation. *Nordic Journal of African Studies, 16*(1), 116–130.

Balogun, O. (2019). *African Philosophy Reflection on Yoruba Metaphysics and Jurisprudence. Xcel Publishers.*

Cleveland Clinic Medical Professional. (2020). *Gut-brain connection.* https://my.clevelandclinic.org/health/treatments/16358-gut-brain-connection#:~:text=Because%20the%20enteric%20nervous%20system,in%20our%20bodies%20and%20in. Accessed Mar 2021.

Delbert, C. (2020). Hey, there's a second brain in your gut. *Popular mechanics.* https://www.popularmechanics.com/science/health/a34934637/gut-brain-science/#:~:text=Hey%2C%20There's%20a%20Second%20Brain%20in%20Your%20Gut&text=New%20research%20reveals%20that%20the,but%20isn't%20well%20understood. Accessed Mar 2021.

Descartes, R. [1641] (1996). Meditation VI'. In *Meditations on the first philosophy* (J. Cottingham, Trans.). Cambridge University Press.

Ducasse, C. (1961). In defence of dualism. In S. Hook (Ed.), *Dimensions of mind.* Collier.

Feigl, H. (1967). *The mental and the physical the essay and the postscripts.* University of Minnesota Press.

Gbadegesin, S. (1983). Destiny, Personality and the Ultimate Reality of human Existence: A Yoruba's Perspective. *A paper presented at the Institute of Ultimate Reality and Meaning.*

Gbadegesin, S. (1991). *Eniyan: The Yoruba concept of a person, in African philosophy: Traditional Yoruba and contemporary African realities* (The African philosophy reader). Routledge.

Gbadegesin, S. (1999). *African Philosophy: Traditional Yoruba Philosophy and Contemporary African Realities.* Chicago: Gateway Publishers.

Green, R. (1981). Central state materialism and consciousness. *Philosophy, 56*(215), 106–113. https://doi.org/10.1017/S0031819100049822

Howard, R. (2023). Dualism. In Zalta, E. N. & Nodelman, U. (Eds.), *The Stanford encyclopedia of philosophy.* https://plato.stanford.edu/archives/spr2023/entries/dualism/. Accessed Mar 2023.

Idowu, B. (1962). *Olódùmarè: God in Yorùbá belief.* Longman Publishers.

Jackson, F. (2008). David M. Armstrong (1926–). In A. P. Martinich & E. Sosa David (Eds.), *Blackwell companion to philosophy: A companion to analytic philosophy* (pp. 413–415). Blackwell Publishing.

Karolinska Institute. (2020). New fundamental knowledge of the 'Abdominal Brain'. In *Neuroscience.* Press Office – Karolinska Institute. https://neurosciencenews.com/ent-neurodevelopment-17376/. Accessed Mar 2021.

Makinde, A. (1984). An African concept of human personality: The Yorùbá example. *Ultimate Reality and Meaning Inter-Disciplinary Studies in the Philosophy of Understanding, 7*(3), 189.

Nellickappilly, S. (2018). Rene descartes: The mind-body dualism. In *Aspects of Western Philosophy,* 10. https://www.academia.edu/12185411/Aspects_of_Western_Philosophy. Accessed June 2020.

Place, U. T. (1956). Is consciousness a brain process? *British Journal of Psychology, 47*(1), 44–50.

Polger, T. W. (2009). Identity theories. *Philosophy Compass, 4*(5), 822–834. Blackwell Publishing Ltd.

Smart, J. J. C. (1959). Sensations and brain processes. *The Philosophical Review, 68*(2), 141–156. Duke University Press.

Vintiadis, E. (2013). Property dualism. In *Introduction to philosophy: Philosophy of mind.* Chapter 4. https://press.rebus.community/intro-to-phil-of-mind/chapter/property-dualism/. Accessed Mar 2021.

Chapter 4
Between Sense-Phenomenalism, Equi-phenomenalism, Quasi-physicalism, and Proto-panpsychism

Ada Agada

Abstract African philosophy of mind is still a developing area of African philosophy. The main issues driving debates in the field include the essential components of the human being (whether this being is wholly physical or partly physical and partly non-material), the relation of the body with the mind or consciousness, whether there is a unifying principle that grounds both body (matter) and consciousness, and whether there is an aspect of the human being that survives biological death. Physicalist theories such as sense-phenomenalism, equi-phenomenalism, and quasi-physicalism have been proposed by some African philosophers as theoretical frameworks for thinking and rethinking the relation of the body with consciousness in the African universe. This chapter examines the plausibility of the three frameworks and argues that the persistence of the quality of subjective experience and the seeming independence of the subjective sphere require a recourse to panpsychism as a theoretical framework that better accounts for the fact of subjective experience. The chapter proposes a moderate version of panpsychism labelled proto-panpsychism as a metaphysical framework that adequately accounts for the phenomenon of consciousness while unifying the African universe of material and non-material entities.

Keywords Physicalism · Quasi-physicalism · Sense-phenomenalism · Equi-phenomenalism · Panpsychism · Proto-pansychism · African philosophy · *Mood* · *Sunsum*

A. Agada (✉)
Centre for Leadership Ethics in Africa, University of Fort Hare, Alice, South Africa

Conversational School of Philosophy, Calabar, Nigeria
e-mail: adaagada@gmail.com

A. D. Attoe et al. (eds.), *Conversations on African Philosophy of Mind, Consciousness and Artificial Intelligence*,
https://doi.org/10.1007/978-3-031-36163-0_4

4.1 Introduction

The worldviews of traditional African societies reveal that these societies have for centuries reflected on the phenomenon of consciousness and the reality of spiritual entities like God. These societies speculated that there must be a hidden or invisible, enduring aspect of the human person that grounds the subjective experience of thinking, feeling, willing, etc. Consequently, these African societies postulated the existence of a soul component of the human being. This chapter briefly but concisely examines some physicalist, quasi-physicalist, and panpsychist responses of a number of African philosophers to the puzzles about the relation of consciousness with matter that are already embedded in the traditional worldviews of African societies. The main focus of the chapter is the African philosophy of mind. However, the chapter will invoke theories propounded by non-African philosophers of mind where such theories help illuminate the issues under discussion.

The physicalist response, represented in this chapter by sense-phenomenalism, equi-phenomenalism, and quasi-physicalism, champions physicalism as an appropriate theoretical framework for understanding the relation between matter and consciousness. Physicalism is the view that reality is fundamentally physical or explicable in the framework of scientific knowledge of the world (see, for instance, Segun, 2019). The quasi-physicalist response championed by Wiredu (1983, 1996) and Kwame (2004) is a moderate version of physicalism that leaves the door open to the possibility that matter has inherent powers to produce invisible effects which may account for the seeming independence of the subjective sphere of experience. The proto-panpsychist response pursues a metaphysical framework that unifies the African universe of material and non-material realities with the postulation of a universal event, or *mood,* which grounds materiality and non-materiality (see Agada, 2019, 2020).

Accordingly, Sect. 4.2 of the chapter highlights the strengths and weaknesses of sense-phenomenalism and equi-phenomenalism, while Sect. 4.3 weighs the merit and demerit of the quasi-physicalist response. Section 4.4 proposes proto-panpsychism as a viable alternative to physicalism and quasi-physicalism for the reason that the former asserts the fundamentality of consciousness, as well as the fundamentality of matter, in a universe where reality necessarily expresses itself as a consciousness-matter unity in the most fundamental event of the universe which is dubbed *mood.*

4.2 Sense-Phenomenalism and Equi-phenomenalism

The great success recorded by science in the last two centuries deeply influenced the thought of philosophers around the world, leading to the eclipsing of religious explanations of the universe. It became fashionable to fit philosophical assumptions within the empirical framework with which science operates. The immediate implication of this trend for the philosophy of mind is the rise in popularity of physicalism which asserts the monistic view that reality is physical. This means there is one basic stuff of the universe and this stuff is physical and ultimately amenable to scientific investigation and explanation. While physicalism has been highly successful in explaining many aspects of the world, it has seemingly met a brick wall where understanding the phenomenon of consciousness is concerned, given the difficulty that comes with reducing consciousness to the body (brain states and neural functions). Consciousness seems to have a freedom quality, or raw feels, that asserts independence of bodily functions. Chimakonam (2019) and Segun (2019) have tried to show that this independence is illusory by simply putting faith in the brute presence of the body.

Chimakonam's physicalist framework, sense-phenomenalism, aims primarily at establishing what he calls a body-centred theory of personal identity, drawing on a presumed African social identification convention that prioritises bodily characteristics over first-person reports of responses to stimuli in the environment. In seeking to achieve this objective, Chimakonam pays critical attention to the phenomenon of consciousness in a manner deserving serious consideration. The hard problem of consciousness, which Chalmers (2015) greatly emphasized in the Western philosophy of the mind, centres on the difficulty of accounting for subjective experience (first-person report of mental states) in purely functional neuro-scientific terms (third-person account of mental phenomena). The intimacy of experience, or the qualia effect, appears to gain a certain level of independence that has led non-reductive philosophers of mind to consider consciousness as either dependent on the body but describable in non-physicalist language or that it is produced by neural processes and then somehow becomes ontologically distinct from the body or that it is just as fundamental in the universe as matter. The second and third possibilities water down physicalism and mark a shift towards panpsychism, the claim that consciousness is fundamental in the universe. Chimakonam rejects all three views. He firmly rejects the hard problem of consciousness and all non-reductive and panpsychist theories of mind in the belief that subjective experience itself is a mirage.

In a fashion reminiscent of David Hume, Chimakonam distinguishes between ideas of reflection and sensation. He reckons that the admissibility of this distinction supposedly demystifies qualia (subjective experience) by accounting for it in terms of what Chimakonam calls *sata*. For him, ideas of reflection arise from the exercise of the imagination while those of sensation follow from the operation of bodily sense organs. Ideas of reflection are "figments of our imagination" while ideas of sensation are *sata,* which refers to "sense-organ-receptible neural codes or information" (2019, 16). The brain receives data or sensory information from specific organs and processes the data before relaying the same to the sense organs. Chimakonam uses the term *sata* to distinguish between information received by the senses from the environment (data) from information processed by the brain and once again received by the sense organs (*sata).* For him, it is this body-mediated function of the sense organs, the sensory reception of processed data, that is mistaken for experience (in the sense of qualia).

Chimakonam's dismissal of subjective experience as a figment of the imagination reveals his struggle to escape reductive physicalism by deploying an eliminativist tactic of condemning subjective experience to unreality, while, paradoxically, assuming that the experiential sphere achieves a form of independence of neural processes. By asserting that experience is an idea or is idea-based, he unwittingly lends credence to the non-reductive intuition that the private status of subjective experience calls for rethinking the assumption that there is a direct correspondence between physical brain states and mental states. Imagining as a form of thinking or reflection is a goal-oriented function that is no longer dependent on a motivating brain state but becomes integral to the aspirations of the whole person. A figment is something not based in reality. If an idea of reflection is not grounded in reality, it will appear that the power to conjure the figment exceeds the powers of the brain as a bodily organ. Subjective experience may well actualize itself in the sense of organizing its processes according to its own inner principles, which are yet to be discovered. This position, which is implicit in the assumption of the ideality of subjective states, is further revealed when Chimakonam denies the brain the power of sensation. He notes that subjective experience does not take place in the *inside;* it does not happen in a place called the mind, and not in the physical brain.

Sensation, that is, subjective experience, happens in the *outside,* somewhere in and around the sense organs. It is worth remembering that for Chimakonam, data are raw objects of the senses while *sata* (a neologism derived from the combination of sense receptivity and data) are ideas, what he claims are mistaken for subjective experience. It is the speed of the neural function of perception of stimuli and reception of *sata* that gives us the impression of internality and the accompanying puzzle of what-is-it-like, according to Chimakonam. Even as an eliminative physicalist, Chimakonam must admit that sensations, as subjective phenomena, are private. Hence, he attributes ideality or unrealness to subjective experience. Private experience can be communicated. For instance, one can describe the pleasure of eating oranges, but it cannot be participated in by the listener. Oranges may be sweet, but each person's pleasure is uniquely their own. The displacement of subjective experience from the presumed mysterious place called the mind to somewhere in and around the sense organs does not solve the problem of qualia, the maligned hard problem of Chalmers, because another mystery is created when we try to identify the site of *sata* actualization in sense organs like the eye or tongue. If Chimakonam insists on his empiricist approach, it will be in order to demand that we be able to empirically observe the phenomenal process of *sata* reception, distinct from the process of neural transmission of data, as it occurs at the site of sense organs. This observation is impossible because experience is a subjective phenomenon. Neural transmission of data from the brain is not itself phenomenal. It is the first-person report that is phenomenal.

The reference to ideas of reflection as figments of the imagination does not help Chimakonam's commitment to strong physicalism. By Chimakonam's account, subjective experience is a shadow, a figment that arises as a result of neural activities. The presumed unrealness of subjective experience is, in fact, its ideality, or privacy. If we assume that the neocortex and thalamus are the parts of the brain responsible for imaginative functions, then we admit that subjective experience has a bodily (brain) basis. Ideas of reflection, and subjective experience specifically, become real rather than mere figments. Consequently, Chimakonam merely avoids mentioning the unmentionable, the hard problem of consciousness, on account of its difficulty. Qualia is not eliminated by merely referring to it as a shadow. The shadow persists and swirls in its special intimate sphere of operation where it somehow asserts the independence of neural processes. Rather than demonstrating the non-existence of something we may call the mind, Chimakonam appears to be simply asserting that reality is fundamentally physical and subjective experience is a necessary function of physical neural processes, a stance embraced by Segun whose commitment to non-reductive physicalism leads him to rehabilitate the qualia element that Chimakonam discards, as I will soon show.

Chimakonam's struggle with the elimination of subjective experience is further revealed in the way he repeatedly uses the term experience (as a private first-person report) even when holding that there is no such thing as experience (as a private first-person report). He notes that: "Since the human brain was not designed to *experience* sensations, the actual *experiences* of the output occur externally at the senses…sata are like shadows of things…they are not the *experiences* of things…" (2019, 16, italics mine). It will appear that the shadowiness of *sata* is not an indication of it being a figment or not existing but rather that the shadowiness indicates a fundamental status of experience that does not oppose physicalist monism but suggests a pan-psychist monism that defends the claim that materiality and non-materiality are two aspects of reality. This reality can be understood in terms of the most fundamental principle or event of the universe which organizes beings in such a way that the shadow (experience) and the presumed substance (matter) accompany each other *necessarily.* Segun attempts to move towards this position; however, like Chimakonam, he is too beholden to physicalism to fully embrace the seemingly dualistic thesis. I will advance the view enunciated above as proto-panpsychism in Sect. 4.4 of this chapter.

Impressed by the private status of subjective experience, Segun deviates from Chimakonam's radical physicalism and asserts that mentality, or consciousness, and body, or matter, are equi-phenomena, one in relation to the other. His notion of equi-phenomenalism, therefore, aspires to reconcile first-person/subjective account of consciousness that privileges privacy and third-person/objective account that reduces consciousness to neural functions in line with current neuroscience. Equi-phenomenalism accords equal weight to the first-person and third-person accounts. According to Segun (2019, 56), equi-phenomenalism is a non-reductive physicalist theory that proposes that mental properties are "*necessary* products of consciousness" and consciousness itself is "a necessary product that must be experienced simultaneously with neural activities." He also asserts that "subjective experiences are necessary products of consciousness" (2019, 56). By stressing necessity, Segun hopes to distinguish his theory from epiphenomenalism, a reductive physicalist theory that barely acknowledges consciousness by making it a mere by-product of brain states. However, there is some confusion in the statement of what consciousness is.

Segun seems to separate mental properties from consciousness when he notes that the former is derived from the latter, thereby implying the ontological independence of consciousness as a kind of mental substance. But he is adamant in his rejection of substance dualism; so, one may infer that Segun is asserting that the sphere of mental properties constitutes consciousness, or subjective experience, and that consciousness itself is a necessary product of brain and neural processes. By mentioning necessity, Segun is referring simply to the simultaneity of the occurrence of subjective experience and brain states, when mental states are "experienced simultaneously with neural activities" (2019, 56). The necessity means that there can be no brain state without a consciousness state, all things being equal. In his words, "the physical processes of the brain will not be possible without their correlate subjective experience" (2019, 60). In asserting the phenomenal equality of states of consciousness and brain states, Segun acknowledges the independent-like existence of subjective experience even as he uses the traditional physicalist framework as a general explanatory framework. Thus, for Segun, consciousness is not ontologically a distinct substance but is rather an unavoidable consequence of brain and neural processes, which is required for physical states to be possible. While equi-phenomenalism deals with the problem of qualia more effectively than sense-phenomenalism by admitting that consciousness is in some way fundamental, fealty to physicalism does not permit Segun to make the bold panpsychist claim that consciousness is a fundamental feature of the universe and not merely dependent on the physical brain. Before I submit the proto-panpsychist claim, I will in the next session briefly examine how quasi-physicalism responds to the possibility of consciousness being a fundamental feature of the world without going far enough to embrace panpsychism.

4.3 Quasi-physicalism

The private status of consciousness, the not-hereness and not-thereness quality of mentalism, motivated Wiredu (1996, 2002) and Kwame (2004) to propose quasi-physicalism as a moderate form of physicalism that can accommodate the possible existence of consciousness forms like spirits in a physical universe. Quasi-physicalism may also accommodate the phenomenon of qualia since it asserts that whereas reality is fundamentally physical, some entities have inherent capacities to manifest in non-physical forms (for instance, God and spirits) and exhibit non-physical or consciousness properties. While consciousness may well be ultimately physical since reality is basically physical, the laws of physics that are claimed to govern the operation of all physical entities and phenomena are not inviolable, according to the quasi-physicalist thesis. To Wiredu (1996, 53), a quasi-physical being is any entity or phenomenon "conceived as spatial but lacking some of the properties of material objects."

The clearest definition of quasi-physicalism is presented by Safro Kwame (2004, 345–346) who notes that: "Quasi-physicalism…stretches the limits of matter or materialism as far as is compatible with what we know or do not know, without embracing dualism. It admits the possibility of quasi-physical objects as belonging to a category between the realm of the obviously physical, i.e. those objects that obey the known laws of physics, and the realm of the so-called spiritual or completely immaterial objects that do not obey any of the known laws of physics." Where Chimakonam adopts a decidedly eliminativist stance and fails to locate consciousness in a physical site (the sense organs), Segun concedes the necessary existence of consciousness. Wiredu goes further yet to admit the logical possibility of consciousness-forms existing in a manner that prompts one to suggest the fundamentality of consciousness within a general physicalist framework, a stance similar to the one adopted by Galen Strawson (2015), a Western philosopher who has defended the compatibility of physicalism with panpsychism. By invoking the laws of physics, Kwame invites us to note that a phenomenon does not have to be directly accessible to the senses to persist within the ambit of physics and be explainable by science. Thus, to say, as the traditional African healer will assert, that there are invisible beings, or spirits, able to influence everyday human activities is tantamount to confessing that it is possible for physical knowledge of the universe to someday become so advanced that what some today consider disembodied consciousness-forms will be explained in intelligible physical language. Thus, quasi-physicalism prepares African philosophy of mind to take the claim of panpsychism seriously, to the effect that not only may consciousness be a necessary product of neural processes (Segun, 2019) but also that it may just as well be intimate with the structure of reality, such that it is everywhere present side by side with physical objects and phenomena (Agada, 2020).

At this point, it is important to briefly show how the concept of quasi-physicalism evolved in African philosophy. The related question of the thinkability and status of disembodied consciousness that interacts with physical phenomena emerged as a focal point of debates in African philosophy of mind, independent of issues in Western philosophy of mind. Quasi-physicalism emerged first as a metaphysical theory aimed at unifying the African universe which is assumed to be a whole of material and non-material parts, physical and spiritual objects. Mbiti (1969) asserted early that the African universe teems with spiritual beings and essences and Gyekye (1995, 72) concurred later when he noted that: "The Akan [African] universe, essentially spiritual, is endowed or charged with varying degrees of force or *sunsum.*" By postulating *sunsum* as a universal vital force underlying and animating everything in the universe, Gyekye seeks to unify the African universe and describe it in terms of a panpsychist monism that seemingly presents the physical as the appearance and arrangement of a fundamental consciousness-form (*sunsum*).

The notion of the fundamentality of *sunsum* as a universal or ubiquitous principle becomes controversial when Gyekye attempts to explain how the *sunsum* constitutes the mind, together with another supposedly non-material element called the *ōkra,* in the specific case of the human being. For Gyekye, the *sunsum* can be understood as referring to any being possessing the power of self-awareness and rationality as well as a universal motive force, which I have already mentioned above. Noting the relation between the mind and *sunsum,* he writes: "As for the mind – when it is not identified with the soul – it may be rendered also by *sunsum,* judging from the functions that are attributed by the Akan thinker to the latter" (1995, 88). The functions include the power of feeling, thinking, imagining, etc. Gyekye (1995, 95) says clearly that it can be predicated of the phenomenon thus: "His *sunsum* is sad." Gyekye refers to the *ōkra* as the soul in the Cartesian sense of a thinking substance distinct from the body.

But since the *sunsum* constitutes the *ōkra,* with the latter being simply a mode of the *sunsum* in the specific case of the human being, it is correct to say the *sunsum* is consciousness considered as fundamental in the universe. The *ōkra* is immortal, according to Gyekye; this implies that the *sunsum* is an eternal principle, as old as the universe. The profound insight from Gyekye that recommends the *sunsum* as underlying all beings in the universe eludes Wiredu who focuses his attack on a presumed dualism in Gyekye that illegitimately introduces Cartesianism into the African philosophy of mind, with the attendant problem of how to explain the interaction of mind and body.

Wiredu rejects Gyekye's interpretation of traditional Akan notions of the mind. He insists that since the Akan regards the universe itself as spatial, nothing in it can assert ultimate independence of the spatio-temporal order; hence, neither the *sunsum* nor the *ōkra* is a pure consciousness-form in the sense of being immaterial (Wiredu, 1983, 1996). Instead, for Wiredu, both principles are quasi-physical, if at all they exist in reality. Even if the notion of *sunsum* is merely a postulate (Wiredu, 2002, 61), there is no way of proving its non-existence. On the other hand, as the seat of subjective experience, we can at least confirm its manifestations when we report our private experiences.

Wiredu is right to question the vagueness of Gyekye's undeveloped panpsychist theory, which seems to deny fundamentality to materiality, but his alternative theory of quasi-physicalism is still beholden to physicalism, just like Segun's theory of equi-phenomenalism. It is incontestable that scientific knowledge of the world is unrivalled by any other kind of knowledge, but one must admit that science has not answered all questions, including the question of why one cannot find qualia (which we unavoidably report in the first person) anywhere in the brain or the sense organs (cf., Chimakonam, 2019) if everything in the world is *ultimately* physical and why there should be qualia at all if the phenomenon is not *necessary.* It will appear that the way of saying that everything is *ultimately* physical, the very invocation of the term *ultimately,* indicates that there is indeed an uneasiness about the problem of subjective experience and that the eliminative physicalist is engaging in some form of dogmatism by rigidly rejecting the possibility of a consciousness sphere existing in fact.

In the next section, I will propose a moderate panpsychist theory that addresses Wiredu's concern about Gyekye's theory of mind, which he believes to have failed in unifying the African universe by making consciousness (*sunsum*) fundamental and, thereby, displacing materiality. In unifying insights from Chimakonam, Segun, Gyekye, and Wiredu, I will propose *mood* as the most fundamental principle in the universe, a unity of equally fundamental poles or aspects (consciousness and matter) of reality that manifests as a consciousness-matter event.

4.4 Proto-panpsychism

Where Chimakonam insists that only what is physical is fundamental, I add that consciousness is also fundamental from the perspective of proto-panpsychism. Where Wiredu, Kwame, and Segun are reluctant to concede to the structural independence of consciousness, by which I mean the arrangement of consciousness types side by side with physical types to complete reality, I unambiguously adopt a panpsychist stance that accords equal value to consciousness, without adding, as Segun does, that consciousness is a necessary product of neural processes. Where Gyekye identifies *sunsum* as the most fundamental principle in the universe and fails to iterate the fundamentality of materiality, I avoid the seeming dualist trap by presenting *mood* as the most fundamental principle in the universe and as a unified consciousness-matter event. I use matter here in the sense of body or that which is physical. Since the most fundamental principle of the universe that informs both consciousness types and physical types is an event, an unintended dualism of the Gyekye type can no longer be assumed because an event is here understood as being in the process of becoming (see Ramose, 1999). Becoming indicates a flux state of affairs characterized by a thing's quest to achieve a different state of existence. With being revealing itself basically as becoming, borders lose their inviolability, such that there is constant interaction between two entity types (consciousness and matter) with the quest for a complete state of reality as the interactive bond between the entity types. This stance, of course, means that both entity types are related. The relation is established by their common origin in what I call *mood,* which is the very expression of being as becoming.

Now, proto-panpsychism should not be confused with Chalmers' panprotopsychism which evolves within the Western philosophy of the mind as a direct response to the qualia problem and which adopts a moderate physicalist position that leaves the door open to the possibility of physical objects having proto-conscious essences (see Chalmers, 2015). Proto-panpsychism emerges within African discourse about the nature of the universe; it is first a metaphysical theory that seeks to unify the African universe of material and non-material beings. In the process of unifying the African universe, however, proto-panpsychism sheds light on the relation of consciousness with matter.

I noted elsewhere that: "Proto-panpsychism accepts that matter is fundamental, but it goes on to accept the claim that mindedness is also fundamental as it co exists with matter to co-constitute that which is ultimately real, *mood* as a singular event" (Agada, 2020, 115). As a proto-mind, *mood* is not pure mindedness. *Mood* "marks the boundary between the physical and the immaterial. Immateriality here does not mean a radical absence of matter but rather indicates the dominant phase of mentalism in a universe that is fundamentally a communion of the physical and the mentalistic in a unity defined as yearning" (Agada, 2020, 111). The reference to *mood* as a proto-mind immediately conveys the idea that one is not talking about something that is wholly mentalistic in the sense of pure consciousness. Rather, the term proto-mind indicates that *mood* is constituted by two states of being, with each state necessary to the structure of reality and, therefore, equally important.

Someone impatient with presumably imprecise language will wonder what yearning means. In the proto-panpsychist perspective, yearning refers to the quest of being for its own full realization in all aspects of growth, a quest which is, tragically, undermined by the tendency for things to degenerate and pass out of existence. The yearning for a full state of being can be understood in terms of an internal and external purpose. An internal purpose tells us about how a thing is organized to fulfil functions without the exertion of conscious intelligence, for instance, the mechanism of digestion in animals and neural processes accompanying environmental stimuli. An external purpose involves deploying conscious effort towards the accomplishment of goals of the type associated with human beings and higher animals, such as seeking a mate or improving one's quality of life.

Whether we are talking about what is physical or focusing on consciousness, yearning is the basis for the organization of physical and consciousness phenomena, precisely because everything is animated by *mood*. When we talk about everything being *ultimately* physical regardless of the fact of mental properties existing in the world, we are, in fact, saying that everything is ultimately *mood,* a communion of the physical and the minded in one universal event. As events, entities do not have a rigid consciousness-matter boundary. Rather, we may talk of the dominant phases of reality. When phenomena are in their dominant physical phase, we say a thing is physical, whereas this thing is actually the consciousness-matter event. When phenomena are in their dominant consciousness phase, we say a thing is immaterial, whereas this thing is actually the consciousness-matter event. The necessity of the existence of consciousness, which sense-phenomenalism discounts and which equiphenomenalism and quasi-physicalism acknowledge, attains the status of fundamentality in the proto-panpsychist perspective.

One criticism that may be directed at proto-panpsychism is pointing out the seeming impossibility of determining the shifting boundary separating consciousness types from physical types. When we see a person experiencing a conscious state, for example, pleasure, we cannot from observation determine how the person is co-constituted by consciousness and matter. We only see the body and we can explain the person's mental state in terms of neural processes. Consequently, it may be argued that proto-panpsychism has only a speculative value. However, this objection discounts the privacy of first-person report and overlooks why there is such a report rather than merely the reality of observable brain activity and neural processes. According to the proto-panpsychist account, brain states and neural processes are not pure physical states and processes. These states and processes involve a thing's quest for the attainment of an internal purpose, which constitutes the thing's yearning, the basis for the violation of the consciousness-matter boundary, and the interaction of the two fundamental aspects of *mood.* As the brain is a manifestation of *mood,* it is not a pure physical type. The brain can only be categorized as a physical organ to the extent that it is *mood* persisting in its dominant physical state. The dormant consciousness state of *mood* is present in the brain in any given brain state. The necessary existence of consciousness means that it anticipates the physical wherever it is found.

4.5 Conclusion

In this chapter, I examined four physicalist and panpsychist theories of mind developed by a number of African philosophers, namely, sense-phenomenalism, equi-phenomenalism, quasi-physicalism, and proto-panpsychism. I argue that while sense-phenomenalism satisfies our commonsense intuition that the human body mediates the process of perception and response to stimuli, it fails to satisfactorily account for the privacy of experience. If one adopts an eliminative physicalist stance and subjective experience cannot be located in the brain, which is a bodily organ, it is unlikely that it is located in the sense organs which are also bodily organs. On the other hand, equi-phenomenalism attempts to fill the gap in sense-phenomenalism by establishing consciousness as a necessary product of neural activities. In a similar manner, quasi-physicalism *ab initio* accepts the claim that reality is basically physical and consciousness types are quasi-physical phenomena. Advancing the trajectory initiated by Gyekye, I argued that a moderate panpsychist position that acknowledges the fundamentality of both consciousness and matter unifies the underlying intuitions in equi-phenomenalism and quasi-physicalism that seem to point to the possibility that consciousness and matter may be individually fundamental in the universe. I presented proto-panpsychism as such a moderate panpsychist theory of mind. I argued that not only does proto-panpsychism account for the seeming independence of the sphere of subjective experience with the endorsement of the claim of the fundamentality of consciousness but also that the theory adequately unifies the African universe of material and non-material phenomena.

References

Agada, A. (2019). Rethinking the metaphysical questions of mind, matter, freedom, determinism, purpose, and the mind-body problem within the panpsychist framework of consolationism. *South African Journal of Philosophy 38*(1), 1–16. https://doi.org/10.1080/02580136.2018.1560589.

Agada, A. (2020). Grounding the consolationist concept of *Mood* in the African vital force theory. *Philosophia Africana, 19*(2), 101–121. https://doi.org/10.5325/philafri.19.2.0101

Chalmers, D. J. (2015). Panpsychism and panprotopsychism. In T. Alter & Y. Nagasawa (Eds.), *Consciousness in the physical world: Perspectives on Russellian monism* (pp. 246–276). Oxford University Press.

Chimakonam, J. O. (2019). A sense-phenomenal look at the problem of personal identity. In J. O. Chimakonam, U. O. Egbai, S. T. Segun, & A. D. Attoe (Eds.), *New conversations on the problems of identity, consciousness, and mind* (pp. 11–32). Springer.

Gyekye, K. (1995). *An essay on African philosophical thought: The Akan conceptual scheme* (Rev ed.). Temple University Press.

Kwame, S. (2004). Quasi-Materialism: A contemporary African philosophy of mind. In K. Wiredu (Ed.), *A companion to African philosophy* (pp. 343–351). Blackwell.
Mbiti, J. S. (1969). *African religions and philosophy*. Heinemann.
Ramose, M. (1999). *African philosophy through ubuntu*. Mond Books.
Segun, S. T. (2019). Neurophilosophy and the problem of consciousness: An equiphenomenal perspective. In J. O. Chimakonam, U. O. Egbai, S. T. Segun, & A. D. Attoe (Eds.), *New conversations on the problems of identity, consciousness, and mind* (pp. 33–65). Springer.
Strawson, G. (2015). Real materialism. In T. Alter & Y. Nagasawa (Eds.), *Consciousness in the physical world: Perspectives on Russellian monism* (pp. 161–208). Oxford University Press.
Wiredu, K. (1983). The Akan concept of mind. *Ibadan Journal of Humanistic Studies, 3*, 113–134.
Wiredu, K. (1996). *Cultural universals and particulars: An African perspective*. Indiana University Press.
Wiredu, K. (2002). Conceptual decolonization as an imperative in contemporary African philosophy: Some personal reflections. *Rue Descartes, 2*(36), 53–64. https://www.cairn.info/revue-rue-descartes-2002-2-page-53.htm

Chapter 5
An Alternative Response to the Knowledge Argument

Clarton Fambisai Mangadza

Abstract Kwasi Wiredu's interpreted view of the Akan concept of mind (adwene), complemented with David Lewis's version of the ability reply, offers an alternative African statement of the ability reply, and, at the very least, in a novel way turns the negative ability reply into a positive reply to Frank Jackson's formulation of the knowledge argument. For Wiredu the mind is not taken as a distinct substance, but rather as a cognitive ability; while for Lewis together with Paul Snowdon's capacity thesis challenge; an ability as 'knowledge-how' is understood as subjective experience, so subjective experience as *a cognitive faculty of the mind,* adds substantive knowledge. Essentially, *adwene* demonstrates an integral aspect of support to the conclusion of Jackson's knowledge argument, where the mind is a cognitive capacity. Thus such support allows an African perspective to shine new light on the knowledge argument, an enduring problem in philosophy of mind.

Keywords Adwene · Quasi-physicalism · Knowledge argument · Ability reply · Subjective experience · Personhood

5.1 Introduction

In this chapter, I argue in support of the knowledge argument against the ability hypothesis. My argument is a non-reductive physicalist offering of a novel hypothesis that adds to the knowledge argument debate. My hypothesis is formulated as an epistemological, as well as a metaphysical, response based, on the one hand, on David Lewis's (1988) ability hypothesis which was actually a negative hypothesis to Frank Jackson (1982) and, on the other hand, on Kwasi Wiredu's (1987)

C. F. Mangadza (✉)
Govan Mbeki Research and Development Centre (GMRDC), University of Fort Hare, Alice, South Africa
e-mail: mangadzafc@gmail.com

A. D. Attoe et al. (eds.), *Conversations on African Philosophy of Mind, Consciousness and Artificial Intelligence*,
https://doi.org/10.1007/978-3-031-36163-0_5

interpretation of the Akan concept of mind.[1] I am not attaching any implicit or explicit tag of value on the two distinct traditions; I am only aiming at addressing how these two can complement each other in an attempt to solve an 'intractable issue'[2] in philosophy of mind.

My argument postulates: if the ability hypothesis is considered in the context of Wiredu's work on the Akan concept of mind, it can in fact, in a novel form, be harnessed to become positive support of Jackson's definitive formulation of the knowledge argument. Let me add a disclaimer, I acknowledge that Jackson has more recently changed his position on the knowledge argument;[3] however, I maintain Jackson's original view (1982, 1986) for the paper, in light of his own recent critique of the old view. Jackson's view that I defend argues, 'you cannot deduce from purely physical information about us and our world, all there is to know about the nature of our world because you cannot deduce how things look to us, especially in regard to colour [red]' (Jackson 1998a, b). The view is presented in classic vivid ways, the story of Fred and the story of Mary (Jackson, 1982, 1986). The story of Mary has been labelled by David Chalmers the 'canonical version of the [knowledge] argument' (Chalmers, 2010: 108). It was Yanyan Zhao (2012: 304) who remarked, how ironic it can be that after 16 years of defending the [successful] knowledge argument, Jackson goes on to announce that he had changed his mind, stating that although his argument contained no obvious fallacy its conclusion – physicalism is false – must be mistaken (Jackson, 1998a, b);[4] I share the remark. Noteworthy, Jackson's current view is not my focus in this chapter: my interest is in seeing how Western debates in contemporary philosophy of mind can be enriched by an African perspective.

The chapter is organised in four parts; first, I restate the version of the knowledge argument as outlined by Jackson (1982). I will not go into the different versions of the argument that date back to nearly a century ago, e.g. CD Broad (1925), Herbert

---

[1] I use *interpreted* to specify that the "Akan concept of mind" is contested, the concept translated '*adwene*' arises from Akan personhood debates, e.g. Kwame Gyekye offers a dualist interpretation of the view, while his fellow Akan Kwasi Wiredu gives a quasi-physicalist interpretation to the Akan theory of mind. I would like to point out that Wiredu's work on the mind is limited, in the main, to his 1987 paper, which evolved from his 1983 paper titled 'The Akan concept of Mind'. In this chapter, I use the 1987 publication as my primary focus from where I get Wiredu's voice. However, I would also like to point out that a few snippets here and there on the Akan concept of mind can be gleaned in other published works by Wiredu that I appeal to in this chapter. See Wiredu (1996, 2002, 2010).

[2] See David Chalmers (2010) *The Character of Consciousness*. Oxford: Oxford University Press; Colin McGinn (1989) "Can we solve the Mind-Body problem?" *Mind.* Vol. xcviii. No. 391.

[3] Jackson (1998a, b) wrote 'Most contemporary philosophers given a choice between going with science and going with intuitions go with science. Although I once dissented from the majority, I have capitulated and now see the interesting issue as being where the arguments from the intuitions against physicalism – the arguments that seem so compelling – go wrong. For some time, I have thought that the case for physicalism is sufficiently strong that we can be confident that the arguments from the intuitions go wrong somewhere, but where is somewhere?' (Jackson, 1998a, b in Ludlow et al., 2004: 421).

[4] See also Robert Van Gulick (2004) 'So many ways of saying no to Mary'.

Feigl (1958), Thomas Nagel (1974), among others. Second, there are many responses to Jackson's knowledge argument that have accumulated over the years; my focus will only be on Lewis's (1988) 'ability hypothesis'. The ability hypothesis is formulated as a negative hypothesis to the knowledge argument. However, in my view, it can be transformed to become favourable to Jackson's original position. The third part introduces Wiredu's quasi-physicalism: a philosophical view arising from within Akan personhood debates.[5] The final part will be what I postulate as the novel 'alternative hypothesis' to the knowledge argument. I see a novel non-reductive promise in the ability reply, if I interpret it and expand it via the interpreted Akan concept of mind, which portrays or understands mind as a cognitive faculty. I propose that subjective experience (SE)/what-its-likeness understood as an emergent mental property, emerging from the physical brain, adds 'real' knowledge to a person's existing knowledge. The hypothesis affirms that subjective experience (SE) is the feeling of what-it-is-like, understood as an emergent mental property, emerging from the physical brain, adds 'real' knowledge to a person's existing knowledge. Through that subjective experience, we gain knowledge of something non-physical/qualia, for instance. I sum up the alternative hypothesis in premise-conclusion.

5.2 The Knowledge Argument

The knowledge argument is framed as an attack on reductive physicalism (RP)[6] and aims to establish as it where that phenomenal conscious mental experience involves non-physical properties. The knowledge argument is about knowledge and not about the metaphysics of the mind. According to Jackson, the central claim of the knowledge argument is that 'one can have all the physical information without having all the information there is to have' (Jackson, 1982: 130). Therefore, the argument suggests the possibility that subjective experience (SE) or qualia of an event or phenomenon adds 'real' knowledge to a person's existing knowledge. Subjective

[5] There are considerable debates regarding the concept of quasi-physicalism; a term that Wiredu coined. Part of the dispute arise from how one of the constituents that unite for Akan personhood, *okra* (a life-giving entity) is understood, while others postulate it as spiritual (non-physical) (Gyekye, 1995; Majeed, 2013) for Wiredu (1987) it is quasi-physical, in other words he does not accept the mind as 'some kind of substance' (Wiredu, 2002: 61). Wiredu says 'far from the *adwene* being an entity, it is a capacity […]' Wiredu (2002: 61).

[6] Physicalism comes in two varieties, viz., reductive (RP) and non-reductive physicalism (NRP). Proponents of these two varieties of physicalism are in agreement that there is one physical substance; but the locus of their disagreement arises from the fact that NRP proponents do not agree that the physical aspect is all there is to mental phenomena whilst RP proponents insist that there is only the physical. Currently, NRP is now the more acceptable formulation of the physicalist perspective in contemporary philosophy of mind.

experience (SE) is understood as (knowledge of) the feeling what it is like to[7] experience something.

The knowledge argument presented by Jackson (1982) is explained by two imaginative examples: (1) the case of Fred, the best tomato sorter ever imagined and (2) Mary the brilliant neurophysiologist, the best there is in her field. The case of Mary, though presented as 'seemingly' an afterthought has become the most popular:[8]

> Mary is a brilliant scientist who is, for whatever reason, forced to investigate the world from a black and white room via a black and white television monitor. She specializes in the neurophysiology of vision and acquires, let us suppose, all the physical information there is to obtain about what goes on when we see ripe tomatoes, or the sky, and use terms like 'red', 'blue', and so on. She discovers, for example, just which wavelength combinations from the sky stimulate the retina, and exactly how this produces via the central nervous system the contraction of the vocal cords and expulsion of air from the lungs that result in the uttering of the sentence 'The sky is blue'. ... What will happen when Mary is released from her black and white room or is given a colour television monitor? Will she learn anything or not? (Jackson, 1982: 130).

There have been several replies that have been offered to the knowledge argument, two are well-known: they are the ability hypothesis and the acquaintance hypothesis. I will focus only on the ability hypothesis, which I aim to transform from being a physicalist reply to a hypothesis that supports Jackson's knowledge argument.

5.3 The Ability Hypothesis

The ability hypothesis in its current form was formulated by 'hardcore physicalists' Nemirow (1980, 1990) and Lewis (1983, 1988).[9] A similar exemplification of the hypothesis was formulated by Earl Conee (1994) and is called the acquaintance hypothesis. Conee (1994) makes the point 'that knowledge consists in acquaintance with the experience' (1994: 136). His argument is that Mary makes epistemic progress when she gets acquainted with the red hue for the first time. My focus is on what I term the 'most popular negative' hypothesis, as devised by Lewis (1988), which is specifically directed at Jackson (1982, 1986). Lewis says Mary does not acquire propositional knowledge but only acquires a capacity; hence, his hypothesis

---

[7] This terminology is due to Thomas Nagel, from his famous what 'What is it like a bat'. Nagel's argument is not a rejection of physicalism and other forms of reductivism. His argument merely shows that they are inadequate since they cannot describe all the facts about experience.

[8] In Jackson (1986), 'What Mary didn't know' an article which has been labeled the formalization of the knowledge argument (Chalmers, 2002: 199), the case of Fred is dropped, and since then, the example has become redundant.

[9] Lewis (1983) clearly credits the general idea of the ability hypothesis to this version by Nemirow (1980) as the precursor of his own statement on the view. Nemirow's version was crafted in a book review of Nagel's (1979) *Mortal Questions*. Notably, the version actually predates Jackson's knowledge argument, the point made was in connection to a version of Nagel's 'knowledge' argument: about the existence of subjective facts.

is referred to as the ability hypothesis. The ability hypothesis is based on the knowledge-that and knowledge-how[10] debate with its roots in Gilbert Ryle's *The Concept of Mind* (1949), which is precisely one of the reasons why it is amenable to become support for Jackson instead of a negative response to him. I will argue that the ability hypothesis may be transformed into a strong argument in favour of the knowledge argument, if read against Wiredu's interpretation of the Akan concept of mind (I will come back to Wiredu below).

Before proceeding let me go into some background details on the ability hypothesis. Nemirow (1990) tweaked his 1980 version in an article 'Physicalism and the Cognitive role of acquaintance' and calls it 'the ability equation' (Nemirow, 1990: 492). The equation summarised states 'knowing what it's like may be identified with knowing how to imagine' (1990: 493). Nemirow argues that the knowledge argument 'rests on shaky inference' (1990: 492), which I think is an assertion he makes hastily. My slight objection on Nemirow's argument relates to the idea of knowing – what-it-is-like which invokes a notion of subjectivity (the aspect of actually being the experiencer, not just imagining it), i.e. the state of being able to control auricular muscle movements to wiggle one's ears. One can ask is this kind of knowledge attainable as an objective fact? If not, can the physicalist defend such knowledge since it would seem to go against physicalism? In my view, failure by Nemirow to clearly demarcate and specify an understanding of knowing-how and his understanding of ability (to imagine) limits his response to the knowledge problem.

Bence Nanay makes a point that is acceptable, the striking response is what Lewis has offered,[11] a response which goes beyond Nemirow's imagining experiences only. Lewis (1988) adds other mental states, viz., remembering and recognising the experiences (as other abilities) hence my particular focus on his version which states,

> [t]he ability hypothesis says that knowing what an experience is like just *is* the possession of these abilities to remember, imagine, and recognize. It isn't the possession of any kind of information, ordinary or peculiar. It isn't knowing that certain possibilities aren't actualized. It isn't knowing-that. It's knowing how (Lewis's *emphasis*, 2004: 100).

The point Lewis is making is that the new experience gained is only capacity: to imagine, to recognise and to remember experiences; in other words, it is expertise

[10] I will explain the distinction in subsequent paragraphs. For now, suffice it to say, there is a distinction to these types of knowledge: *knowledge-that* (propositional knowledge) and *knowledge-how* (practical knowledge).

[11] Bence Nanay would not agree with my assertion that Lewis's response is striking, in his view Nemirow, Lewis and D.H. Mellor's versions of the ability hypothesis, he labelled as AH1, AH2 and AH3, in his view, '(AH2) and (AH3) need to be discarded: we are back with (AH1). But we have seen that (AH1) in itself will not do [...]' (Nanay, 2009: 704–705). He suggests: 'the ability to discriminate' (Nanay, 2009: 705): 'knowing what it is like to experience E is having the ability to distinguish imagining or having experience E from imagining or having any other experience' (*ibid.*). The scope of my argument does not cover this comparative analysis of the different versions of the ability hypothesis; I rather aim at consolidating what Lewis has offered.

(*knowing how*), not factual or propositional knowledge (*knowing that*). I will complement this epistemologically rooted view, with Wiredu's metaphysically inspired quasi-physicalist view which I introduce below (with disclaimers on the epistemological and metaphysical, as given earlier).

5.4 Interpretation of the Akan Concept of Mind

Wiredu (1987)[12] has offered an interpretation of the traditional Akan view of the mind (*adwene*),[13] mind understood as 'the function of thought' (Wiredu, 1996: 16), that is the view that the mind does not exist in the body, but rather it is a cognitive capacity, this view emerges from within personhood debates among the Akan of West Africa. The word 'mind' is translated as '*adwene*' in Akan (Wiredu, 1987: 157), which is referring to mind, interpreted as having a 'non-substance character' (*ibid.*). The determination of mind as a cognitive capacity is implicit in the Akan language and their corpus of communal beliefs: for the Akans, 'mind [*adwene*] is intellectual [...] just for thinking' (Wiredu, 1987: 172, 2004: 204). It is on this view of the mind that the philosophical upshot of Wiredu, termed quasi-physicalism is based.[14] Note Wiredu's view is a non-substance view that is similar to, but distinct from, what Ryle offered.

As a non-substance theory, the view is not peculiar to Wiredu's interpreted Akan view. Ryle (1949) in *The Concept of Mind,* also advocated a non-substance theory. However, these two are not equivalent. The interpretation of mind (*adwene*),[15] advocated by Wiredu (1987), clarifies that *adwene* 'is never mentioned in any enumeration of entities that unite to constitute a person' (Wiredu, 2004: 16). His emphasis is that the cognitive aspect of the mind (*adwene*) is never thought of as an entity, since 'if mind were thought of as an entity, this omission would be totally explicable' (ibid.).

Personhood for the Akan broadly consist of a few constituents: *nipadua* (body) and *okra* (a life-giving principle), together with *sunsum* (that which gives a person's personality its force). In other words, a person in Akan consist of 'physical (bodily) and extra-bodily entities' (Majeed, 2014: 44). The extra-bodily refer to two logically distinguishable entities – the *sunsum* and *okra* while the bodily refer to *nipadua*. I mention these constituents that unite to establish personhood for clarification purposes, since it is from within these debates that a better understanding of

[12] 'The Concept of Mind with Particular Reference to the Language and Thought of the Akans'.

[13] As translated into the Akan language.

[14] The use of the term quasi-physicalism in this chapter is not meant as a label for Wiredu's theory of mind. In coining the term quasi-physicalism Wiredu, in my view, uses the term to structure Akan metaphysics of the person and the relation to the world. Consequently, I am using the term quasi-physicalism to refer to Wiredu's logical construction of the theory of mind.

[15] It is important to clarify that 'mind' and 'thought' are equivalent as the noun forms of the verb *dwen* (to think).

Wiredu's interpretive philosophical take on *adwene* is brought out. Notably, there is no uniformity among the Akan on these debates: there are camps pitting Wiredu on one end, and on the other end Kwame Gyekye, with several acolytes on both sides. Gyekye is dualistic in his views whilst Wiredu's view is classified quasi-physicalism (Kwame, 2004; Majeed, 2013). In essence Wiredu rejects subjective experience. My take, however, is that if Wiredu's quasi-physicalist perspective is brought to the ability hypothesis; an alternative fortified hypothesis may be formulated so as to become a positive hypothesis to Jackson. I will now move on to the formulation of my alternative response.

5.5 A Novel Alternative Response to the Knowledge Argument

The driver of my argument is a combination of Wiredu's quasi-physicalism with Lewis' version of the ability hypothesis and, at the very least, in the process, to formulate a positive African philosophical statement of the ability hypothesis – that is, turning the ability hypothesis into a positive hypothesis to support Jackson's knowledge argument.

Arising from the two outlines earlier, the basis for my argument is that for Wiredu the mind is not taken as a substance distinct from the body, but rather as a cognitive ability, while, for Lewis, now together with Paul Snowdon (2003) an ability as 'knowledge how' is understood as subjective experience. In introducing Snowdon (2003) here I aim to structure a link that will assist me in constructing my argument.

Snowdon (2003) presents a reaction to Ryle's established epistemological view, restated thus:

> [T]here are at least two types of knowledge (or to put it in slightly different way, two types of states ascribed by knowledge ascriptions) identified, on the one hand, as know (or state) which is expressed in the 'knowing that' construction (sometimes called, for fairly obvious reasons, 'factual' knowledge) and on the other, as the knowledge (or state) which is ascribed in the 'knowing how' construction (sometimes called 'practical' knowledge) (Snowdon, 2003: 1).

Snowdon's approach on the knowing-how and knowing-that debate introduced an alternative perspective on Ryle's epistemological view. Such an alternative reading forms a part of my argument that gets support from Snowdon's challenge of the Rylean established view. Snowdon's take, which I discuss below, argues that there is compelling evidence to be advanced to motivate for a slight shift away from the 'standard view' (Snowdon, 2003: 2), which only affirms Ryle's view.

The prevailing response strategies to the knowledge argument focus on the metaphysical aspect. For my hypothesis, I bring two (metaphysical and epistemological) philosophical paradigms together. On one side is the epistemological argument, which brings out the bridge between Snowdon and Lewis as I will show below. The 'epistemological argument' develops an argument for claiming why *subjective experience* (SE) *is know-how* and, following Snowdon, why it is knowledge. On the other side (in the other section) is the 'metaphysical argument' appealing to Wiredu's interpreted Akan theory of mind and is summarised thus: *mind is a function, the function of thinking*. On this side, I consider Lewis augmented by Wiredu's quasi-physicalism. The rationale is that since Wiredu's view is non-reductive: that is the perspective that the mind is a cognitive faculty and not a materially existing entity or substance, but indeed also not reducible to the body.[16] This would in this case make Wiredu's quasi-physicalism view plausible and pertinent when added to Lewis' ability hypothesis.

I propose the following logical formulations, in premise-conclusion, which I will explain in detail in the subsequent paragraphs as my argument. Starting with the *epistemologically* inspired argument:

1. Subjective experience (SE) is knowledge-how (KH) (Lewis).
2. Knowledge-how (KH) is knowledge (K) (Snowdon).
3. Therefore, subjective experience (SE) is knowledge (K).

And the *metaphysically* directed argument:

1. (a) Subjective experience (SE) is ability (imagine, recognise and remember) (Lewis)
   (b) Ability is imagining, remembering and recognising (Lewis)
   (c) Imagining, recognising, remembering is thinking (common sense)

Interim Conclusion: Therefore, subjective experience (SE) is thinking (1a–c).

2. (a) Thinking is a mental activity (Akan: *adwene* 'mind' and *dwen* 'to think')
   (b) Mind is a function of thought, a cognitive faculty, made possible by the brain: having a brain is a pre-requisite for thinking/having a mind (Wiredu)

Second interim conclusion: Therefore, thinking emerging from the brain as a cognitive function is a mental property (from 2a and 2b).

Final conclusion: Thus, subjective experience is a mental property (From interim conclusions above).

To explain the logical formulations, on one side is the 'epistemological' argument and can be summarised thus: *knowledge-how is knowledge*. When considering this view, I consolidate Lewis (1988) with Snowdon's (2003) 'capacity thesis challenge'. As pointed out earlier, it is a challenge to Ryle's (1949) familiar epistemological know-that and know-how distinction.[17]

[16] Wiredu is not explicit on this non-reductive view; the interpretation I credit to Wiredu is through the philosophical lens of Safro Kwame and Haskeei M. Majeed. See Kwame (2004: 25–30) and Majeed (2014: 56–61).

[17] Cath (2019: 1) has pointed out that the distinction between two components of knowledge-how: the negative claim (*anti-intellectualism*) and the positive claim (*abilitism* or *dispositionalism*), which for a period of time was uncontested and taken as philosophical orthodoxy, is far from that straightforward facade. The scope of this discussion is something beyond what I aim to achieve so I will not go into a detailed epistemology debate on the distinction.

Without restating Ryle's famous view, which has received good mileage in the literature; which Snowdon (2003) labels a 'positive thesis' in his *The Presidential Address*: 'Knowing how and Knowing that: A distinction reconsidered'. According to Snowdon (2003), and I agree with him, the decades old Rylean argument benefits from an unchallenged taking for granted of the distinction in epistemology between knowledge-how and knowledge-that. Snowdon captures Ryle's view and characterises it into a view he calls '*the Standard View*' (*author's italics* Snowdon, 2003: 2). According to him his take on the standard view is only a 'useful stalking horse' (*ibid.*). I think Snowdon is very modest to label his effort only that since in my view, his interpretation deserves more credit. It is a game changer interpretation of Ryle's argument.

The standard view can be characterised as affirming two propositions. The first one is a negative thesis: 'knowing how is disjoint from knowing that' (*ibid.*). Snowdon labels this Ryle's disjointness thesis (DT):

> Knowing how does not consist in knowing that some proposition is true or that some fact obtains; knowing how cannot be reduced to or equated with (any form of) knowledge that (*ibid.*).

The second proposition is what Snowdon (2003) gives as Ryle's positive thesis: 'knowing how is 'practical' knowledge'. Snowdon has labelled it capacity thesis (CT),

> Knowing how to G does in fact consist in being able to G, in having the capacity to G. Knowing how ascriptions ascribe abilities or capacities to do the mentioned action (*ibid.*).

Due to my current scope of argument, I will reserve a discussion of the DT (disjointment thesis) for another occasion and focus on the CT (capacity thesis). The purpose of focusing on CT is to show that knowledge-how is knowledge and not only limited to ability or capacity. This will become clearer when I apply Snowdon's CT discussion to Lewis's negative ability hypothesis, transforming it to show that subjective experience (SE) is knowledge-how, and thus knowledge, contrary to Lewis (1988).

The capacity thesis (CT) that had been accepted and read in a particular way was given to a different guise. Specifically, Snowdon warned that 'when know how, as it is often is, is described as "practical" knowledge' (ibid.) only, it would suggest a somewhat dangerous way to express the CT claim since:

> 'Practical' applies unproblematically to knowing how in that the content of such knowledge relates, at least usually, to *practice*. Thus, knowing how to G concerns the practice of G-ing, just as knowing the date of the Battle of Hastings concerns mediaeval history. It is quite clear, though, that from this obvious sense in which knowing how is practical that it does not follow that it is practical in the sense affirmed by CT. It does not follow that the presence of knowing how consists in the presence of a *practical capacity* (*author's italics ibid.*).

That challenge to the way of expressing the CT by Snowdon breached the gauntlet on what had become considered as the accepted way or what had for years 'remained part of conventional wisdom in philosophy' (Snowdon, 2003: 1). The challenge thereby precipitated an alternative understanding of interpreting CT away from the accepted standard account.

Now let me try to explain my interest in the CT. For brevity, the CT is expressed as follows: 'S knows how to G if and only if S can, or is able, to G' (Snowdon, 2003: 8). A capacity (or ability) as we are aware within the Western view is taken as knowledge-how (practical knowledge). However, this 'familiar approach' (Snowdon, 2003: 2) within the Western context is turned on its head by Snowdon's discussion of the CT, for the following reason. The interpretation of the CT, implying that knowledge-how is just a capacity, is what worries Snowdon (2003); he labels it a dangerous interpretation. And, Snowdon warns against the interpretation as I have already pointed out. In motivating his stance against such an interpretation, he aims to show that there is another applicable interpretation of the CT, that argues for an alternative suggestion that seeks to affirm that knowledge-how is not only capacity but is also propositional knowledge. I will make this point clearer when I discuss the counterexamples in the next section.

Thus, the novel alternative hypothesis I propose is nested within the following context: subjective experience (SE) as imagining, remembering and recognising is taken *as* ability by Lewis, but following Snowdon, ability is knowledge. Wiredu explains mind as a function of thought, which, following Lewis, means there is a link between mind and having the ability for subjective experiences. In the following sections, I will elucidate in some detail Snowdon's epistemologically directed argument followed by Wiredu's metaphysically situated argument.[18]

5.6 The Epistemological Argument: Lewis and Snowdon

Lewis (1988) as a reductionist via his established ability hypothesis has negatively adjudicated Jackson's (1982) knowledge argument. His negative hypothesis is summed up thus, knowledge-how is only an ability (to remember, recognise and imagine). I argue that such a negative take on the knowledge problem can be reviewed in different light if a specified interpretation of know-how is applied. I will refer here to views of Snowdon (2003), Yuri Cath (2019) and Joshua Habgood-Coote (2019), respectively, on reviewing the status of knowledge-how, with the

[18] A disclaimer, I am not saying the Snowdon is only epistemological, nor do I imply that Wiredu is only metaphysical.

focus here on Snowdon, while noting that both Cath[19] and Habgood-Coote[20] have related views that endorse Snowdon's position.

As mentioned earlier, Lewis phrases the ability hypothesis in a way that implies that there is no new knowledge gained when Jackson's Mary leaves the room; in the sense that subjective experience (SE), as knowledge-how, is not viewed as new knowledge (subjective experience (SE) as something non-physical that comes out of the physical), which implies that he is not a property dualist. Property dualists exemplify non-reductive physicalism (NRP) with Jackson as a prime example. As a non-reductive physicalist, Jackson would insist that mental properties are something over and above physical properties. But, on the contrary, Lewis, as a reductionist, does not allow that mental properties are different in kind from physical properties and views the former as ontologically reducible to the latter. Hence, he is against Jackson's property dualism and is in defence of reductive physicalism (RP).

I hold that he offers a fairly successful view when he argues against phenomenal knowledge under the interpretation of knowledge-how. However, I would like to reassess his contribution by reconsidering the ability hypothesis in the context of Snowdon's interpretation of knowledge-how. The problematic issue is that Lewis sees phenomenal experience as an ability *only* and equates knowledge-how with an ability. A J Ayer (1956) states,

> For someone to think that he knows something when he really does not know it, it is not enough, [...], that he should be mistaken about the character of his mental state: for if his mental state were what he took it to be, that is a state of knowledge, he could not be mistaken about the fact which it revealed to him. If this view were correct, then being in a

[19] Cath (2019) has weighed in with another approach that acknowledges, but shifts from the traditional Rylean argument; 'accounting for the relationship between knowledge-how and action' (Cath, 2019: 9). The shift is to understand the intelligence of knowledge-how without appealing to knowledge (Cath, 2019: 6). For Cath there are grounds for an argument that says 'knowledge-how has a different *epistemic profile* from knowledge-that' (*ibid.*), which allows a window for viewing know-how not just in terms of a capacity. And, Habgood-Coote's (2019) approach has also sought to illuminate Ryle's traditional knowledge-how distinction. What he calls a 'compromise position', a position that seeks to synchronize claims about knowledge-how "as a kind of propositional knowledge" (Habgood-Coote, 2019: 86) and knowledge-how taken 'to be a kind of ability' (*ibid.*). see also Cath (2009).

[20] Joshua Habgood-Coote (2019) has also expressed what he calls the *Interrogative Capacity View*: 'knowledge-how to do something is a certain kind of ability to generate answers to the question of how to do it' (Habgood-Coote, 2019: 86). He says, '[...] combining a propositional object with an abilitative relation makes the view uniquely well-placed to defuse the tension between semantic theory and the practicality of knowledge-how, and allows it to illuminate the relation between knowledge-how, propositional knowledge, and abilities' (Habgood-Coote, 2019: 88).

Habgood-Coote (2019) argues that 'knowledge-how is not identical with *just* any ability to answer a how-to question' (*my emphasis ibid.*). I think Habgood-Coote to his credit has made an important point that I agree with, knowledge how is 'not a distinctively practical kind of knowledge' (Habgood-Coote, 2019: 93) only; instead in a simplified way, knowledge-how is knowledge. That suggest that being able to perform (ability) entails already the possession of certain other forms of knowledge-that. The position is similar to what Snowdon (2003) put across as the positive CT, which also forms part of his analysis to re-evaluate the danger as arising from such an interpretation, that limits knowing-how to capacity only.

> mental state of this kind would be a sufficient condition for having knowledge. And if, in addition, one could not know anything to be true without being in this state, it would be both necessary and sufficient (Ayer, 1956: 15).

The above view can be summarised as follows: being in a certain cognitive state is being in a mental state, and being in that state is a sufficient state of knowledge. Ayer (1956) objects to that by seeking a closer consideration of what the nature of possession of knowledge amounts to. According to him, does possession of knowledge only mean showing a performance that confirms possession of such knowledge? Either to (1) oneself as the one possessing the knowledge or (2) as displayed to others? For example, if we take historical facts; I know some facts of history, but those facts are available to me only 'on rare occasions when I call them to mind. I know them at this moment even though I am not thinking of them' (*ibid.*).

Let us consider the following example; I could not be thinking about the day Pope John Paul II died (April 2, 2005) right now but I know that date, despite me not actively musing about it presently. What Ayer (1956) argues for is that once I think harder about it, I can remember the correct date. Which suggests that there can be aspects of knowledge we can identify as knowledge not only because one is presently exercising it, so the point is

> [t]he verb 'to know' is used to signify a disposition or, as Ryle puts it, that it is a 'capacity', verb. To have the knowledge is to have the power to give a successful performance, not actually to be giving one (*ibid.*).

Snowdon's (2003) revamped analysis of the CT positions an interpretation of knowing-how that challenges the view of CT as ordinarily affirming 'that the presence of knowing how consists in the presence of a *practical capacity*' (*ibid.*). For him, capacity (practical knowledge) is not only knowledge-how. To try to make the point explicit, let's turn to some counterexamples. Snowdon (2003) has proposed five counterexamples that seek to show that the 'possession of the capacity (or ability) to G is not a necessary condition for knowing how to G' (Snowdon, 2003: 8). I will only give one here from Snowdon, since all the five counterexamples apply mutatis mutandis.

> I know how to make Christmas pudding, and have done so frequently. Alas, a terrible explosion obliterates the world's supply of sugar, so that no one is able to make it. I still know how to but, like everyone else, cannot (*ibid.*).

This counterexample in my view does not offer a clear-cut view on how knowledge-how is knowledge, but it does at least not imply that knowledge-how consists of a practical ability *only*. I think – having the ability to bake a cake, implies that one has propositional knowledge and not just an ability, as even if one does not have the ability anymore, one does know what it means to bake a cake. Another example, imagine an artisan who gets unlucky in a horror traffic accident and both hands are amputated, the artisan retains the knowledge of his trade, and only loses the capacity to apply the knowledge. The point I am illustrating is to say that knowledge is not *only* based on the subject being able to show, teach, or tell (or otherwise convey) us how to do something – Ayer's point above. There is no assumption that the knowledge to be acknowledged at present 'entails that it can be passed on by the knower […]' (Snowdon, 2003: 9). The critical point to hold on to is that the CT argues against knowledge-how as a capacity (only) and points to what I am attempting to affirm; that the ability hypothesis is actually a positive hypothesis favourable to Jackson's (1982) knowledge argument. Recall, I am offering a defence of the knowledge argument from the ability hypothesis.

So, now, bear in mind that Lewis implies that knowing-what-it-is-like is the ability to place oneself in a state representative of an experience. That implies understanding an experience means that one can remember, recognise and imagine the experience (Lewis, 1988: 18) which equates for Lewis to knowing-how. This understanding of an experience implies, in its turn, now following Snowdon (2003), that because you know how to experience, you have knowledge (of the experience). If we consider the experiencing of red by Mary, we can say she has the knowledge of what-it-is-like (subjective experience) to see the red fire truck, and that means she is able to see red. The know-how as knowledge comes before – or, if we push Snowdon's argument, independently of – the ability: ability as remembering, imagining and recognising our subjective experience (SE) for the experience it is, according to Lewis.

5.7 The Metaphysical Argument – Lewis and Wiredu

Shifting to the metaphysical argument; in my view, in this context, the ability hypothesis (if brought to converse with Wiredu's quasi-physicalism) offers potential to be fortified so as to become a positive hypothesis to Jackson. The Akan perspective of the mind – the view that the mind does not exist in the body, but rather that it is simply a cognitive capacity (Wiredu, 1996: 16) – is a 'nonsubstance conception of mind' (Wiredu, 1987: 160).[21] It is the view that human mind is a *function*, viz., the function of thinking, not the source of thought, in other words, the mind is 'conceived as the functional *capacity* of the brain' (*author's italics* Masolo, 2010: 244). As I have pointed out in the above footnote, the view is unlike functionalism or property dualism,[22] which focus on causal properties.[23] To be clear, arguing that the mind is a cognitive faculty may also seem to be in support of reductive physicalism (RP) as per identity theorists. Identity theorists state that mental states are identical

[21] The view is different from functionalism, an account of the theory of mind that says the essential or defining feature of any type of mental state is the set of causal relations it bears to (1) environmental effects on the body, (2) other types of mental states and (3) bodily behaviour (Churchland, 1985: 36).

[22] Property dualism is the view that, while there is only one kind of substance (viz., matter), the matter referred to can have two kinds of properties (viz., physical and mental).

[23] The point is functionalists stress that what is important about mental states is not how they are realized (i.e. as physico-chemical states) in the brain, but – according to David Armstrong (1968) and other central states materialists-rather the role they play within the causal system.

to neurophysiological states. The point I stress is that mind for the Akan is viewed as a cognitive faculty, and, as such it is also not reducible to the physical; for the Akan it emerges from the physical (Wiredu, 1987: 161). Significantly, I argue that Wiredu's quasi-physicalism offers a non-reductive perspective of the mind: the conception of mind as a cognitive faculty and not a materially existing entity or substance, but indeed is also not reducible to the body. By appealing to quasi-physicalism Wiredu, in my view, is able to make sense of Akan belief in such metaphysical entities like God, the soul and ancestors. Hence, I postulate and position my interpretation of Wiredu's theory of mind (an Akan-inspired theory) as benefitting from a quasi-physicalist perspective which points us in the direction of affirming subjective experience (SE) debates.

Phenomenal experience (qualia) allows a context for a positive response to Jackson's knowledge argument against reductive physicalism (RP), specifically, in defence of some form of dualism: property dualism. Property dualism is a kind of mixture of dualism and physicalism in the sense that it, unlike substance dualism, states only matter exists, but does support the view that two categories of properties (mental and physical) exist. Property dualists as such claim that there are two essentially different kinds of *property* out in the world (Robinson, 2017: n.p.). Burwood et al. (1999: 8) refer to the view as 'modern physicalism' and in many ways a direct 'inheritor' of Descartes' work. Jackson (1982, 1986) exemplify a 'modern dualist' because he seems to support that some limited form of dualism must be true (Cooney, 2000: 9); however, he does not endorse substance dualism; instead, in his scheme of things only phenomenal properties or 'qualia' are non-physical, meaning that only some aspects of our mental lives need be non-physical.

Phenomenal experience is a cognitive epistemic ability that qualifies to provide propositional knowledge. Recall, Jackson (1982) is arguing that there are some non-physical properties that escape the reductive physicalist story: reducing the mental to the physical – what type identity theorists[24] affirm – 'that every mental state is identical with some state in the brain' (Braddon-Mitchell & Jackson, 1996: 91). For Jackson, to recap,

> [...] the material or physical story about us is not the complete story about us, because it leaves out the sensory part, the 'redness of reds' part (Braddon-Mitchell & Jackson, 1996: 127).

A point that those in the non-reductive physicalist camp affirms, and I do not disagree with.

In general, Jackson's (1982) original position means the phenomenal side (the mental) of psychology, e.g. sensation of red colour experiences, the sound of D minor guitar key, the savoury flavour of dumplings and so on, is left out (*ibid.* 128).

---

[24] Smart's (1959) identity thesis, given as a "contingent statement, [...] A is identical to B [...]" (Smart in Robinson (Ed.), 1998: 190). Such a statement suggests that all the properties of either A or B are in common. Rosenthal (1991) has expressed it as follows, "[...] every mental state, such as a sensation of red, is also a physical state. Since states count as mental or physical in virtue of having properties that are mental or physical, mental states have both mental and physical properties" (Rosenthal, 1991: 162).

While not being a reductive physicalist about it, my view is to argue for a non-reductive view (token-identity theory), thus if I am not successful it implies that subjective experience (SE) is an ability, and that Lewis refutes Jackson. So, potential affirmation of ability theorists as positive support for Jackson (1982) has to be based on something more than the 'Western' version of the ability hypothesis, as we need an epistemological and a metaphysical refutation of the negative ability hypothesis.

In my view, Wiredu's (1987) quasi-physicalism is a form of property dualism: in terms of the interpreted Akan concept of mind, that is, mind as cognitive faculty irreducible to the physical, and thus allows the possibility of subjective experience (SE), but not in the reductive physicalist manner (mind is what the brain does), but rather in the property dualist manner that views subjective experience (SE) as a mental property. Therefore, Wiredu's (1987) interpreted Akan view that is quasi-physicalist has been demonstrated as a viable positive hypothesis to the knowledge argument when *merged*[25] with the negative ability hypothesis as presented by Lewis (1988). As a result, although the ability hypothesis modestly challenged Jackson: it is unconvincing and actually facilitates a gap that turns out as support of the knowledge argument. To restate, on the one hand, the ability hypothesis as directed to Jackson's non-reductive physicalism (NRP) is about having knowledge-how, as an ability; whilst on the other hand, according to Wiredu (1987), the mind is understood as a cognitive faculty which can also be shown to be knowledge-how, in other words an ability. I argue that knowing-how, in the sense of what-it-is-like-to can be new knowledge, following Snowdon (2003). In that way, Jackson is defended epistemologically. To clarify the context of the metaphysical defence: subjective experience (SE) is thinking, following Lewis (1988), but by appealing to Wiredu (1987), we see that thinking is a mental event (mind is a function of thought), and so subjective experience (SE) is a mental event.

Thus, subjective experience (SE), as a mental event or property (metaphysical argument), is an ability (knowing how) that is equivalent to the propositional knowledge (knowing that) (epistemological argument).

5.8 A Concluding Synthesis of the Two Arguments

As I conclude, Jackson's knowledge argument is an argument against reductive physicalism (RP), that is, it is a doctrine that asserts the view that everything that exists is *not* the sum of its physical properties only. As argued earlier, the ability hypothesis forms an integral part of the replies to Jackson's knowledge problem, especially since the negative ability hypothesis to it (Lewis) claims there is no new

[25] The idea of a merger is about offering an argument that shows that both sides – *as people* – can augment each other, on the basis of mutual equality and recognition, in the quest to solve a philosophical issue that has been portrayed as mainly a Western philosophical issue, while it has always been considered in African thought as well.

propositional knowledge that Mary adds, only that she achieves 'possession of certain abilities' (Braddon-Mitchell & Jackson, 2007: 138). Recall, the abilities referred to here are that she can imagine sensing red and is able to recognise red simply by looking at a red object presented in daylight (*ibid.*). In addressing such a hypothesis to Jackson's anti-physicalist stance, I refined the 'negative ability hypothesis' by (1) benefitting from Snowdon's relook of CT to show that subjective experience (SE) is knowledge and (2) that subjective experience (SE) is mental (as it is the cognitive faculty of thinking and mind is a function of thought – Wiredu).

As already noted, my argument benefits from a double-pronged description; one is an epistemological argument and the other is a metaphysical argument (with disclaimers for both arguments). The epistemological argument brings together Lewis and Snowdon to show that subjective experience (SE) is knowledge. My approach showed that knowing-how is knowledge, based on the assumption that *subjective experience (SE) is knowledge-how*. The assumption is embedded on the reassessment of Lewis by applying aspects of Snowdon's ground-breaking challenge to Ryle's capacity thesis (CT). And that leads to the conclusion that subjective experience (SE) is knowledge. The metaphysical argument appealed to Wiredu's Akan interpreted quasi-physicalist view to show that subjective experience (SE) is a mental property, emerging from the physical brain *amene*. Therefore, my defence of Jackson's knowledge argument is based on tentatively showing that subjective experience (SE) is an emergent property which contributes new knowledge, which validates property dualism, his non-reductive physicalism (NRP). I, therefore, conclude that Jackson's property dualism/NRP is defendable, and as such leads to the conclusion that the knowledge argument can be justified. In other words, my novel proposal strengthens Jackson's hand by showing that the negative ability hypothesis can be support for Jackson's knowledge argument.

Finally, my argument in premise-conclusion form is as follows:

If the knowledge argument is sound, then subjective experience (SE) is knowledge (assumption for epistemological argument):

1. Subjective experience (SE) is knowledge-how (assumption plus Lewis).
2. Knowledge-how is knowledge (assumption plus Snowdon).
3. Thus, the knowledge argument is sound (1, 2).
4. Therefore, subjective experience (SE) is knowledge (1, 2, 3).

If quasi-physicalism is true, then subjective experience (SE) is an emergent mental property and property dualism is true (assumption for metaphysical argument):

1. Subjective experience (SE) is an ability (e.g. thinking) (Lewis).
2. Thinking (as a cognitive ability) is an emergent property (common sense plus Wiredu).
3. Thus, quasi-physicalism is true (1, 2).
4. Therefore, subjective experience (SE) is an emergent mental property and property dualism is true (1, 2, 3).

If subjective experience (SE) is knowledge and property dualism is true (assumption for synthesis), then the knowledge argument is validated:

1. Property dualism is true (metaphysical argument).
2. Subjective experience (SE) is knowledge (epistemological argument).
3. The ability hypothesis validates the knowledge argument (synthesis) (1, 2).

Thus, subjective experience (SE) or qualia (diverse mental states, e.g. hearing D minor, seeing red, feeling pain and so on), understood as a cognitive faculty of the mind (following Wiredu added to Lewis' ability hypothesis), which emerges from the physical brain (following Wiredu), adds 'real' knowledge to a person's existing knowledge base because subjective experience (SE) as knowledge-how is knowledge too, following Snowdon.

References

Armstrong, D. M. (1968). *Materialist theory of the mind.* Routledge/Kegan Paul.

Ayer, A. J. (1956). *The problem of knowledge.* Penguin books.

Braddon-Mitchell, D., & Jackson, F. (1996; 2007). *Philosophy of mind and cognition: An introduction* (2nd ed.). Blackwell Publishing.

Broad, C. D. (1925). *The mind and its place in nature.* Routledge/Kegan Paul.

Burwood, S., Gilbert, P., & Lennon, K. (1999). *Philosophy of mind.* University College London Press/Taylor and Francis.

Cath, Y. (2009). The ability hypothesis and the new knowledge-how. *Noûs, 43*(1), 137–156. Retrieved from http://www.jstor.org/stable/40267332

Cath, Y. (2019). Knowing how. *Analysis*, 1–17. https://doi.org/10.1093/analys/anz027

Chalmers, D. J. (2002). *Philosophy of mind: Classical and contemporary readings.* Oxford University Press.

Chalmers, D. J. (2010). *The character of consciousness.* Oxford University Press, Inc.

Churchland, P. M. (1985). Reduction, qualia, and direct introspection of brain states. *The Journal of Philosophy, 82*(1), 8–28. Retrieved from https://www.jstor.org/stable/2026509

Conee, E. (1994). Phenomenal knowledge. *Australasian Journal of Philosophy, 72*(2), 136–150. https://doi.org/10.1080/00048409412345971

Cooney, B. (2000). *The place of the mind.* Wadsworth/Thomas Learning.

Feigl, H. (1958). The cognitive roles of acquaintance. In H. Feigl, M. Scriven, & G. Maxwell (Eds.), *Concepts, theories, and the mind-body problem* (Minnesota studies in the philosophy of science: Volume II, pp. 370–497) University of Minnesota Press.

Gyekye, K. (1995). *An essay on African philosophical thought: The Akan conceptual scheme* (Revised edition). Temple University Press.

Habgood-Coote, J. (2019). Knowledge-how, abilities, and questions. *Australasian Journal of Philosophy, 97*(1), 86–104. https://doi.org/10.1080/00048402.2018.1434550

Jackson, F. (1982). Epiphenomenal qualia. In P. Ludlow, Y. Nagasawa, & D. Stoljar (2004) (Eds.), *There's something about Mary: Essays on phenomenal consciousness and Frank Jackson's knowledge argument* (pp. 39–50). The MIT Press.

Jackson, F. (1986). What Mary didn't know. In P. Ludlow, Y. Nagasawa, & D. Stoljar (2004) (Eds.), *There's something about Mary: Essays on phenomenal consciousness and Frank Jackson's knowledge argument* (pp. 51–56). The MIT Press.

Jackson, F. (1998a). Mind and illusion. *Royal Institute of Philosophy Supplement* (2003), *53*, 251–271. https://doi.org/10.1017/S1358246100008365

Jackson, F. (1998b). Postscript on qualia. In P. Ludlow, Y. Nagasawa, & D. Stoljar (2004) (Eds.), *There's something about Mary: Essays on phenomenal consciousness and Frank Jackson's knowledge argument* (pp. 417–420). The MIT Press.

Kwame, S. (2004). Quasi-materialism: A contemporary African philosophy of mind. In K. Wiredu (Ed.), *A companion to African philosophy* (pp. 343–351). Blackwell Publishing Ltd.
Lewis, D. (1983). Postscript to 'Mad pain and Martian pain'. In D. Lewis (Ed.), *Philosophical papers* (Vol. 1, pp. 130–132). Oxford University Press.
Lewis, D. (1988). What experience teaches. In P. Ludlow, Y. Nagasawa, & D. Stoljar (2004) (Eds.), *There's something about Mary: Essays on phenomenal consciousness and Frank Jackson's knowledge argument*. The MIT Press.
Lewis, D. (2004). An argument for the identity theory. In J. Heil (Ed.), *Philosophy of mind: A guide and anthology*. Oxford University Press.
Majeed, H. M. (2013). A critique of the concept of quasi-physicalism in Akan philosophy. *African Studies Quarterly, 14*(1 & 2). http://www.africa.ufl.edu/asq/v14/v14i1-2a2.pdf
Majeed, H. M. (2014). The problem of destiny in Akan and Yoruba traditional thoughts: A comparative analysis of the works of Wiredu, Gyekye and Gbadegesin. *Journal of Philosophy and Culture, 5*(1), 43–66.
Masolo, D. A. (2010). *Self and community in a changing world*. Indiana University Press.
Nagel, T. (1974). What Is it like to be a Bat?. *The Philosophical Review* 83(4). Duke University Press on behalf of Philosophical Review. Retrieved from http://www.jstor.org/stable/2183914
Nagel, T. (1979). *Mortal questions*. Cambridge University Press.
Nanay, B. (2009). Imagining, recognising and discriminating: Reconsidering the ability hypothesis. *Philosophy and Phenomenological Research, LXXIX*, 3.
Nemirow, L. (1980). Review of *Mortal Questions* by Thomas Nagel. *The Philosophical Review, 89*(3), 473–477. http://www.jstor.org/stable/2184400. Accessed 06 June 2018, 13:29 UTC.
Nemirow, L. (1990). Physicalism and the cognitive role of acquaintance. In W. G. Lycan (Ed.), *Mind and cognition: A reader* (pp. 490–499). Basil Blackwell.
Robinson, H. (2017). Dualism. In E. N. Zalta (Ed.), *The Stanford encyclopaedia of philosophy* (Fall 2017 Edition). https://plato.stanford.edu/archives/fall2017/entries/dualism/
Robinson, D. (Ed.). (1998). *The mind*. Oxford University Press.
Rosenthal, D. M. (Ed.). (1991). *The nature of mind*. Oxford University Press.
Ryle, G. (1949). *The concept of mind*. Reprint, Aylesbury: Penguin, 1990.
Smart, J. J. C. (1959). Sensations and brain processes. In B. Cooney (Ed.), *The place of mind*. Wardsworth.
Snowdon, P. (2003). *The presidential address: Knowing how and Knowing that: A distinction reconsidered*. https://core.ac.uk/download/pdf/73772.pdf
Van Gulick, R. (2004). So many ways of saying No to Mary. In P. Ludlow, Y. Nagasawa & D. Stoljar (Eds.), *There is something about mary. Essays on phenomenal counsciousness and frank jackson's knowledge argument*. MIT press.
Wiredu, K. (1987). The concept of mind with particular reference to the language and thought of the Akans. In G. Fløistad (Ed.), *Contemporary philosophy: A new survey* (pp. 153–179). Martinus Nijhoff Publishers.
Wiredu, K. (1996). *Cultural universals and: An African perspective*. Indiana University Press.
Wiredu, K. (2002). Conceptual decolonization as an imperative in contemporary African philosophy: Some personal reflections. *Rue Descartes, 36*(2), 53–64. https://doi.org/10.3917/rdes.036.0053
Wiredu, K. (Ed.). (2004). *A companion of african philosophy*. Wiley-Blackwell.
Wiredu, K. (2010). The Ghanaian tradition of philosophy. In K. Wiredu & K. Gyekye (Eds.), *Person and community: Ghanaian philosophical studies* (Vol. I). CIPSH/UNESCO. The Council for Research in Values and Philosophy.
Zhao, Y. (2012). The knowledge argument against physicalism: Its proponents and its opponents. *Frontiers of Philosophy in China, 7*(2), 304–316. Retrieved from http://www.jstor.org/stable/44259407

Chapter 6
Epistemological Implications of Chimakonam's Theory of Sense-Phenomenalism

Maduka Enyimba

Abstract Sense-phenomenalism according to Chimakonam is a 'body-only-model' of personal identity which holds that an individual's identity is determined by the physical features that are sensually perceptible by other humans in society. I argue in this work that this theory has some implications for the theory of knowledge. First, it leads to the belief that we can only gain knowledge through the 'other', which further suggests that the individual cannot know himself/herself except through the *other*. Second, I contend that Chimakonam's leaning on Menkiti's community-based conception of personhood, with its obvious limitations, to substantiate his theory, is problematic. Finally, I suggest that this view would also encourage epistemic marginalization and racial discrimination based on bodily features. I show that this further complicates the problem of social epistemology, self-knowledge and the question of what part of the human system knowledge resides.

Keywords Sense-phenomenalism · Chimakonam · Menkiti · Social epistemology · Self-knowledge · Racial discrimination · Epistemic marginalization

6.1 Introduction

In this essay, I will examine Chimakonam's sense-phenomenal theory of personal identity and expose some of its inherent limitations. Identity is a social factor, and a person's identity lies in their bodily features. This is the position of Chimakonam in an essay titled 'A Sense-phenomenal Look at the Problem of Personal Identity' (2019a, 11–32). What Chimakonam contends in that paper is that identity is not a psychological or metaphysical property, it is rather a social property that is configured based on perceptible data. In other words, identity is not an individual-based

M. Enyimba (✉)
Department of Philosophy, University of Calabar & Conversational Society of Philosophy, Calabar, Nigeria

A. D. Attoe et al. (eds.), *Conversations on African Philosophy of Mind, Consciousness and Artificial Intelligence*,
https://doi.org/10.1007/978-3-031-36163-0_6

judgment, but a community-based judgement. This brings to mind Menkiti's proposal in his 'Person and Community in African Traditional Thought'. Here, Menkiti proposes a community-based conception of personhood, in which a person is identified as a person through the community (Menkiti, 1984, 171). In other words, a person's identity is a function of the society or community in which s/he lives. This further means that a person's identity is a socio-physical matter perceptible by others in the community.

This is similar to the physicalist account of the nature of personal identity projected by scholars such as Bernard Williams (2000, 154–156). According to this account, it is the brain or the body that determines a person's identity. Their emphasis is on the body or the brain as a continuation of the same brain of yesterday. Though Chimakonam subscribes to this physicalist account of personal identity, his approach differs remarkably (Enyimba, 2021a, 6). He draws attention to the parts of the body that are concrete and perceptible. In other words, his theory of sense-phenomenalism excludes the brain as part of the criteria of personal identity and focuses on tangible body parts.

I will argue that a careful analysis of the theory reveals three major implications for the theory of knowledge. First, one cannot claim to have knowledge of him/herself except what has been impressed on him/her by others (the community); hence, knowledge becomes a social or communal phenomenon. Second, since knowledge is a social construct, the brain or the mind cannot access knowledge of any kind except what the body perceives. This reduces knowledge to only the empirical, and it invariably suffers the setbacks of empiricism. Third, Chimakonam's sense-phenomenalism unconsciously encourages epistemic marginalization of individuals based on their bodily features, and by extension fosters racial discrimination based on skin colour and other body marks or features.

Against this backdrop, I contend that the sense-phenomenal theory of identity reduces epistemological issues and knowledge acquisition in particular to empiricism at the exclusion of other legitimate sources of knowledge. It also creates room for the epistemic marginalization and racial discrimination of the other as it deepens the dichotomy between the self and the other, and this consequently may deter the progress of the epistemic enterprise. Thus, I begin with a critical overview of the main thrust of the theory of sense-phenomenalism. Next, I articulate some of the implications of the sense-phenomenal theory of personal identity for epistemology.

6.2 Sense-Phenomenalism: A Critical Overview

Sense-phenomenalism is a new theory of personal identity developed by Chimakonam to answer the question of personal identity based on the bodily features of the given person. It was articulated to demonstrate that the problem of personal identity entertained by scholars like Descartes (1968, 106–107), Hume (1993, 326), Chalmers (1995, 202) and Menkiti (1984, 172) is resolvable within the confines of a person's physical traits or features, and as recognized by the community which s/he belongs. Chimakonam aims at refuting earlier and contrary theories on the nature of personal identity and presenting a fresh theory, namely, sense-phenomenalism. In order to achieve this avowed aim, he reasons that as a social property erected on the basis of sensible data, if one insists on the duality of a human being, then, personal identity is located in the body (Chimakonam, 2019a, 12). The author employs analogies and some thought experiments to substantiate his arguments/positions.

Accordingly, Chimakonam deflates the psycho-metaphysical criterion of personal identity which holds that the mind's contents such as the disembodied thoughts and memories are the custodian of personal identity. In other words, who we are is determined by our memories, consciousness or thoughts (Quinton, 2000, 157–162; Locke, 1894, Sec. 9). Chimakonam's reason for rejecting this criterion of personal identity is that it troubles human imagination with a sort of confusion that prevents the mind from seeing the real thing.

The next criterion or theory of identity dismissed by Chimakonam as untenable is the survivalist criterion presented by Partif and Vessey (2000, 163–168) and Dennett (1993, 327–333). According to this criterion, a person's survival, no matter how many times over, is the determinant of personal identity. For Chimakonam, the complexity of this criterion may force one to avoid any investigation into personal identity. Moreover, it suggests that one person could have multiple identities which is quite an uncomfortable idea to contemplate.

Of particular interest is Chimakonam's discontent with Chalmers' version of consciousness-theory or mind-content-theory of identity. Chalmers' approach to the nature of personal identity and of the mind-body problem is such that he makes a gradual movement from the brain, which is material to a non-material entity he describes as 'conscious experience'. Consciousness for Chalmers involves such activities as the ability to discriminate, categorize, react, integrate information or deliberately control behaviour, differentiate wakefulness and sleep (1995, 200–201), etc. This could be likened to Hume's reasoning that what we call self, consciousness or person is not any one impression, but a bundle or collection of different perceptions, such as heat, love, hate, pain and pleasure, which succeed each other with an indispensable rapidity and are in a constant change. And for Locke, the consciousness of the self, which is the constituent of personal identity, involves conscious pleasure, pain, happiness or misery (1952). Chalmers considers all of these aspects of consciousness as not constituting any serious problem to the question of identity. For him, the main problem, otherwise known as the hard problem lies with the idea of conscious experience, which is the inner feeling of images and sensation of reality. This is where Chimakonam takes on Chalmers' rendition.

Following other critics of Chalmers, such as McGinn (1989), Dennett (2005), Churchland (1995), etc., Chimakonam describes the hard problem as making little or no sense. He rejects the idea of qualia or subjective experience as suggested by Chalmers' position. He explains that every perception of such qualities as redness and smell is the same for all humans under normal circumstances. So, apple tastes the same to all and colours appear the same to all (Chimakonam, 2019b, 15).

The question at this point, which Chimakonam needs to answer, is what constitutes a 'normal circumstance' and who determines what passes for a normal circumstance? The implication of the phrase normal circumstances is that there are certain circumstances under which perception of certain qualities of say, redness, the taste of an apple, etc. differ across persons. In such circumstances, the idea of subjective experience is established and as such Chimakonam's rebuttal of subjective experience and/or qualia (as not qualified to be called experience) is seriously challenged.

Chimakonam insists that the feelings of love or hate, for instance, are not experiences, but ideas from either reflection or sensation. While reflection is mere imagination, sensation is sata. By sata, he means sense organ receptible neural codes or information (Chimakonam, 2019b, 16). This sata, he explains is what the brain sends back as a finished product to the sense organ. With this the sense organ is made to perform two basic functions, namely, perception of data and reception of sata (Chimakonam, 2019b, 16). Based on this, he denies the existence of qualia or subjective experience and affirms the existence of sata. For him, sata are created from data in the engine of the mind in such a manner that when we perceive anything with any of our five senses, sense data is relayed to the brain through relevant channels where the relevant brain cells transform them into sense receptible format called sata (Chimakonam, 2019b, 16). According to him, the rapid nature of this process misleads one in thinking that the experiences of these sensations occur inside the mind whereas it is external. Thus, for him, the brain reads, decodes and recodes sense data into sata, but nothing like perception occurs in the brain or mind, and if perception does not occur in the brain or mind, then it makes no sense to talk about the so-called conscious experience (Chimakonam, 2019b, 18).

Now as interesting as Chimakonam's argument may appear, certain challenges present themselves before him. First, if the brain does not perceive or experience as Chimakonam would want us to believe, how, and with what instruments, organs or qualities does it apprehend (read, decode and recode) the data before it sends it to the senses as sata? This suggests that there might be some perceptual qualities or organs possessed by the brain (mind) with which it apprehends sense data and processes them before sending them to the sense organs as sata (following Chimakonam's rendition). The point is that the brain could not have engaged in these activities without the help or instrumentality of perceptible qualities or organs of the brain. In other words, all sense organs are connected to the brain, which interprets sensations. For example, the eyes, skin, tongue, ears and nose are all connected to the brain. Without this connection, we are unable to tell what sweetness or bitterness tastes like, what white or orange colours look like or what fragrance smells like. Moreover, another challenge with Chimakonam's position is that his argument presents a poor understanding of how the human nervous system works. At this point, one is immediately reminded of an exposition of the nature of the mind through the different functioning of what Immanuel Kant (1966, 45) describes as the categories of the mind which actively participates in the processes of acquiring knowledge (Enyimba, 2012, 15).

Second, the sense in which Chimakonam employs the notion of sensation and reflection is not quite clear. Is it in the Humean or Lockean sense? Though he makes reference to Hume's ideas of reflection which come through the exercise of our imagination and ideas of sensation which come through the operations of our sense organs (see Chimakonam, 2019b, 15); it appears to be more akin to Locke's version of sensation and reflection:

> what we imagine when we close our eyes like being tangled up with the spouse of our dream or the sound that appears to echo inside when someone rings the door bell, or the feeling that seems to swell inside when we feel love or hate, *are not experiences. They are ideas from either reflection or sensation.*[1] The first are figments of our imagination and the second, for lack of a better characterization are 'sata'... I believe that the sense-perceived 'data' changes structure when it reaches the brain and gets processed into finished products. This is because what the brain sends back to the sense organs for reception are not raw data, they are processed products which I have dubbed sata... (Chimakonam, 2019b, 16).

What is suggested in the above excerpt is that knowledge begins with experience and that its basic ingredient is idea, which comes from the senses. It is through the process of sensation that the sense-perceived data are sent to the brain, which processes them as finished goods, and returns them to the sense organ, which in turn receives them as sata. It is pertinent to note that a reference to the fact that our experiences are ideas from either reflection or sensation is at the same time an acknowledgement of the fact that there exist ideas that result from the internal functioning of the mind or brain. This line of thought might have led Locke to divide the source of knowledge into two, namely, sensation and reflection. While sensation is the act of immediate awareness of external objects through the media of the senses, reflection refers to the activity of the mind on the data supplied by the external senses (Locke, 1952, 95). Where Chimakonam and Locke differ with reference to the ideas of sensation and reflection is that, while Chimakonam's submission may suggest that the mind (brain) is a receptacle of ideas, Locke insists that the mind is active, and its activity involves compounding and abstracting, putting ideas together, breaking down complex ideas etc. Basically, for the two scholars (Locke and Chimakonam), the basic building blocks of knowledge, therefore, are ideas received into the mind through the five sense organs. This makes both scholars empiricists.

Thus, Chimakonam's theory of sense-phenomenalism appeals to the five sense organs. It is based on the empirical perception of an individual by others or in the community. Sense-phenomenalism, for him, does not consider the content of a person's mind or any other mental property in determining his/her identity. Chimakonam appeals to the African conception of personhood espoused by Menkiti (1984, 171–172, 2018, 162) to argue that personal identity is a public or social issue, not a private one. Accordingly, it is evident in how we know and identify a person in the community. Mental properties/qualities such as rationality, will, memory and consciousness have nothing to contribute in matters of personal identity of a person, but the bodily features of that person which is also used to recognize or identify him/her by others in the community.

[1] Emphasis is mine.

To further buttress his argument and substantiate the veracity of the sense-phenomenal theory of personal identity, Chimakonam employed a thought experiment, which he tagged mental surgery (Chimakonam, 2011, 197–204, 2019a, 21–29). Here Chimakonam narrated an incident of a mind transplant that occurred between two human beings, namely, a certain Prof. Momoh (Sagittarius) and Mr. Jonathan (Venus). The essence of the narration is to demonstrate that personal identity does not reside in the mind/soul/brain, but in the body which is visible to other members of the society and by which they can recognize and identify the said person.

Thus, following a successful mind transplant, Prof. Momoh's mind was removed and planted in Mr. Jonathan's body, while Mr. Jonathan's mind which was also removed was planted in Prof. Momoh's body. From then, Prof. Momoh who now owns the mind of Mr. Jonathan began to think and act like Mr Jonathan oblivious of his bodily changes. He soon began to have problems and confusion with, and among his peers, family members and intellectual community, who recognize him as Prof. Momoh by virtue of his bodily features, but cannot match them with the thoughts, behaviours and experiences (which are those of Mr. Jonathan who they do not know) that he expresses towards them. The point is that the entity whose body is old and weak, and recognized and described by others in his community as the old wise Prof. Momoh, thinks of himself as Mr. Jonathan – a young, vibrant and aspiring scholar.

Similarly, the same problems and confusion confront Mr. Jonathan whose body houses the mind of Prof. Momoh. While he acts and thinks of himself as an old, weak, wise and seasoned Professor Momoh, his body which feels light, young and vibrant like a teenager is recognized and identified by his supposed friends, family and community members who refer to, and describe, him as simply Mr Jonathan. He is plunged into confusion and a crisis of identity. Again, the question arises; is he the old wise Prof. Momoh as he thinks and believes he is, or is he the young vibrant Mr Jonathan, as those who think they know him say he is? Thus, Chimakonam employs the theory of sense-phenomenalism to respond to this personal identity question by arguing that irrespective of which mind is in which body, the body features of the two entities that are recognized and identified by members of their family and community as Prof. Momoh or Mr. Jonathan, respectively, are what constitute who they are – their personal identity. Thus, for Chimakonam, personal identity lies in the bodily features of a person and which are visible and identifiable by others around him/her. If this is taken to be true, what possible implication could this have for epistemology? Does a person's knowledge of oneself not count in matters of personal identity? What could be the possible consequences of defining a person's identity or essence in the light of the knowledge of others? I shall attend to these and similar questions subsequently.

6.3 Epistemology, Sense-Phenomenalism and Personal Identity

What is it about me without which I would not be me? Is it the knowledge I have of myself or the knowledge others have of me? Is who I am dependent on others' perception of me, or my perception of myself? Can I have knowledge of myself by myself, or can I have knowledge of myself only through what others know about me? A cursory look at the above questions reveals that the problem of personal identity has some epistemological undertones (Enyimba, 2021b, 118). When we raise these sorts of questions, we put in perspective such epistemological issues as self-knowledge and social knowledge (otherwise known as social epistemology). This is what can be regarded as the 'epistemology of personal identity'.

Epistemology is basically the systematic study of the nature, sources, extent and limitations of human knowledge. What we know, how we know it and how sure we are of what we claim to know are of essence in epistemic discourses. In this regard, how we know a person's identity and how sure we are of our knowledge claim, is more epistemological than metaphysical, psychological or neuro-philosophical. In this section, Chimakonam's sense-phenomenalism is examined from the ambience of social epistemology and the idea of self-knowledge.

Social epistemology interrogates the social dimensions of knowledge by construing epistemology as a collective achievement. It is a study of epistemic properties of groups or social systems (Goldman, 1976, 771–791). In other words, social epistemology entails that knowledge is a community or social fabrication and not something given out there to be discovered. Self-knowledge, on the other hand, connotes the knowledge of one's own sensations, thoughts, beliefs and other mental states. This suggests that one can legitimately claim to have some knowledge of his or herself. One can possess information about his/her internal states, ideas, thoughts, imaginations and so on. Following this, sense-phenomenalism finds a place within the circumference of social epistemology. This means that one may legitimately refer to the theory of sense-phenomenalism as an aspect of social epistemology, which is opposed to the problem of self-knowledge. Like sense phenomenalism, social epistemology would suggest that our knowledge of a person's identity is based on social, communal and public qualities and properties. The implication of this for the epistemology of personal identity is very grave.

Sense-phenomenalism is empirical in its approach to our knowledge of personal identity. Empiricism as an epistemological theory holds the view that authentic knowledge is gotten mainly by sense experience through the five sense organs. So, like empiricism, sense phenomenalism rejects innate ideas, intuition and other sources of acquiring knowledge of self and the other that is not sensual.

One major challenge that confronts any empirical theory is the question of whether the individual has no role to play in the acquisition of knowledge and whether knowledge comes from experience alone. Empiricism does not consider the individual who actively experiences the experience in the knowledge acquisition process. Cornelius Benjamin (1943, 13) refers to this individual as the 'active experiencer', and when s/he is excluded it becomes difficult to appreciate the type of knowledge empiricism presents.

Moreover, the senses are prone to deception and misinformation as it concerns what we may claim to know. Without allowing the subject to participate in the knowledge process, the outcome may be a lopsided knowledge claim that is exclusive of other necessary ingredients that could give us holistic knowledge. For example, when Sagittarius's (the entity with Jonathan's mind and Momoh's body) social community perceived him as Momoh by virtue of their empirical observation of his physical body, they were deceived or mistaken in calling him Momoh, which caused a lot of confusion among them. Had they allowed the entity to participate in their knowledge of him and had they known that that entity was carrying a different mind; his dual personality would have been open to them. Again, they would not have insisted on identifying him as Momoh, since upon such revelation of his mind's content, he could not have rightly been called the person they know as Momoh. The same is applicable to Venus (the entity with Momoh's mind and Jonathan's body). But Chimakonam's sense-phenomenalism just like social epistemology and to a large extent empiricism would insist that the social community of Sagittarius, as well as that of Venus, were correct in their knowledge of who they are respectively. Thus, Sagittarius and Venus have no right to the knowledge of themselves; instead, they were forced to accept the knowledge of others about them. This logically leads to another epistemic challenge orchestrated by the sense-phenomenal theory of personal identity – knowledge as discriminatory.

A strict adherence to sense-phenomenalism would imply that one cannot have the capacity of knowing oneself by oneself except through others. In other words, one cannot claim to have knowledge of himself or herself outside what has been presented to him/her by others (the community). Hence, the important place of self-knowledge in the knowledge acquisition process is grossly undermined. Knowledge then becomes discriminatory as it deepens the dichotomy between the self and the other. This is an instance of epistemic marginalization, a situation whereby a person's knowledge production (either of his/her self or of an external object) is rejected on the grounds of the person's physical features or that the person has no such ability or right.

The above type of occurrence is what Miranda Fricker (2007) refers to as epistemic injustice. According to Fricker, there is a distinctly epistemic kind of injustice that plays itself out in two specific dimensions, namely, testimonial and hermeneutical. These represent a form of a wrong done to someone in his/her capacity as a knower (2007). Sagittarius and Venus were wrongly treated in their capacity as knowers. While testimonial injustice arises when a prejudiced hearer attempts to discredit a speaker's words; hermeneutical injustice takes place when one finds oneself in an unfair, disadvantageous point as a result of a lack of interpretative resources to make sense of his/her social experiences. Epistemic injustice is inherently subconscious and plays itself out in our daily lives when we disapprove of the knowledge of others and impose our own knowledge and interpretation of reality on them. One sees these two forms of epistemic injustice play out when one approaches the problem of personal identity from the perspective sense-phenomenalism.

As testimonials, the words, explanations, reactions, and indeed the self-knowledge expressed by Sagittarius and Venus, respectively, were discredited, disregarded and dismissed as false and meaningless by members of their social environment due to their prejudices and presupposition of who they believe Sagittarius and Venus were. While hermeneutically, they were placed at a disadvantage because of the lack of interpretative resources to make sense of their internal experiences and what was going on in their minds which the members of their community could not physically perceive.

No wonder Sagittarius and Venus were not given the opportunity to express their knowledge of themselves, and when they eventually did in their respective social environment, they were not taken seriously, it did not matter to the 'others' (the community). The knowledge of others of them was sacrosanct. In fact, by virtue of the sensual perception of others of them, their freedoms were restricted. This is one of the major challenges with Menkiti's communitarian conception of personhood, which is one of the launch pads of Chimakonam's sense-phenomenal theory of personal identity. Menkiti's communitarian theory of personhood, which states that it is the community that qualifies a person to be a person, denies the individual his initiative, freedom and rights to be who and what s/he wants to be, and pursue what s/he wants without undue interference from the community (the other). As such sense-phenomenalism like Menkiti's communitarian theory shrouds the individual within the community. The individual seems to lose his/her self to the community. This is rather detrimental to not only personal development and communal development but also to epistemic development.

The point being made here is that this type of condition created by a theory such as sense-phenomenalism might encourage such social ills as racial discrimination and other forms of discrimination against the *other*. If personal identity is to reside in the bodily features of a person such as colour, height, size and body marks then Chimakonom's sense-phenomenal theory of personal identity may give impetus to racism, ethnocentrism and other forms of social discrimination.

Articulating reasons why the racial politics of colour-branding should be discontinued, Chimakonam (2019b, 1–4), in another paper, raises such questions as is it correct to profile or brand different people with colours? Do the symbolic meanings of different colours correctly describe the attributes and attitudes of the people they are used to categorize? His answer is no. In the same vein, and as regards the idea of personal identity by bodily features, one might rightly ask, is it correct to locate a person's essence in his/her body features or attribute? Do the bodily attributes of a person correctly represent his personality or identity? The answer should be a vehement no following the preceding arguments. However, sense-phenomenalism responds in the affirmative, which is why it might be seen to inadvertently encourage colour branding and other forms of racism. According to *Encyclopedia Britannica* (1981), racism is the theory or idea that there is a causal link between inherited physical traits and certain traits of personality, intellect or culture and combined with it the notion that some races are inherently superior to others. This is the type of reasoning that led Western scholars of the like of Hegel (1975), Hume (cited in Eze, 1998), Kant (cited in Eze, 1998) and Levy-Bruhl (1947) to describe

Africans as primitive, illogical and having no philosophy simply on the basis of their bodily features, such as skin colour. How does a person's bodily feature (skin colour) translate to his/her personhood or personality? How can a person's essence be a function of his physical features without unknowingly putting him/her through some form of harm, victimization or discrimination or the other? This is exactly what Chimakonam's sense-phenomenal theory of personal identity portends.

In a critique of Chimakonam's earlier article on personal identity, Peter Bisong (2014, 50) canvasses the view that personal identity resides in consciousness because it is consciousness that differentiates human beings from non-human animals. According to him, this is not to say that the body is not a criterion of personal identity rather what it implies is that personal identity resides more in the consciousness than in the body. The body could only serve as a criterion when the consciousness is lost, but when consciousness is regained, the body ceases to be the criterion. What Bisong suggests here is that the body is simply a temporary criterion of personal identity. While one may sympathize with Bisong's submission, one might not be incorrect to observe that the individual consciousness alone might not be adequate enough as a criterion of personal identity. Hence, a combination of both individual consciousness and body features is very suggestive.

Similarly, Segun (2019, 33) introduces equiphenomenalism as an explanatory model of consciousness. He argues that the problem of consciousness cannot be adequately addressed by a strict adherence to a materialist/physicalist account of consciousness that rejects subjective conscious experiences. What Segun's equiphenomenalism implies is that a combination of subjective and objective (first person and third person) accounts of consciousness is useful in understanding personal identity. Hence, identity does not involve or depend on external bodily features alone, but also on the mind. This is why as I stated earlier, Sagittarius' and Venus' real identity would have been assessed if the content of their minds were combined together with their external bodies in the attempt to identify the person for which these properties were attributes. This would have prevented the confusion, deception and mistaken identity that confronted them and their community (friends and families) on their arrival from the hospital. Thus, if an individual is a composition of physical (biological) and non-physical properties or features, why the emphasis on the physical body or the brain at the exclusion of the mind or consciousness as Chimakonam (2019a) and Attoe (2019), respectively, suggests?

If we go along with Chimakonam that sata are created from data in the mind, then the important role of the mind (which is an intangible entity) in the formation of knowledge of a person's identity or knowledge of any kind cannot be neglected. This means that the epistemology of personal identity is not all a physical matter, the mind is involved largely in performing a crucial function in the entire process contrary to Chimakonam's supposition that perception does not occur in the mind. This is because the process which the mind undertakes in reading, decoding and recoding sense data into sata involves a substantial form of perception. To this extent, one might agree with Segun (2019, 33) that conscious experiences cannot be jettisoned in any attempt at making sense of personal identity. If this suggestion is neglected by theories of personal identity such as sense-phenomenalism, it might give impetus to epistemic injustice, marginalization and socio-racial discrimination of one form or the other against persons based on their physical traits that are perceptible to others at the expense of their internal experiences and contents of their mind.

6.4 Conclusion

Does it matter what society thinks it knows about me? What is the relevance of society to the knowledge of who I am? Could I still know myself and be myself without society's dictates? Is my identity, personality or essence social, personal or both? Could society take me for whom I am, and not who it thinks I am? What possible epistemological implication would other people's knowledge of me that is based on my physical features alone have on me? Would I not be misjudged, misunderstood, misrepresented, mistaken for another and possibly discriminated against because of what and whom my community presumes I am? Where lays my knowledge of myself by myself? Is it of any consequence or importance? These fundamental philosophical questions constitute the epistemology of personal identity. The questions of personal identity when closely analysed are fundamentally epistemological in nature. As such theories of personal identity, such as sense-phenomenalism as presented by Chimakonam, which repose a person's essence and identity to the perceptible body features only, are prone to racial discrimination, epistemic injustice and marginalization.

References

Attoe, A. D. (2019). Proto-phenomenalism as an explanatory model to the mind-body problem: A neurophilosophical inquiry. In J. O. Chimakonam, U. O. Egbai, D. A. Attoe, & S. T. Segun (Eds.), *New conversation on the problems of identity, consciousness and mind* (pp. 67–94). Spinger.

Benjamin, C. (1943). The essential problems of empiricism. *Philosophy of Science, 10*(1), 13–17.

Bernard, W. (2000). The self and the future. In T. Furman & M. Avila (Eds.), *The canon and its critics: A multi-perspective introduction to philosophy* (pp. 154–156). Mayfield.

Bisong, P. B. (2014). Jonathan Chimakonam's concept of personal identity: A critical reflection. *Filosofia Theoretica: Journal of African Philosophy, Culture and Religions., 3*(1), 50–66.

Chalmers, D. (1995). Facing up to the hard problem of consciousness. *Journal of Conscious Study,* 2, 200–219.

Chimakonam, J. O. (2011). Mental surgery: Another look at the identity problem. *Filosofia Theoretica: Journal of African Philosophy, Culture and Religions., 1*(1), 195–208.

Chimakonam, J. O. (2019a). A sense-phenomenal look at the problem of personal identity. In J. O. Chimakonam, U. O. Egbai, D. A. Attoe, & S. T. Segun (Eds.), *New conversations on the problems of identity, consciousness and mind* (pp. 11–32). Springer.

Chimakonam, J. O. (2019b). Why the racial politics of colour-branding should be discontinued. *Phronimon, 20,* 1–24.

Churchland, P. M. (1995). *The engine of reason, the seat of the soul: A philosophical journey into the brain*. MIT Press.
Dennet, D. C. (1993). Precis of conciousness explained. *Philosophy and Phenomenology Research, 53*(4), 889–892.
Dennett, D. (2005). *Sweet dreams: Philosophical obstacles to a science of consciousness*. MIT Press.
Descartes, R. (1968). *Discourse on methods and the meditations* (F. E. Sutclife, Trans.). Pengiun.
Encyclopedia Britannica. (1981). Vol. 15. William Benton Publisher.
Enyimba, M. (2012). Epistemological implications of Kant's notion of space and time. *European scientific journal, 8*(24), 186–194.
Enyimba, M. (2021a). New conversations on the problems of personal identity, consciousness and mind. *South African Journal of Philosophy, 40*(1), 117–120. https://doi.org/10.1080/02580136.2021.1885909
Enyimba, M. (2021b). How sense-phenomenal theory of personal identity might legitimate racism. *Dialogue and Universalism, 31*(1), 177–190.
Eze, E. C. (1998). Modern western philosophy and African colonialism. In E. C. Eze (Ed.), *African Philosophy: An Anthology* (pp. 214–220). Blackwell Publishers.
Fricker, M. (2007). *Epistemic injustice: Power and the ethics of knowing*. Oxford University Press.
Goldman, A. I. (1976). Discrimination and perceptual knowledge. *The Journal of Philosophy, 73*(20), 771–791.
Hegel, W. F. G. (1975). *Lectures on the philosophy of world history*. (H. B. Nisbet, Trans. Cambridge University Press.
Hume, D. (1993). The self. In J. Fienberg (Ed.), *Reason and responsibility* (pp. 324–326). Belmont.
Kant, I. (1966). *Critique of pure reason*. Anchors Books.
Levy-Bruhl, L. (1947). *Primitive mentality*. University of France Press.
Locke, J. (1894). *Essay concerning human undersatnding*. Vol. 1. Clarendon Press.
Locke, J. (1952). *Essay concerning human understanding* (M. Adler, Ed.). Great Books.
McGinn, C. (1989). Can we solve the mind-body problem. *Mind, 98*(391), 349–366.
Menkiti, I. (1984). Person and community in African traditional thought. In R. Wright (Ed.), *African philosophy. An introduction* (3rd ed., pp. 41–55). University Press of America.
Menkiti, I. (2018). Person and community. *Filosofia Theoretica: Journal of African Philosophy, Culture and Religions, 7*(2), 162–167.
Partif, D., & Vessey, G. (2000). Brain transplant and personal identity: A dialogue. In I. Furman & M. Avila (Eds.), *The canon and critics: A multi-perspective introduction to philosophy* (pp. 163–168). Mayfield.
Quinton, A. (2000). The soul. In I. Furman & M. Avila (Eds.), *The canon and critics: A multi-perspective introduction to philosophy* (pp. 157–0163). Mayfield.
Segun, S. T. (2019). Neurophilosophy and the problem of consciousness: An equiphenomenal perspective. In J. O. Chimakonam, U. O. Egbai, D. A. Attoe, & S. T. Segun (Eds.), *New conversations on the problems of identity, consciousness and mind* (pp. 33–65). Spinger.

Chapter 7
Traditional African Philosophy of Mind and World: Facilitating a Dialogue

Patrick Giddy

Abstract This chapter is a preliminary to the development of a philosophy of mind and world that has learned from the African traditional understanding of the human person. The objective is to frame the discipline by reference to the norms internal to philosophy as a social practice, thus facilitating dialogue across traditions. The obstacle lies in the oversight of such normative framing in the more dominant Analytic approach to the philosophy of mind, for which science and scientific method is paradigmatic. By the nature of things, there is in the framework of science no resources for thematizing the one doing the science, the person or agent treated not as one object among others but presupposed to science as a human project. The key point is the determination of 'objectivity', which is, in that tradition, contrasted with the subjective world that is the reality of the human person as they experience themselves. The African insights into how persons grow (as subjects) through the natural and personal environment undercut this dualism. To show this, and to mitigate a misrepresentation of the African insight into the spiritual reality of the person in terms of a dualism, the African traditional categories of mind and world, predating the rise of science, have to be translated into a register that is self-consciously in dialogue with a scientific and secular culture. I take as my example the Thomism-influenced African philosophy of mind of Placide Tempels.

Keywords Analytic philosophy of mind · Notion of objectivity · Dualism · Person as agent · Lonergan · Tempels · African traditional thought

P. Giddy (✉)
School of Religion, Philosophy and Classics, University of KwaZulu-Natal, Durban, South Africa
e-mail: jpgiddy@gmail.com

A. D. Attoe et al. (eds.), *Conversations on African Philosophy of Mind, Consciousness and Artificial Intelligence*,
https://doi.org/10.1007/978-3-031-36163-0_7

7.1 Introduction

This chapter is a preliminary to the development of a philosophy of mind and world that has learned from the African traditional understanding of the human person. The preliminary work is necessary if 'African Philosophy' is not to be side-lined as a curiosity and if the discipline is to play a real role in the dialogue that characterizes philosophical method. At the heart of the discussion is the African cultural notion of the person as intersubjectively empowered. This carries the implication that in the African approach the philosophy of mind will always be framed by a set of normative ideas. This metaphysics of the person – for example, denying any determinism – does not at first glance sit easily with the dominant standard Analytic approach to mind and world. In this latter approach, the influence is overwhelmingly that of science and scientific method, as French philosopher Luc Ferry, looking across the channel, has remarked (2011, 202). Within the framework of science, there is by the nature of things no resources for thematizing the one doing the science, the person or agent treated precisely not as one object among others but, of course, presupposed to science as a human project.[1] It will routinely overlook, or misinterpret as a dualism, the African traditional understanding of the spiritual reality of the person. What is needed for a preliminary framing of African philosophy of mind is to clear this up by unpacking the notion of 'objectivity' that, it will be argued, is at issue.

Happily, no dubious metaphysical leap of faith is envisaged here, for the one tradition to meet the other. In the uncontroversial notion of philosophy as a social practice – 'a coherent and complex form of socially established cooperative human activity' (MacIntyre, 1981, 175) with internal goods that operate as standards of excellence – we have a picture of the participant as tied into a normative journeying from apprentice to expert or 'professed'. You cannot be a proper participant without appreciating those standards (easy in a practice such as the game of soccer, much more difficult in the practice of family life). Getting to this appreciation is a growth moment for the novice or apprentice to the practice.[2] The ineluctability of the framing normativity here can be seen to be isomorphic with the normativity attached, in the broader context, to the African notion of the person or 'muntu'. Denying this normativity, in the case of the philosopher, amounts to a performative self-contradiction, or self-stultification: you are in fact declaring yourself out of the game (see Sect. 7.6, below).

I begin (Sect. 7.2) with an introductory sketch of how, within the frame of the standard approach to philosophy of mind, one can misconstrue the African

[1] Marilynne Robinson sums up the problem of this philosophical approach, without irony, in the title of her book, *Absence of mind* (2010).

[2] A child may read a novel in order to complete the assignment set by the teacher, but that day when, long after dark, the child is found with her bedside light on reading for its own sake – this is the moment when the child is now a reader, a full participant in the practice. A further point is that the way the practice conceives of its internal goods may, over time, be 'systematically extended'. This means that any philosophy of mind (say, the traditional African) may well be enriched through a confrontation with alternative traditions.

traditional notion of the spiritual reality of persons as a form of dualism. The situation does, however, also make a demand on African philosophy of mind, a tradition of thought predating the rise of science, to re-express itself in our new cultural context. And this is to the good, as the insights from the social sciences may amplify the traditional intuitions concerning the intersubjective conditions for personal growth.

In presenting some foundational notions of a philosophy of mind that has absorbed the African cultural insights into persons, I take my cue from Placide Tempels, one of the African philosophy pioneers (Sect. 7.3). There is a remarkable congruency of Tempels' version of African thought with some philosophical ideas of Thomas Aquinas. Tempels was a Catholic priest and would have studied Thomism at seminary. However useful we find the formulations of Aquinas' appropriation of Aristotelean thought, our very different context demands more, namely an approach that is self-consciously in dialogue with the culture dominated by science. For this reason, I will introduce a version of the pre-modern approach of Tempels that has learnt from the existentialists' move, in reaction to the emphasis on science, to recapture the subject at the heart of philosophy. Following the lead of Canadian philosopher Bernard Lonergan, I focus on an ambiguity attaching to the idea of 'objectivity' (Sect. 7.4) and I outline a more nuanced understanding of this notion that allows for a proper thematization of the person and subject. This is a key preliminary to the dialogue of the two traditions.

Contemporary European philosophy has not been completely unaware of the problems associated with the tendency to obliterate the subject and agent in the dominant philosophy of the modern period. Not all philosophy of mind is Analytic. An obvious example of this awareness is the existentialist approach, reacting against 'scientism', and it helps to see (very briefly!) why it does not get to the root of the problem (Sect. 7.5). I introduce, with the African traditional notion of personhood in mind, a way of translating the ideas of Tempels (and of African thought before the encounter with European culture) into a language that speaks directly to philosophical assumptions characteristic of an age of science. The normativity attached to being a person is expressed, in Lonergan's thought, in the notion of the self-appropriation of the subject and agent. This fundamentally undercuts any dualist interpretation of the spirituality of the person (Sect. 7.6).

Finally, in Sect. 7.7, we turn to the restructuring of the basic questions in the philosophy of mind, to take into account the African traditional insights into the human person. As foil for the discussion, I take Thomas Nagel's classic of introductory philosophy of mind (1987), *What does it all mean?*

7.2 An African Traditional Approach to Human Spirituality: Not a Dualism

The central 'given' in African traditional philosophy of mind, to be further unpacked, is the human person or subject as able to take hold of itself. This is a crucial datum in African philosophy and in African traditional culture the person is seen, in the first place, within a normative frame of reference – a boy or girl is initiated into and encouraged to grow towards an objective ideal of what it is to be, for example, a Mosotho man or woman. Placide Tempels highlights the centrality of this idea: 'It is the living *muntu* who, by divine will, is the norm of either ontological or natural law… [and] equally the norm of language, grammar, geography, of all life…' (Tempels, 1959, 121–2). But, suggests Ndaba, the neo-logical-positivist school of philosophy – the Analytic, to use a more general term – is unable to capture this life-world of the African (2001, 37). Why is this? The answer lies in the absence, in the Analytic discussions, of this crucial 'given'. And this, as already mentioned, could issue in the thought that the African understanding of mind and world is a form of dualism: there is the body, and there is also the soul or mind. But this would be to (mis)read the past through the lens of the categories of thought characteristic of modernity and associated with the rise of science. In order to see this, one has to trace the dominant way mind and world are seen in Analytic philosophy, the philosophical school most pressurized by science's self-understanding, and which I will try to show, disallows according to the status of 'real' to anything not subject to scientific methods (Kim, 2005). By the nature of things, that includes the subject or self (the doer of science, presupposed to science itself) and the kind of self-knowledge that is at issue when one talks about growing as a person. Something like the soul, simply added to the 'bodily reality', is then seen as un-real, or at least of no consequence to our normal way of seeing things.[3]

There is another reason for not interpreting African traditional thought as dualist. By taking on the task of breaking the reductionism that characterizes the understanding of the intersubjective formation of the person, African thought can deepen its own insight into the fact and norm of *ubuntu*, through the way the human sciences unpack the levels of interpersonality. Each person, after all, has a mix of motives, both other-centred (the *ubuntu* ideal) and selfish, and unless bolstered by the concrete modes in which the former is developed and the latter inhibited, the ideal could seem simply of cultural interest.

The reductionism I am referring to, and its intimate connection to dualism, is familiar to philosophers. It is built into courses in introductory philosophy, perhaps in particular in Anglophone cultures. It is 'in the genes' of modernity to think in this way, the securely true objective world out there, and the subjective world of my conscious experience. Factors outside this subjective world can and do influence me (my class positioning in society, or my gender, and so on) in ways that I might not be aware of, but it would be contrary to this received wisdom to think that they could in any way be thought to *enhance* my freedom to be myself.

This leads to a third point, not dealt with in this discussion but indicating the importance of following this line of research. The human person in the European – and, through cultural colonization, to some extent global – tradition as it has come

[3] If only bodily things are real, the question arises as to the status of how we *experience* the world (the sunset as sublime rather than the sunset as refracted light), how to deal with the evidence of 'qualia'. This is termed by philosophers in the Analytic tradition, 'the hard problem of consciousness' (Solms, 2019).

down to us, is characterized by the capacity for freedom, and the absolute centrality of this idea is given expression in the liberal democratic structures of government. Human rights are all about respecting the capacity of each individual for freedom. Yet because of the philosophical framework that has accompanied this valuable insight into human persons, the freedom remains at an abstract level, its ethical potential unrealized, the social structures of centrifugal individualism tied to a skepticism about human transcendence through growth in self-knowledge and in less conflictual habitual dispositions.

A new way of framing this tradition is needed, and I want to suggest here the potential of an African traditional understanding of mind and world to meet this need. That the latter predates the scientific revolution is to its advantage: it is not stuck in the problematic dualism of the objective world mapped by scientific theory and the subjective world that is the reality of the individual person as they experience themselves. Problematic because it seems to lead to at least two unhappy conclusions: the reduction of the subjective reality to determination by pre-personal forces uncovered by the sciences (giving rise to the 'intractable problem of free will'); or the dualism of the free subject alongside the determinism of the objective world, a view sometimes associated with religious faith, in the sense of hanging on to the reality of something more than the physical world. In contrast, the idea of growing as a person (subject) through the objective social and human environment of the subject is central to African traditional thought. It is an understanding of transcendence, but not at all implying a dualism.

The absolutely crucial preliminary task for African philosophy of mind, then, is, starting from the intuition sketched above, to pull apart the standard introduction to the philosophy of mind that is caught up in a framing of philosophical questions that arise from the particular conditions of modernity but arguably cannot on its own terms challenge itself. I have pursued this line of thought in a number of publications without particular reference to the African thought context (2009, 2016), and this has been paralleled by unpacking a cognate direction in ethics, virtue ethics (1997). I have also, with many others, been interested in how traditional African culture conceptualizes the human person (2002). The former critique of standard philosophy, I now want to suggest, not only allows for but also embraces the specific way African tradition thinks of the person. To use a military metaphor, these two lines of research can be seen as a two-pronged or pincer movement that closes down on its target. What is the target? It is, proximately, the contemporary outline (only an outline) of a non-dualist understanding of the person, or the mind, sourced in African traditional thought, and which is justified by the clarification of a certain ambiguity, even incoherence, in the Analytic strain of thought concerning the notion of objectivity – and which I take to be the chief obstacle to this understanding. It is, remotely, the facilitation of a dialogue, one that, as I have suggested, may truly assist modernity to better frame its leading ideas and values.

7.3 Tempels' Bantu Philosophy: Categories of Mind and World

According to Tempels, the metaphysical substratum for the western philosophical tradition is that of 'being' while for the African traditional mind it is 'active force'.[4] Force is not something 'out there' simply to be observed in a neutral way; rather it is at once a reality and a value: things find their fulfillment, their natural end, in the actualization of what they potentially are. And since persons are part of nature – not standing over against nature – their actualization is also a value for us. Union with how nature is, is a value. And nature tends towards the augmentation of force.

Nature and persons are seen as very much more integrated than is the case for the western thinker. There is a spirit ('living force') which runs through the whole of the cosmos, as Bernard Matolino reminds us, the 'divine force, celestial or terrestrial forces, human forces, animal forces, vegetable and even material or mineral forces' (in Matolino, 2011, 338). Things are thought of not in terms of what they are but rather how they act: force is not an accidental predicate of some or other static being, thought of in a neutral way apart from how it acts. Rather, 'force is the nature of being, force is being, being is force.'

Tempels' interpretation seems to resonate with other African philosophers. For example, Camerounian intellectual Achille Mbembe writes in *Le Monde* (December 15, 2019; my translation) that

> Western philosophers of the subject… start from the idea that there is something that is intrinsic to us, fixed and stable and unvaried. Creator of himself, a person gets his identity from himself, and because he has a reflexive consciousness and an interiority, he is distinct from all other living species.

In contrast, for traditional African thinkers, the identity of the person was more dispersed. What was important

> was not the self as such, but the manner in which one composed and recomposed oneself, each time in relation to other living entities. In other words, personal identity was nothing other than the process of becoming, within the tissue of relationships of which each person was the living sum.

Matolino, however, is critical of Tempels' approach to African metaphysics. 'Whereas being is a fundamental category in Western thought,' Matolino argues (2011, 338), 'its equivalent in African thought is some dubious concept of force gleaned from magic and irrational fears' and that it is 'illogical and mystified'. There are basically two points of criticism here. First, in what way can we show that magic, and a fortiori witchcraft, are not implied by the logic of this way of thinking? Secondly, does not this whole idea of external forces operating on persons stem from primitive fears in the face of things beyond one's control? Would that not undermine responsibility and, indeed, ethics as such?

---

[4]In this section, I am drawing largely on my paper (2012a) (and, related to this, see my 2012b and 2013.)

The first point seems unfair to Tempels. It is true that he uses the term 'magical' to describe the influences of forces upon one another. However, he clarifies that if we want to keep the term 'magic', 'it must be modified so that it is understood in conformity with the content of Bantu thought' (1959, 59). Such modification will show up, Tempels argues, that magical practices exhibit 'contradictions of the healthy principles of his [i.e. the African person's] own philosophy'.

Tempels himself does not allude to his own philosophical background but we can, as mentioned already, note a similarity of Bantu philosophy as he describes it with Thomistic metaphysics, originating in Aristotle's hylomorphism. Whereas Plato thought of things in terms of their (static) essence and their (changing) appearance, the essence lying behind the appearance, Aristotle saw that the essence (form) was what made the thing what it is, and to describe it is to specify what the form is a form *of*, i.e. its 'matter'. But matter is never something existing of itself, it is matter *of* a particular form. Every being is properly described in terms of how it is becoming itself, form out of matter, so that matter is the potential for that being to become actual. How it is becoming itself we call its characteristic 'act of being', for example, growth in a plant, sensitive living in a non-human animal, knowing and responsible acting in a human being. The dynamic of all things can be captured conceptually by means of the categories of form, matter, and act. The African world of living forces has something in common with this strand of philosophy – hence not at all self-evidently irrational, as Matolino judges it to be.

This whole conception can be further clarified if we follow the strand of thought in the European philosophical tradition that has articulated, with Hegel and others, a shift from substance talk to subject talk. That is to say, a shift from the impersonal third-person description of humanity – characteristic of Caesar's own narration of his part in the Gallic wars, for example – to first-person descriptions that are, clearly, also intersubjectively accessible, as when one reads a contemporary autobiography. This will introduce the idea of fuller or more comprehensive levels of being. So far as the *substance* (the being) of 'human nature' is concerned, it does not matter if one is asleep, awake, inattentive or alert, exercising intelligence or looking blankly into space, considering carefully how best to act or reacting without thought. But from the point of view of the *subject* this is absolutely crucial. One moves to a different level of existing, from asleep to being awake, to applying one's powers of observation, to asking intelligent questions about the data, to considering the plausibility of one's idea and so not jumping to a conclusion: these actions involve the virtues, but they are also one's very being, one's level of existing. That it is indeed a question of a higher level of being comes out clearly when one considers how, in coming to hold a new belief on the basis not of influencing factors but on the grounds of having a good reason for it, one achieves a 'new self': myself holding the new belief. And this is through my own agency, the exercise of my capacity to 'double' myself, to hold my own beliefs in consideration. Similarly, in the case of actions taken responsibly. This is, clearly, a notion very far from mystical or magical.

The second point raised by Matolino is that the metaphysics of 'force' is generated out of irrational fears. It is true that Tempels develops his ethics on the basis of how every person is always, as he says, 'in intimate and personal relationship with other forces acting above him and below him in the hierarchy of forces. He knows himself to be a vital force, even now influencing some forces and being influenced by others' (1959: 103). The growth of force occurs through the positive influence of others who are more 'persons' than oneself.

But Tempels emphasizes the *normal*, not mysterious or mystical, nature of this transaction of forces, far removed from superstition. 'One force will reinforce or weaken another. This causality is in no way supernatural in the sense of going beyond the proper attributes of created nature. It is, on the contrary, a metaphysical causal action which flows out of the very nature of a created being' (1959, 59).

Nevertheless, it could seem that if a personal force outside me determines my very being, I am to that extent diminished, and I should fear this, as hostile to me. A writer who has expressively addressed this question is Augustine Shutte (1995). If the transaction is envisaged on the model of the natural sciences, this is indeed the case; the more A operates as a force on B, the less work B does. However, there are other models, in particular the way that one person influences another person so as to empower them: here, the *more* influence (of the correct sort) A has on B, the *more* work B is empowered to do in their own self-actualization. Explaining the notion of 'interpersonal causality' Shutte writes: 'The more you are involved *in a strictly personal way* in the production of my act, the more the act is my own' (1995, 92). This is because the influence of the more matured, integrated personality on my own results, through my identification with that person, in myself affirming a less conflicted set of wants in myself.

7.4 Modernity, Science, and the Problem of Objectivity

We turn now to the question of the encounter of this metaphysics of the human person with the more dominant tradition. It is quite common for African thought, out of fairness, to be allocated a place in the curriculum, the specialization termed 'African Philosophy'. This can happen while philosophy ('as such!') goes its merry way, just as it used to. Our understanding of philosophy as a social practice is aimed at undercutting this tendency. Our suggestion is that there is a normative set of standards applicable to anyone participating in the social practice. If these standards are systematically obscured, as they arguably are in the dominant practice, this will disallow anyone from raising the question of a perhaps *better* set of foundational questions in the philosophy of mind.

A confusion about objectivity is central to the failings, as we see them, of the dominant approach to the philosophy of mind. The subject – it is supposed – in general experiences something different to what is actually the case in the objective world. The internal incoherence of this is immediately evident: the statement purports to say something objective here, and not just confined to the subjective world as experienced by the speaker. In this and the following two sections, this confusion will be carefully traced and unpacked.

To suggest there should be a norm of being human – even worse, an African norm – that frames philosophical questions would seem a case of reverse cultural imperialism. But this misunderstands what is being proposed. The problem is clear: when Plato suggested a normative human nature, his thought was that this lies in the role played by reason in a person's life, ruling over desire. His interlocuter, Callicles, was quick to respond: without desire you might as well be dead (*Gorgias*, 492e). The norm, in other words, seems to have something arbitrary about it. Why not opt rather for desire? 'Reason' as central to our human nature is not self-evidently true. Would this be the case for any suggested norm of being human?

On the other hand, let us return to the idea of a social practice. Practices do have framing normative structures. They have objective standards attaching to the realization of their internal goods. You are not a proper soccer player if you think you can systematically disregard the offside rule. You are failing to be a true participant. And in our own case, we are suggesting the set of standards simply to be a participant in the practice, a normativity transcending any particular way that one might participate.

In a sense, the move being suggested here goes back to the origins of philosophy in classical Greek thought: in his celebrated cave metaphor, Plato describes human knowing as an existential journey, a journey of personal growth. What obscures this framing of philosophy is the idea that, as personal, it is seen as not something 'objective' or of metaphysical import. Wittgenstein famously believed that there was nothing of philosophical interest in this line of questioning, in other words only empirical psychological facts: 'the will *as a phenomenon* is of interest only to psychology' (2001, para. 6.423, my emphasis).

However, the Canadian philosopher Bernard Lonergan has put his finger on the root of the problem: the ambiguity in the notion of what 'objective' actually means. This ambiguity stems from an unavoidable duality in human knowing. He notes (1970, 251-253) the kind of 'objectivity' relevant for any biological organism confronting and tasked with dealing with what's out there, not flying into a windowpane, in the case of the ibis. And he contrasts this with the attainment of objectivity through our capacity to reflect on and evaluate the accuracy of our ideas, and how we suppose things to be. The organism – and this is the case with the new-born infant too – lives in a world of immediacy, dominated by biological ends. With the acquisition of language, we however also live in a mediated world – encountered not in terms of biological needs but through meaning. We can think, because we can unlike the pre-linguistic toddler grasp things in the mind without grasping them with the fingers or the mouth. By invoking their names, we can simply hold them in mind without them being present. When your dog pricks up his ears on hearing your name spoken in a conversation while you are still at work, he looks around to identify you. But your name is being used here not at all to point to you but to bring you to mind. The dog plays no active part in this conversational world.[5]

[5] An anonymous referee remarks here, 'We cannot know what it is like to have a dog's subjective experience'. This viewpoint is standard in the dominant tradition of the philosophy of mind: it refers back to Nagel's (1979) famous essay, 'What is it like to be a bat?' An objective description,

If we focus only on the former sense of objectivity, we might think what is real are 'bodies', i.e. 'out there' (Lonergan, 1972, 238–9). But more coherently, what is real is whatever we come to critically judge actually is the case on the basis of the evidence – 'bodies', to be sure, but also, for example, minds, atoms, transactional forces, personal growth, and so on.

A key factor in this whole historical development is the shift from what one might term a common-sense culture to one in which meaning is 'controlled' not by sheer volumes of additive experience (the sage) but by theory and science (Lonergan 1972, Chap. 4, 1988, Chap. 16). As an example of this shift, we can take the classic case of Newton's dissent from the common-sense idea that bodies have a natural tendency to fall down. Newton disagreed: all change – whether from a stationary position to movement or from uniform motion in a straight line to something else – must be explained by the intervention of outside forces. The key idea is that of inertia. Treat all physical reality, he suggests, as nothing like our experience of intentionally aiming at something (the stone 'wants' to reach stability) but as inert. The upshot of this new approach is the contemporary conventional wisdom that sees the universe in terms of a dualism of the purposive, end-directed, reality of free personal subjects choosing for themselves and the non-purposive causally determined reality of objects that is the proper domain of science.

Such major cultural shifts can lead to widespread scepticism about truth and value objectivity. Common sense is discredited in favour of the real, scientific facts of the case. But even science is seen as socially constructed (Boghassian, 2006), and by this is meant, not objectively true, but relative to some person's viewpoint.

Common sense relates things to us, from our perspective, while theory, science, relates things to one another, the difference between saying 'it is heavy' and specifying the weight in kilograms. In a sense, the latter can be termed, in the title of Nagel's book, 'the view from nowhere' (Nagel, 1989). But it is not really a *view* at all. Newton struggled with the problem of relative and absolute motion; he postulated an absolute space-time viewpoint. But we do not need this absolute point for viewing the world. Viewing, or touching, or sensing do not give us knowledge, but only evidence. We need an insight into the evidence that yields how things actually are. The rain falls and the sun dries out the rain. But only insight into what is captured in the concepts of evaporation and precipitation give us an understanding of what is actually going on. Objectivity is not a matter of having the perfect (detached!) view of things, but rather of continuing to ask further questions until the evidence is

Nagel says, can only abstract from the particularities of the organism's subjectivity (1979, 174). This shows a confusion about 'objectivity' that supposes we have immediate subjective knowledge of our own selves which we can then infer of other selves, but this does not apply to organisms with different sense apparatus. In fact, all we have in our own case is an immediate awareness: *knowledge* of ourselves, just as knowledge of others, is a question of making sense of the data, and judging the possible accuracy of our grasp of how things are. Because we can use our imagination and intelligence, a woman can enter into the subjective life of a man (the great novelists!), an ethologist into the subjective life of a dog, or a lioness. See, for example, Midgley (1995, 231–2) and Coetzee (1999, 54).

accounted for and a reasonable judgement can be attained (Lonergan, 1970, Chap. 10).

Having this kind of consciousness or awareness of ourselves implies an ineluctable tendency to ask questions. This posing of questions, an openness to my reality, is emphasized by existentialists. And this implies that there is a transcendent normative framework that makes me me. When I judge some understanding as probably true, it is I myself taking hold of myself; similarly, a considered action marks me as the one who chooses that kind of action, as responsible. The conditions for rising up to this set of standards that mark what we are furnish the normative framework for philosophy as a social practice.

7.5 Contemporary European Thought on 'the Subject'

Existentialist philosophy is the most well-known of the reactions to the thinned-out philosophical agenda of modernity, and an obvious candidate for framing a future philosophy of mind open to the African traditional insights into the human person. For Kierkegaard (1968, 181), the highest truth is what he terms 'subjectivity'. In the existentialist approach, philosophy needs to say something about what it is to be a self-conscious subject faced with the need to make something of oneself, to 'be oneself' (Romano, 2019).

The name Sartre is synonymous with the idea that no objective account of the person can replace the existential awareness of one's open choice to determine one's own life. This openness, the 'pour-soi' or 'for-itself', is defined by the phenomenon of being conscious. But this determining of oneself seems doomed to be frustrated, as Sartre explains in the opening section of *Being and nothingness.* Here, Sartre argues that consciousness, as consciousness *of* something, is always directed towards an object, and being directed outward, contains nothing – in the sense of having as it were *another* object 'in the mind'. At the same time, he says, it is clearly *conscious* of itself as being conscious of the object – the contrary would be 'absurd' (1969, xxviii). However, since consciousness always is directed upon an object *other* than itself, it cannot grasp itself, because it is not itself an 'object': 'there is no inertia in consciousness', as there is in bodily things (1969, 104). For this reason, we are not able to take hold of ourselves in the way that we have outlined above, the way suggested in the African normative idea of being a person become more of a person, more consistent in our choices of action, for example.

This idea that we do not have the ability to objectify ourselves, and so the possibility of making something of our lives can be traced back to Hume and Kant. Hume (1740/1969) discredits the idea that one can come to a belief on the grounds that one's reasons for the belief are, in fact, sound. As he explains (*Treatise*, Bk 1, Part 3, Sect. 8): 'When I give the preference to one set of arguments above another, I do nothing but decide from my feeling concerning the superiority of their influence.' The belief 'arises immediately, without any new operation of reason or imagination'. Kant ([1783]/1966), objecting to Hume's reductionism, puts the spotlight not on passive sensing, feeling, but on our active capacity to formulate ideas. He argues, against Hume, that there is a reality that is the mind or the self, the 'transcendental unity of apperception'. The mind, however, is framed by a finite number of structures determining how those ideas are formulated. Kant has forgotten the element of holding our ideas reflectively, judging their possible objectivity. All we can hope for is 'universal necessity', that is to say, agreement (*Prolegomena*, para.19).[6]

7.6 Lonergan and Self-Appropriation: Framing a Dialogue

It is Lonergan's insight into the ambiguity around the notion of objectivity that allows us to take forward the existentialist focus on the subject or person. Our target is framing a possible dialogue that undercuts the practice of side-lining African traditional thought. For this, a normativity transcendent of particular cultures needs to be put in place. This is done when one thinks of this normativity in terms of the internal goods of the social practice.

The technical term for the kind of argument used in establishing these 'rules of the game' is 'retortion'. The argument turns, Lonergan remarks (2001, 317), 'upon what no subject can avoid':

> You cannot avoid experience. You cannot avoid trying to understand… If you want to play the fool, to play being stupid, still you do that intelligently. Again, you cannot avoid the exigencies of your own reasonableness… If you were to renounce your reasonableness you would find yourself asking reasons for it.

There is an internal demand of the subject (the participant in the practice) to bring these norms of intelligence and reasonableness to conscious awareness, to appreciate and 'appropriate' this way of being.

The existentialist turn to the subject is thereby amplified, to its benefit. The questioning characteristic of the new openness to becoming oneself has a natural end. *Being self-conscious* does not imply I lack a human nature, as Sartre thought. I can develop in accordance with my nature as a questioning being, faced with obstacles or blocks or tasks to be met well or badly. The activation of my questioning is not without an effort. My judgement of the adequacy or otherwise of my insights has to overcome pressures towards laziness or failing to admit the possibility of an oversight. It is always a struggle to accept, from anonymous journal referees of one's manuscript, that sections could be better expressed. This struggle is even more pronounced in the case of my judgement that such-and-such is the best course of action, all things considered, and of course it takes effort to conform my will to that judgement. The motivation of that effort is a further interesting question.

---

[6] Similarly, on Kant, see Kitcher (2006). She mentions, on the other hand, those contemporary writers who remain followers of Hume's denial of any reality to 'the self', such as Derek Parfit and Daniel Dennett (Kitcher, 2006, 199). For an account of how Kant's account of subjectivity differs from that of Lonergan, see Lonergan (1993, 1996).

The foundational question in the philosophy of mind is not:

What are the conditions of possibility for knowing anything at all?

which seems to invite a too static set of conditions, whereas we are trying to capture what it is to be the dynamism – the norm of 'muntu' – somewhat enacted but not at all fully so; but

What am I doing when I am knowing?

In other words, we do not pretend that we are not already aware that we do make judgements about our own ideas, and come to own our beliefs, or at least some of them. This undercuts the conventional starting question in the philosophy of mind, how can I be sure that I know anything at all (Is it all a dream?). Now, on the contrary, we can see there is, in the reframed question, a necessary normative dimension.

7.7 Philosophy of Mind and World: Shifting the Questions

We can now give an example of how, with this normative framing of the philosophical practice, an African-influenced philosophy of mind will shift the fundamental questions.

It is convenient to follow some of the issues put forward in Nagel's (1987) classic of introductory philosophy in the English-speaking world.[7] The first question, as already indicated, concerns the problem of knowledge, framed as: Can we get from 'in here' – our mind – to 'out there'? This is only a coherent question if we assume the aim of knowledge is to get to what is 'out there'. If by 'out there' is meant simply what is the truth of the matter (rather than simply imagined), then the problem dissolves into the development of reasonable judgements. However, if by 'out there' is meant what does not involve the subject, it is a misleading concept of the real. In the process of trying to reach knowledge, the aim is a reasonable judgement of the accuracy or otherwise of our ideas in the light of the data furnishing evidence. The aim is the appropriation of our capacity for a heightened self-presence and cognitional self-transcendence. In other words, the framing question has to do with the fulfilment of our humanity – in our African suggestion, this is captured in the term *ubuntu*. How is this possible? How is it linked to the human sciences? How has our understanding of it changed since the rise of modern science? These are, contrary to Nagel, the more interesting questions.

Nagel asks whether other minds exist. This is an offshoot of the above problem: if we assume, with Descartes, some special exceptional inner knowledge of our own self, then we might ask what about other selves (as opposed to their obviously real bodies)? But if the capacity for self-consciousness develops only through others, the

[7] The first three topics are: How do we know anything? other minds, and the mind-body problem. This is followed by discussions of the meaning of words and of free will. Similarly, in other textbooks, for example, Pinchin, 2005; Salazar, 2019.

reality of my own self is not at all something like an inner 'thing'. It is affirmed simultaneously as real and as a norm (I can achieve it more and more). We discover our own self in intersubjective causality, in the sharing of ideas and the personal influence of one person on another.

Is there an intractable problem of free will? If every event has a cause, then so too must so-called free choices. If an action is caused, it is determined. The problem lies in the fact that our entire social set-up, in particular our legal system, seems to *assume* the capacity for free choice and responsibility, that is to say, precisely *not* being determined. But how is this explained? It is implausible – an anomaly – to suggest that that there is a magical power of choice operating apart from the conditioning factors uncovered by the human sciences, by psychology, sociology and ethology.

Our normative framing of philosophical discussion on the human person can clear this up. No magical power is invoked. The norm of 'having a good reason' for an action is a constitutive ('internal') element in philosophy as a practice, and it is similarly constitutive of doing science, when one determines (reasonably!) the particular cause of an event. The two 'causalities' are not in conflict. There is, however, a real, though not 'intractable' problem of free will, and that is the problem of how the essential human capacity for free self-disposition translates into a real, effective freedom. In the philosophy of mind, this would be the more fruitful question.

I mentioned at the start that an African philosophy of mind, in contrast to the more dominant tradition, will always be framed by a set of normative ideas, focussed on what it is to be a person. We can, finally, suggest something of the background to this conflict between the two traditions. It has to do, to simplify, with a general understanding of modernity in terms of simply subtracting from the whole set of objects of belief (spirits, gods, miracles, myths, and so on) of a previous age, to reach the natural (material, bodily, scientific) residue underneath. It is that previous age that is the cultural milieu of African traditional philosophy of mind. The feeling is, however, that we are now free from this, we are enlightened. Putting aside that world of transcendence as a matter of principle would seem to be largely a prejudice. On the contrary, I would suggest, along with Charles Taylor (2007, 151–4) and Marcel Gauchet (1996), for an understanding of modernity as deriving from an appropriation of human subjectivity that has its roots in what Taylor (2012) and others term the 'axial age' of the major religious traditions (the prophets in the Hebrew religion, the Upanishads and Gautama Buddha in the Indian culture, for example), where outward conformity is criticised in favour of an inner authenticity of human faith and the norm of self-appropriation developed above.

African philosophy of mind can point to a recovery of human transcendence, and this is big with implications for broader matters. To give just one example, in the African traditional thought-world, social connectedness is a higher value than that of procedural equality (Jakobsen-Widding, 1995). This is because, as we have seen above, the effective human ability to act ethically (to be a full person) is dependent on the action of others on one, and one's own receptivity to such action. Again, it is Matolino who expresses well the response of modernity: could Tempels not see, he asks, that all peoples, in this case African peoples, can indeed 'go beyond their culture to see timeless values such as equality, justice and fairness' (2011, 340). Whatever one's answer, it is clear that changing the metaphysical agenda allows for these kinds of interesting questions, in the context of a world opening up to a plurality of cultural ideals.

References

Boghassian, P. (2006). *Fear of knowledge: Against relativism and constructivism*. Oxford University Press.

Coetzee, J. M. (1999). *The lives of animals*. Princeton University Press.

Ferry, L. (2011). *A brief history of thought* (T. Cuffe, Trans.). London: HarperCollins.

Gauchet, M. (1996). *The disenchantment of the world* (O. Burge, Trans.). Princeton University Press.

Giddy, P. (1997). A communitarian framework for liberal social practices? *South African Journal of Philosophy, 16*, 150–157.

Giddy, P. (2002). African traditional thought and growth in personal unity. *International Philosophical Quarterly, 42*, 315–327.

Giddy, P. (2009). Objectivity and subjectivity: Rethinking the philosophy syllabus. *South African Journal of Philosophy, 28*, 359–376.

Giddy, P. (2012a). The ideal of African scholarship and its implications for introductory philosophy: The example of Placide Tempels. *South African Journal of Philosophy, 31*, 504–516. https://doi.org/10.1080/02580136.2012.10571790

Giddy, P. (2012b). 'Philosophy for children' in Africa: Developing a framework. *South African Journal of Education, 32*, 15–25. https://doi.org/10.15700/saje.v32n1a554

Giddy, P. (2013). Can African traditional culture offer something of value to global approaches in teaching philosophy? *Acta Academica, 45*, 154–172.

Giddy, P. (2016). Human agency and weakness of will: A neo-Thomist discussion. *South African Journal of Philosophy, 35*, 197–209. https://doi.org/10.1080/02580136.2016.1167346

Hume, D. ([1740] 1969). *A Treatise of human nature*. Penguin.

Jakobsen-Widding, A. (1995). 'I lied, I farted, I stole…': Dignity and morality in African discourses on personhood. In S. Howell (Ed.), *The ethnography of moralities*. Routledge.

Kant, I. ([1783] 1966). *Prolegomena to any future metaphysics* (P. Lucas, Trans.). Manchester University Press.

Kierkegaard, S. (1968). *Concluding unscientific postscript*. Princeton University Press.

Kim, J. (2005). *Physicalism, or something near enough*. Princeton University Press.

Kitcher, P. (2006). Kant's philosophy of the cognitive mind. In P. Buyer (Ed.), *The Cambridge companion to Kant and modern philosophy* (pp. 169–202). Cambridge University Press.

Lonergan, B. (1970). *Insight. A study of human understanding* (3rd ed.). Philosophical Library.

Lonergan, B. (1972). *Method in theology* (2nd ed.). Darton, Longman and Todd.

Lonergan, B. (1988). Dimensions of meaning. In B. Lonergan (Ed.), *Collection* (Collected works of Bernard Lonergan, Vol. 4, Chap. 16). University of Toronto Press.

Lonergan, B. (1993). The theory of philosophic differences. In B. Lonergan (Ed.), *Topics in education* (Collected Works of Bernard Lonergan, Vol. 10, Chap. 7). University of Toronto Press.

Lonergan, B. (1996). Philosophical positions with regard to knowing. In B. Lonergan (Ed.), *Philosophical and theological papers 1958–1964* (Collected works of Bernard Lonergan, Vol. 6, Chap. 10). University of Toronto Press.

Lonergan, B. (2001). *Phenomenology and logic. The Boston College lectures on mathematical logic and existentialism* (Collected works of Bernard Lonergan, Vol. 22). University of Toronto Press.

MacIntyre, A. (1981). *After virtue*. Duckworth.

Matolino, B. (2011). Tempels' philosophical racialism. *South African Journal of Philosophy, 30*, 330–342. https://doi.org/10.4314/sajpem.v30i3.69579
Mbembe, A. (2020). Les métaphysiques africaines permettent de penser l'identité en mouvement. *Le Monde*, December 15, 2019. Accessed August 29, 2020, from https://www.lemonde.fr/afrique/article/2019/12/15/achille-mbembe-les-metaphysiques-africaines-permettent-de-penser-l-identite-en-mouvement_6022959_3212.html
Midgley, M. (1995). *Beast and man* (Revised Ed.). Routledge.
Nagel, T. (1979). What is it like to be a bat? In T. Nagel (Ed.), *Mortal questions*. Cambridge University Press.
Nagel, T. (1987). *What does it all mean?* Oxford University Press.
Nagel, T. (1989). *The view from nowhere*. Oxford University Press.
Ndaba, W. J. (2001). *An African philosophy for dialogue with Western philosophy – A hermeneutic project*. Unpublished PhD thesis, University of Fort Hare.
Pinchin, C. (2005). *Issues in philosophy. An introduction* (2nd ed.). Palgrave Macmillan.
Robinson, M. (2010). *Absence of mind. The dispelling of inwardness from the modern myth of the self*. Yale University Press.
Romano, C. (2019). *Etre soi-même*. Gallimard.
Salazar, H. (Ed.). (2019). *Introduction to philosophy of mind*. Rebus Community. Accessed June 15, 2020, from https://press.rebus.community/intro-to-phil-of-mind
Sartre, J. P. (1969). *Being and nothingness* (H. Barnes, Trans.). Washington Square Press.
Shutte, A. (1995). *Philosophy for Africa*. Marquette University Press.
Solms, M. (2019). The hard problem of consciousness and the free energy principle. *Frontiers in Psychology*. Accessed June 15, 2020, from https://doi.org/10.3389/fpsyg.2018.02714
Taylor, C. (2007). *A secular age*. Belknap.
Taylor, C. (2012). What was the axial revolution? In R. Bellah & H. Joas (Eds.), *The axial age and its consequences* (pp. 30–46). Belknap.
Tempels, P. (1959). *Bantu philosophy* (C. King, Trans.). Présence Africaine.
Wittgenstein, L. (2001). *Tractatus logico-philosophicus* (D. F. Pears & B. McGuinness, Trans.). Routledge Classics.

Part II
Conversations on Africa and Some Major Themes of the Fourth Industrial Revolution

Chapter 8
Transhumanism, Singularity and the Meaning of Life: An Afrofuturist Perspective

Ojochogwu S. Abdul

Abstract Transhumanism, a movement promoting the possibility and desirability of using science and technology in overcoming fundamental human limitations, could be conceived as a type of philosophy of life that emphasizes a meaningful and ethical approach to living informed by reason, science, progress, the value of existence in our current life, and the eventual goal of human enhancement. Related to transhumanism is the concept of the Singularity described as a future period during which the pace and impact of technological change will be so rapid and deep that human life will be transformed irreversibly. The projections and implications of transhumanism and the singularity phenomenon raise many important philosophical questions and possible new answers concerning human nature, intelligence, and the meaning generally of life. In this chapter, we examine both philosophies and apply analytic argumentation in demonstrating that they affect or provide meaning of life at individual, species and cosmic levels. Furthermore, with assessment of meaning of life in some particular African conceptions, the chapter employs a perspective of Afrofuturism and engages in critical reconstruction and creative imagination of African thought-systems in conversation with other intellectual traditions to propose a view connecting transhumanism, singularity and meaning of life within a futuristic African philosophical context.

Keywords Transhumanism · Singularity · Meaning of life · Afrofuturism

O. S. Abdul (✉)
Department of Philosophy, Prince Abubakar Audu University, Anyigba, Kogi State, Nigeria
e-mail: oabdul@kogistateuniversity.edu.ng

A. D. Attoe et al. (eds.), *Conversations on African Philosophy of Mind, Consciousness and Artificial Intelligence*,
https://doi.org/10.1007/978-3-031-36163-0_8

8.1 Introduction

What, if any, is the meaning of life? Is there a reason why we, as individuals or as an entire human species, are here? What, if any, is the point of the Universe? The question "what is the meaning of life" is arguably the most profound question of human existence, and as a meaning-seeking species, humans have understandably pondered this deep existential question for millennia, with tons of stories, religions and philosophies produced in the quest for answers.

At several points in the human history of ideas, this search into life's meaning and efforts at possible answers has been tied to one conception or the other of human nature. Answering the question "what is the meaning of life?" is therefore further complicated by the problematic question "what does it mean to be human?" and responding to the latter, however difficult, remains necessary to elicit views of human potential, purpose and destiny which essentially provide insights into addressing the former.

Transhumanism, as a scientistic yet transcendence-seeking alternative to the humanistic, minimalist, and reductionist animal account of human nature (Hopkins, 2005), presents a conception of human nature as improvable and consequently holds an expansive view of humanity as beings with a potential and purpose to take charge over their destiny and the evolutionary process in striving towards transcendence and/or the perfection of humans and the world. In this character, transhumanism, and the related singularity concept, may therefore be understood as containing answers, or approaches to finding answers to meaning of life questions.

The philosopher Anders Sandberg (2015) availed the transhumanism literature with what might be considered seminal work on the subject-matter of transhumanism and meaning of life upon which this chapter shall also lean heavily, albeit with an analytical approach, in the development of some of its sections. However, whereas Sandberg's work concentrates and draws majorly from the Western philosophical tradition, this chapter shall attempt at novelty by bringing transhumanism and singularity into engagement with some particular African conceptions of meaning of life, and by further presenting a proposal for the re-conceptualization of the transhumanism, singularity and meaning of life connections within a context of Afrofuturist philosophical thinking. The methodology applied in undertaking and presenting this proposal consists basically of a critical reconstruction of cultural and philosophical resources from the African past in, first, synthesis with creative imagination on the African present and future, and, second, in conversation with ideas from other non-African (particularly Western) traditions, to weave an Afrofuturistic narrative on "meaning of life" locatable within the project for a new era of African philosophy.

In executing our task therefore, the chapter proceeds from an initiatory section describing the transhumanism and singularity concepts to a brief but relevant exposition of "meaning of life" in several Western and African philosophical perspectives, and following which the concepts are connected in a preceding section that gets to explore the transhumanism, singularity and meaning of life relationships. In latter sections, the philosophy of Afrofuturism is introduced especially as to be applied in the chapter's context, and which subsequently launches the discussion into the culminating aspects proposing an Afrofuturist perspective on transhumanism, singularity and meaning of life.

8.2 Transhumanism and the Singularity

Transhumanism, broadly speaking, is the view that the human condition is not unchanging but improvable, that it can and should be questioned, and it can and should be changed using applied reason (More, 2013). In Max More's explanation, transhumanism includes life philosophies that seek the continuation and acceleration of the evolution of intelligent life beyond its current human form and limitations using science and technology, and guided by life promoting principles and values (More, 1990). More (2013, 4) also describes transhumanism as:

> …as a type of nonreligious philosophy of life that rejects faith, worship, and the supernatural, instead emphasizing a meaningful and ethical approach to living informed by reason, science, progress, and the value of existence in our current life.

For Bostrom (2005, 202–203), another prominent thinker within the philosophy, transhumanism is:

> … an outgrowth of secular humanism and the Enlightenment. It holds that current human nature is improvable through the use of applied science and other rational methods, which may make it possible to increase human health-span, extend our intellectual and physical capacities, and give us increased control over our own mental states and moods.

The "applied sciences" at work here consists of transformative advancements in the neurosciences, genomics, robotics, nanotechnology, computers, and artificial intelligence. Going by the potentials presented by these sciences and technology, transhumanism therefore emphasizes not only the possibility, but also the desirability (and to some extent "normativity") of using these means in enhancing human existence. Indeed transhumanists, as Schneider (2008, 1) characterized:

> …share the belief that an outcome in which humans have radically advanced intelligence, near immortality, deep friendships with AI (artificial intelligence) creatures, and elective body characteristics, is a very desirable end for both one's own personal development and for the development of our species as a whole.

In agreement with the longing to transcend the "animal account" of the human condition, Bostrom (2003) emphasizes the importance to transhumanism of exploring transhuman and posthuman modes of existence. This exploration is desirable since there are reasons to believe some states in this realm hold great value, nearly regardless of the value theory to which one subscribes (Bostrom, 2008). Transhumanism, in his conception, has this exploration as its core value and then derives other values from it.

Related to transhumanism is the concept of the Singularity. Since the 1990s, a Singularitarian subculture has emerged within the transhumanist movement predicated on anticipation of the dramatic abruption of history by technological acceleration, with most Singularitarians, e.g. Hans Moravic (1988, 1998) and Ray Kurzweil (2005), focusing on the emergence of super-human machine intelligence as a product of the radical technological changes. The singularity concept refers to intelligence explosion and technological creation of superintelligence that will bring about total change in our human society. The singularity will represent the culmination of the merger of our biological thinking and existence with a technology, resulting in a world that is still human but that transcends our biological roots (Kurzweil, 2005).

Kurzweil writes of the singularity as a future period during which the pace and impact of technological change will be so rapid and deep such that the human life will be transformed irreversibly. According to him, evolution throughout all time could be characterized as progressing through six epochs, each one building on the previous one. He says the four epochs which so far have occurred are Physics and Chemistry, Biology and DNA, Brains, and Technology. The Singularity, he predicts, will occur with the next epoch: The Merger of Human Technology with Human Intelligence. For this futurist, once this Singularity arrives, the answer to the question 'What does it mean to be human?' and 'What are the limits of human knowledge?' will be answered in ways as-yet-unimaginable (Kurzweil, 2005). After the Singularity, Kurzweil (2005) says the final epoch will happen, in which we will eventually permeate the Universe with intelligence, causing the Universe itself to 'awaken'.

Transhumanism and the singularity raise many important philosophical questions, among which are the potential consequences of a transformation in human bodies and minds, an intelligence explosion, and evolution and expansion in intelligent life which force us to think hard about what it means to be human, about God and religion, nature and society, values and morality, consciousness and personal identity, the nature of reality, the meaning of life and purpose of the universe. In effect, the projections and implications of Transhumanism and the Singularity phenomenon reenact several of the hardest traditional questions in philosophy and raise some new philosophical questions as well. Conversely, they also pave way for possible new answers concerning human nature, intelligence, values, and the meaning generally of life.

8.3 Meaning of Life: Western and African Philosophical Perspectives

Meaning of life discussions is becoming, in recent decades, a distinct topic of interest among philosophers notably of the Anglo-American analytic tradition, but also expected to receive increasing attention in the philosophical literature of other traditions. When speaking of "life's meaning," at least more than one mode of enquiry gets to be involved, for when we ask what (if anything) makes life meaningful we might be asking what could make human life in general (the entire human race or species) meaningful, on the one hand, or we could be enquiring into what could make a particular human life meaningful, on the other. While the latter enquiry entails a search into the meaningfulness of the life of a human person (Attoe, 2020), the former would involve seeking to answer questions such as whether there is a purpose for which humanity was created, or what the human race as a whole could do to connect with something greater than itself (Metz, 2005). A third enquiry, beyond the individual and human species level, may entail probing the "meaning of life" as relating to all of space-time existence, i.e., what is the meaning of it all? At this stage, meaning of life questions could be taken as involving inquiry into meaning and purpose at a grand cosmic level. In my own view, meaning may be understood rather simply as "the point of it all," and as well a construct of an intelligible and valuable account and narrative for actions and experiences; whether we are talking, in parts or/and in whole, about my life, your life, their lives, all human lives, all life, and ultimately, the "life" of the universe itself.

Most Anglo-American philosophers writing on life's meaningfulness engage in attempts to develop and evaluate theories which seek to capture all the particular ways that a life could obtain meaning. On a metaphysical basis, these theories are broadly divided in terms of which kinds of properties are held to constitute the meaning. Supernaturalist theories are views which maintain that a certain relationship with a spiritual realm is mandatory for meaning in life to be constituted. This view requires the existence of God or a soul, and as well a person's appropriate relationship with them for one's life to be meaningful. Anything to the contrary would render a person's life meaningless. Herein for God-centered views especially, fulfilling God's purpose for us and helping God in realizing his/her/its plan for the Universe is the basis for a meaningful life. On the other hand, naturalist theories are views that meaning can be derived in a thoroughly physical world devoid of any spiritual realities, and as understood by us through our best scientific explanations. In this case, regardless of a possible divine source of meaning, certain ways of living in a purely physical universe would be sufficient for obtaining it (Metz, 2013).

Furthermore, Metz (2013, 10–11) executes a helpful task by presenting a succinct survey of more recent views of diverse philosophers on those values that objectively meaningful conditions involve and consist in, views which include: Nozick's idea of transcending the limits of the self to connect with organic unity; Bond's idea of realizing human excellence in oneself; Singer's idea of substantially improving the quality of life of people and animals; Dworkin's idea of overcoming challenges that one recognizes to be important at one's stage of history; Mintoff's idea of realizing goals that are transcendent for being long-lasting in duration and broad in scope; and Metz' own idea of contouring intelligence towards fundamental conditions of human life. Worthy of note also is that while majority of those writing on life's meaning consider discussions of it centrally to indicate a positive final value that the life of a particular individual can manifest, others (e.g., Munitz, 1986; Seachris, 2009) believe and have written substantially in defense of the view that what is of key interest is the meaning of the human species or universe as a whole. Indeed as humans, we are often drawn to the widest standpoints of reflections on our existence, into the universal perspective, and in questioning who we are, what we do, why we are here, where we are going, and what our place is in the grand scheme of things, we are confronted with conditions which take our concerns about meaning beyond a terrestrial focus and render them as often cosmic in scope. As expressed by Berger (1967, 27), many, while in the endeavour of seeking life's meaning, are engaged in the attempt of locating it "within a sacred and cosmic frame of reference" of labouring to fathom the link "between microcosm and macrocosm." We furthermore here find explanation for why God, transcendence, and several other religious ideas are frequently considered germane to meaning of/in life.

Within the African philosophical tradition, one could assess and work with a handful of theories of life's meaning, as presented in recent times by scholars carrying out critical assessments of resources in the tradition. In the 2020 Special Issue of the *South African Journal of Philosophy* on African conceptions of the meaning of life, a number of scholars presented plausible theories of meaning from the perspective of African philosophy. These include conceptions of meaning (or meaningfulness) as: the pursuit or achievement of moral excellence and the expression of moral virtues (Molefe, 2020); as grounded (from the traditional Yoruba perspective) on the sufficient conditions of material comfort symbolized by monetary possession, a long healthy life, children, a peaceful spouse, and victory over life's vicissitudes (Balogun, 2020); choosing to live as a person (as construed in the African sense of personhood) until death, and where "living as a person" entails establishing harmonious relationships of identity and solidarity with others as such that optimal human flourishing on Earth is promoted (Okolie, 2020); meaningfulness as based on life, love and destiny, with the destiny view as the most plausible African theory of meaning (Mlungwana, 2020); meaningfulness as tied (in the Yoruba view) to the quality of life, social status, moral conduct and the particular context of death of an individual (Olujohungbe, 2020); and meaning as depending on the transcendentalism of vitalism with God as the ultimate guarantor of meaning (Agada, 2020).

Metz, also writing in this watershed publication, evaluates two theories of meaning; viz. vitality and community, which are grounded on some indigenous (specifically sub-Saharan) African philosophical traditions. According to one view, a life is more meaningful, the more it promotes *community* with other human persons, whereas according to the other view, a life is more meaningful the more it promotes *vitality* in oneself and others (Metz, 2020). Attoe (2020) does a taxonomy of African theories of meaning as may be extracted from a range of writings on the subject and presents four, viz.: the African God-purpose theory; the vital force theory; the communal normative function theory; and the consolationist theory of meaning (Attoe, 2020).

All these African theories, importantly, approach the question of meaning majorly at the individual level, i.e., what confers meaning on the life of a given individual, and not on the species as a whole.

8.4 Transhumanism, Singularity and the Meaning of Life

Not much exists currently in philosophical literature, Western and otherwise, providing investigation into possible links between transhumanism and meaning of life. In this regards, the work undertaken by Anders Sandberg in his *Transhumanism and the Meaning of Life* (2015) could be considered a path-finding and very helpful collection and analysis of views bothering on the subject. In this section, I shall essentially be relying substantially on that delivery by Sandberg in presenting a brief discussion on available philosophical views concerning transhumanism, singularity and meaning of life.

With an early reference to Sebastian Seung, Sandberg brings in the description of transhumanism as having accepted the post-Enlightenment critique of reason but "yet not giving up on using reason to achieve grand ends that could give meaning to life individually or collectively" (2015, 3). As Seung (2013, 273) states:

> The "meaning of life" includes both universal and personal dimensions. We can ask both "Are we here for a reason?" and "Am I here for a reason?" Transhumanism answers these questions as follows. First, it's the destiny of humankind to transcend the human condition. This is not merely what will happen, but what should happen. Second, it can be a personal goal to sign up for Alcor, dream about uploading, or use technology to otherwise improve oneself. In both of these ways, transhumanism lends meaning to lives that were robbed of it by science.
>
> The bible said that God made man in his own image. The German philosopher Ludwig Feuerbach said that man made God in his own image. The transhumanists say that humanity will make itself into God.

Upon this background, Sandberg (2015, 4) goes on to show that Seung neatly summed up three strands of transhumanism: transhumanism as a way of improving one's own life (what Sandberg calls "individual transhumanism"), transhumanism as a project dedicated to the betterment of humanity ("terrestrial transhumanism"), and transhumanism as a project with the purpose of achieving the potential of life in the universe ("cosmist transhumanism").

It is necessary to indicate here that it is a matter of debate if transhumanism actually seeks to address matters of the meaning of life. It could be argued (especially from an orientation seeking to distance transhumanism from characterization as a religion) that transhumanism, being merely a philosophical defense of humanity's right to control its own evolution, is neither interested in nor offers any answers about the ultimate purpose and nature of existence. Hence, transhumanism has no business with meaning of life questions. However, as Sandberg (2015, 4) expresses, "By considering the possibility of creating or becoming something superhuman, transhumanism forces meaning of life questions to the foreground as engineering targets." This, he says, "leads to an interesting intersection between transhumanism and questions concerning universal values" and followed up with the question: "How is the meaning of life understood in transhumanist thought?" (Sandberg, 2015, 4).

To begin with individual transhumanism, the individual transhumanist story is commonly expressed as ambition to live a life supported by enhancements in order to achieve better health and mental capacity, refined emotions, new abilities, longevity, and perhaps become a posthuman. Responding to a survey conducted by Sandberg (2015), several self-described transhumanists, when asked about their views on the meaning of life, gave answers which were predominantly rooted in a naturalistic subjectivist and existentialist outlook. For these transhumanists, there was no supernatural world imbuing meaning to existence, but all believed that thinking beings can experience meaningful states—if only meaningful to themselves. The respondents also clearly expressed many things they *experienced* as meaningful, and this for some included finding meaning in being a small part of something very big, i.e., humanity on its way to becoming a cosmic civilization that will achieve the dreams of Fedorov and Tipler (Sandberg, 2015).

Several individual transhumanists are embracing of the idea of human enhancement. However, not much of the arguments over human enhancement so far have bothered on meaning of life. Nonetheless, one area where human enhancement discussions run in parallel with meaning of life discussions is life extension. Arguments do exist which essentially seek to detract from the aim or condition of extended life spans any chance of meaningfulness on the grounds of boredom. Williams (1973), for example, contends that immortality (in the sense of living forever and never dying) would necessarily be an unappealing condition for the kind of creatures that humans are. He and other philosophers (Nussbaum, 1994; Ellin, 1995, 311–12; Belshaw, 2005, 82–91; May, 2009; Smuts, 2011; Kagan, 2012) make charges against immortality to the effect that it would necessarily be boring, and with this "Necessary Boredom Thesis" present an extended case of immortality as consequently resulting in meaninglessness of life. These claims, however, have been duly responded to with counter-arguments to the effect that immortality can be experienced with happiness, significance, and without necessarily yielding to boredom (Fischer, 1994; Wisnewski, 2005; Bortolotti & Nagasawa, 2009; Chappell, 2009; Quigley & Harris, 2009, 75–78; Fischer & Mitchell-Yellin, 2014).

In another variation of the life extension and meaning of life discussion, Kass (2001), for example, argues that immortality would make life meaningless on the basis that the finitude of life somehow imbues it with meaning. On the other hand, Tolstoy's (1983) argument maintains there must be something worth doing for life to be meaningful, but actions without permanent effects on the world do not eventually matter, therefore in order for life to have meaning it requires some ability to have permanent effects. This, as the likes of Metz (2003) would qualify, could be seen as an argument for an immortal soul (or God's eternal remembrance). Transhumanism can however refute this by claiming that Tolstoy's argument merely shows that we should aim for an infinite lifespan, without souls being necessary. Herein can also be found grounds for the argument advancing the priority of our striving for vastly extended life-spans and expanding into the universe in order for our lives to have any meaning (Sandberg, 2015). By this necessity, we may therefore in transhumanism have, as Weijers (2014) suggests, what enables us to lead truly meaningful lives in a physical universe.

The terrestrial transhumanism story on its part is a story on the human species level, about humanity, or perhaps our own current civilization. Commonly this is narrated as a story of technological progress leading to a series of technologies, e.g., biotechnology, life extension, cognitive enhancement, nanotechnology, artificial intelligence, brain–computer interface, whole brain emulation, and space colonization, with transformative effects on the human condition. The new technological capabilities, be they occurring automatically or as an outcome of deliberate effort, enable humans to become enhanced transhumans and eventually posthumans. Singularitarians Kurzweil (2005) and Moravec (1988) are prominent exponents of this form of transhumanism.

How does this progress towards enhanced transhumans and posthumans yield meaning or purpose? This, as could be deduced through the ideas of some transhumanist thinkers (e.g., Ettinger, 1972), comes in a form of meaning through the cumulative growth attained in the process of long-term and successive discovery of solutions to humanity's problems. Given the requirement for long-term enquiry in unraveling answers to some of humanity's oldest, deepest and most difficult philosophical problems, and the possibility that mere human intelligence is not enough, it is arguable that we need to develop human enhancement in that it would entail life extension if we are to stay around long enough to find out the answers to these problems. On another hand, it could also be that these problems will not be solved at all until, using cognitive enhancements and artificial intelligence, we can develop minds (posthuman or artificial) smart enough to unlock them. The interim goal of becoming able to fully discover meaning by generating higher and greater forms of intelligence therefore provides (some) meaning for the ambitions of terrestrial transhumanism (Sandberg, 2015). Furthermore the idea—both in theistic and secular versions—of "doing God's work" in perfecting creation or humanity also features prominently in this terrestrial strand of transhumanism.

Moreover, while there might be posthuman states of great value, there are also potential existential risks posing threats of acutely negative or even no value to the future of humanity and life. Arriving at the posthuman state hence would require not just technological process, enhancements and discovery, but also avoidance of existential risks. The existential risk issue which transhumanists talk about is, in the words of Sandberg (2015, 12): "…not so much an issue about the meaning of life as it is an issue about the prevention of the loss of meaning." For if humanity goes extinct, then this could amount to the loss of all the meaning generated by past and present generations, as well as the loss of all future generations alongside the value they would have created. Beyond this, the erasure of the valuer (beings who experience and have notions of value) could also mean the elimination altogether of value. Sandberg (2015, 12) points out:

> If consciousness or intelligence is lost, it might mean that value itself becomes absent from the universe.

Moving on to the cosmist transhumanist story, here we encounter a narrative occurring at the largest scale: Life first emerges on Earth, and then followed by intelligence. Intelligence takes on a technological character, masters the natural world, and eventually reaches out to colonize space, converting resources in its environment along its spread into things of value to it: spacecrafts, biospheres, cultures and minds (Sandberg, 2015). There are several endings to the cosmist story. One ending is that the entire universe becomes intelligent, i.e., "wakes up," as Kurzweil (2005) puts it, while another scenario envisions intelligence becoming increasingly interconnected and coordinated, ending in a single super-mind or super-social organization (de Chardin, 1959; Tipler, 1994). In either case, the intelligence-dominated universe will be filled with minds protecting life and intelligence, controlling and manipulating the contents of the universe in order to survive or reach unification (Sandberg, 2015).

It is not uncommon to come across in transhumanist cosmology the view that the universe is impersonal and purposeless, but since life and mind, as contrary to mere matter, have potential for meaning, Geraci (2010) suggests that the expansion of life into the universe and the gradual conversion of matter into mind can be a way of providing the universe with meaning. The more we spread life and intelligence across the universe, the more we imbue it with meaning, especially going by reasons to believe a universe rich in life and mind would consequently have more value (Sandberg, 2015). In addition to giving meaning to the universe, this programme of expansion of life and intelligence by humans across the universe likewise contains a promise to provide significance and meaning to humankind itself. Sandberg (2015, 15) explains:

> Cosmist expansion is a way of responding to our apparent insignificance. We may be small and contingent, yet potentially important by triggering the great Cambrian explosion of future species.

An extreme form of life taking control of the universe is represented by Tipler's "Omega Point" cosmology (Barrow & Tipler, 1988), a term borrowed from Teilhard de Chardin (1959). Tipler (1994) describes a scenario where intelligence expands across the universe, achieves infinite information and processing power, and then on to ultimately taking the character of God. Tipler's Omega Point was understood as the future physical cause of the universe. While individual beings had free will their actions would eventually lead to the emergence of the Omega Point, and acting to bring about this Omega Point is the meaning of the world. A number of Singularitarians also express views connected to this scenario. In the "Global Brain" scenario propounded by Smart (2005), Stock (1993) and Bloom (2000), collective intelligence will emerge as all human beings get linked to one another and to machine intelligence in the unfolding global telecommunications web. The "Global Brain" will include all or most of humanity, and come as a climax of social progress. A number of Singularitarians consider this scenario as similar to de Chardin's (1959) idea that humanity would evolve into the global "noosphere," leading to the "Omega Point" of union with God.

The human prospects of technological progress towards posthumanity and the creation and spread of more life and superintelligence to both establish our future in the universe, and as well give a cosmist meaning to our species, the universe and life could be woven into a grand narrative accounting for why we are here in the vast expanse of space and time. In this scenario, we may therefore have what could be the ultimate meaning and purpose of all individual humans, the entire human species, all life, and the cosmos itself.

8.5 The Philosophy of Afrofuturism

An emerging inspiration for advancement in African civilization in the twenty-first century and beyond is the philosophy, culture and movement of Afrofuturism; a cultural aesthetic, philosophy of science, and philosophy of history that combines science fiction with African mythologies, storytelling, traditions and history. Afrofuturism explores the developing intersection of African and African Diaspora culture with technology, re-imagines the past, science and the future from a black and African perspective, and envisions what peoples of African origin can be. The philosophy and cultural movement promises to inspire new technologies, ideas and sociopolitical changes, and conveys a bold sentiment that the future will belong to Africa and its storytellers, even bearing the torch for the world to follow, especially so if fact follows fiction.

As applied in this chapter, Afrofuturism shall comprise of a developing model in African philosophy featuring the combination of critically re-constructed resources from the traditional African past with ideas of modernity, science, technology, creative imagination, reason, progress, and visions of the future. In what follows next, it is this approach which therefore shall be informing much of the content wherein I attempt an Afrofuturist perspective on the subject of transhumanism, singularity and meaning of life. Being an exercise essentially in futurist thinking, my presentation would hence consist intentionally of a combination of descriptive, reconstructive and imaginative analysis, and in which case diverse elements as aforementioned shall be synthesized to deliver on an Afrofuturist philosophical chart in plumbing ideas on transhumanism and life's meaning.

8.6 An Afrofuturist Perspective on Transhumanism, Singularity and Meaning of Life

Transhumanism and the Singularity may come across firstly as strange and very new concepts to African thinking, but when assessed through the lens of Afrofuturism we stand to find that the transhumanist and singularity concepts can be located within, and are not fundamentally alien to the African world after all.

Indeed the ancient human dream of enhancing and transforming ourselves in order to overcome our all-too-human limitations is not historically absent in Africa. An insight into diverse African myths and legends would yield stories of the craving for immortality or about heroic figures displaying superhuman powers, and steeped in many ancient African cultures are such body and mind enhancing practices as physical and mental training, physical modification for cosmetic, religious or other functions, and the use of stimulants for mind-altering and intelligence enhancement. Among the Yoruba of Nigeria, for example, the use of medicinal plants for memory enhancing and anti-aging is widespread. Local remedies for memory loss and aging are described as *Ogun isoye* (memory enhancement drug) and *Ajidewe* (wake up and feel younger/remaining young forever), respectively, which are sometimes used by people as food or in form of medicine which modify the functioning of the central nervous system (Babawale et al., 2016). The medicinal preparation of *Ogun isoye* was a traditional form of nootropics used by Ifa trainees to aid memory (with links also to notions of intelligence), whereas *Ajidewe* could be seen as the traditional idea of the "elixir of life," or what is today termed life extension.

On another subject, i.e., as concerning the human relationship with robots (machines), several ancient African mythologies and traditions likewise included what could be understood as the concept and creation of artificial, animated beings. Plausibly re-interpreted as African practices of robotics, this act could be traced back to ancient Egyptian/Nile Valley culture where statues were "animated" or "brought to life" in ritualistic ceremonies called the "Opening of the Mouth," then on through continent-wide traditional African animist culture in which statues were created to house energies and perform certain tasks in manners similar to robotics, and all the way down to contemporary decades where this African animist tradition of robotics has been inspiring new manifestations of the craft of African automation in fact and fiction.[1]

The modern formulation of transhumanism and singularity as philosophies and movements however calls for much present and future work on the part of African and African Diaspora thinkers to develop a uniquely modern African transhumanist and singularity philosophy, bringing in this bid some concepts from the body of traditional African ideas which can still contribute to human flourishing in the contemporary African world into synthesis with reason, science, technology, the notion of progress, and in dialogue with ideas from other non-African philosophical traditions, as a task within the new generation of construction in African philosophy. Afrofuturism could lead the way for such project.

With this programme of transhumanism[2] in Africa and among the African Diaspora still in view, I will proceed now to briefly consider talk of meaningfulness within the African philosophical system. To engage in the task at hand, I shall adapt from Metz (2020) two prominent (naturalist/secular) theories as informed by the sub-Saharan African philosophical tradition, i.e., the views of community and

[1] For more accounts on a history of African robotics, see the book: Khnum-Ptah to Computer: The African Initialization of Computer Science.

[2] Important to note is the case that although transhumanism arguably parades representatives of religious/spiritual views, the brand of transhumanism which I here have in mind and promote going forward in this chapter is in deliberate terms that of the secular and naturalist wing of the philosophy and movement. This is so intended for an appreciable level of correspondence to be pursued and hopefully achieved between the stated naturalistic version of transhumanism and the secular/naturalist African theories of meaning deployed subsequently in the analysis.

vitality, in exploring "meaning of life." Though there is, according to Metz, a third intellectual source, i.e., the imperceptibility view, which several African philosophers (e.g., Balogun, 2008; Igbafen, 2017) have maintained remains central in conceptions of life's meaningfulness within African thought, I shall again take a cue from Metz in downplaying (or overlooking) this rather supernaturalist approach of the imperceptible realm in discussing life's meaningfulness (see Metz, 2020, 115–116). Furthermore, of the two other African theories (besides "communalism" and "vitalitism") as contained in Attoe's (2020) taxonomy, i.e., the African God-purpose and consolationist theories of meaning, the former shall not concern us in this present chapter as it does not fall within the naturalist scope of applicability intended here.[3] The latter theory, however, being originally Agada's (2015) consolationist theory, in its account of the continued evolution of the universe and the yearning for and attainment of perfection as the meaning of life, shall also be included in our theoretical engagements albeit with a secularist tweak.

The naturalist/secular African theories of community and vitality which shall be mainly deployed here in assessing meaning of life will be so applied basically at the individual level, but also (with some amplification and rethinking) at the human species and cosmic level. The latter effort will be undertaken with a proposal that the two theories hereby employed could be expanded into an argument that the ultimate purpose of the human race is the promotion of life itself and community among the species and across all of the natural world and universe. Finally, based on its principal factor of "yearning," I shall within a naturalist framework also briefly involve the consolationist view, and apply this (in)to an Afrofuturist perspective on transhumanism and meaning as derived through cosmic evolution and the striving for perfection.

According to the community view, a life is more meaningful, the more it promotes community with other human persons (Metz, 2020). The community view can be expressed by the African philosophy of Ubuntu which pervades almost all parts of the African continent and is integrated into all aspects of day-to-day life. Ubuntu promotes interconnectedness of everyone to each other and to the world around them, the view that no one exists in isolation, for we are all part of a larger circle, a large system we both affect and are affected by. We must therefore always be conscious that we are part of a larger community and system, and with the enrichment and progress of the community and system, we will enhance as well. As this philosophy gives, meaning of life is derived from this idea of belongingness and interconnectedness. Attoe (2020) provides valuable insights on this African communal, complementary and interconnected view of meaning at even the universal scale where he writes:

[3] It is plausible to anticipate though that as discussions on transhumanism and meaning of life from African perspectives progress arguments are likely to be put forward especially from the theistic view of "doing God's work" in perfecting humanity and the world as grounds for drawing connections between the African God-purpose theory of meaning and transhumanism. I will rather, however, leave that narrative endeavour to the labours of (current or/and emerging) African thinkers in the supernaturalist camp of the transhumanism and meaning discourse.

> …to fully understand how communal normative relationships can be purveyors of meaning, one must have a full understanding of African views on such relations. Key to this understanding for many thinkers is the metaphysical understanding of the universe as a complementary whole. For most traditional African thought systems, the universe is often thought of as an interconnected whole, with each constituent seen as missing links of a mutually complementary whole.

Still, along this line of thought, Iroegbu (2005, 442) also expresses: "the purpose of our life is community-service and community-belongingness".

Another major strain of African normative thought appeals to the fundamental value of vital- or life-force. According to the vitality view, a life is more meaningful the more it promotes vitality in oneself and others. Expounding on this vital force view, Metz (2020, 119) says:

> Traditionally, it has been conceived as being an imperceptible energy that has come from God and that inheres in everything in the universe in varying degrees and complexities. However, an appeal to vitality to ground a theory of meaning in life is powerful even if it is understood in strictly perceptible or physical terms, which I shall sometimes call "liveliness".

Upon some further background analysis, Metz goes on to render a vitalist theory of meaning as such that a human person's life is more meaningful the more that she promotes liveliness in herself and others (Metz, 2020). We also get further qualifications of this vitalist view of meaning in Attoe (2020), where he opines that:

> ….one can think of this theory of meaning as a possible candidate for a theory of the meaning of life, not merely *in* life. This is mainly because by tailoring one's life towards the goal of continually enhancing one's vital force (even after death as an ancestor), one encounters a coherence and rationale that is needed for any life as a whole to be considered meaningful.

With these African theories of meaning advanced as such, I shall, primarily (though not exclusively) with a Metzian standpoint on the theories in mind, next explore how possible links could be formed between them and Sandberg's (2015) three strands of transhumanism: i.e., individual transhumanism, terrestrial transhumanism, and cosmist transhumanism. This exercise shall be undertaken in the eventual hope of proposing an Afrofuturist perspective on transhumanism, singularity and meaning of life.

The individual transhumanist story, to begin with, could be understood from the African vitalist viewpoint in connecting with meaning of life. For Dzobo (1992), the methods of acquiring vital force involve engaging in activities that express an individual's creative power and productivity. Acquiring and enhancing one's vital force would therefore consist of lifelong projects which present meaning-making sources for our lives (Attoe, 2020). To relate hence, the individual transhumanist perception, typically described as ambition to live a life supported by enhancements in order to achieve better health and mental capacity, refined emotions, new abilities, longevity, and perhaps become a posthuman, constructively links up with a drive for an optimal life as the ultimate goal of being in the world which lies at the essence of the vitalist theory of meaning. As Sindima (1989, 544) says of an African worldview, "[t]he African world is concerned with fullness of life, since it is in its fullness that life's meaning is realized. Fullness of life is realized when human potential and possibilities are allowed to reach their maximum".

The appeal to the African philosophical concept of vitality, or liveliness (understood in strictly perceptible or physical terms)[4] can also dovetail with how human enhancements relate with the meaning of life, especially where life extension is brought into focus. Going by the vitalist theory of meaning that a human person's life is more meaningful the more it promotes liveliness in herself, life extension therefore would suitably, or could be evaluated to, come across as desirable to that vitalist intuition for more and more life as a path to attaining meaning. Here again, we might be reminded of earlier raised positions that living forever or at least for extended periods may only result in boredom and consequently render life meaningless, but one can defend against this thinking through such arguments, as had been earlier presented in this paper (see above) that immortality (or some forms of it at least) could be experienced with happiness, significance, and need not succumb to boredom, or that, as according to Metz (2013), even if immortality were a case of boredom, it is worth questioning still whether boredom in the first place is truly sufficient for meaninglessness.

In addition, transhumanism's response to Tolstoy's (1983) argument for permanence in the claim that the argument merely shows that we should aim for an infinite lifespan for our lives to have any meaning can also be appreciated from the African vitalist approach on the basis of how transhumanism could grant meaning to life by virtue of striving to ensure infinite extension and the presence of liveliness in persons.

Still, in re-interpreting vitality theory, new outlooks could be encountered wherein the focus gets redirected into developing vitality (using technology) in oneself and others to the point where one's vital force is so strong and lasting as to become; in place of the traditional African goal of "ancestor," an enhanced transhuman and eventually posthuman. The meaningfulness of life thence that derives from the African concept of the "living-dead" is transferred and hereby gained through the condition of enhancing one's vitality to the attainment of an infinitely living posthuman.[5]

Furthermore, and still on individual transhumanism, where personal meaning is found in being a small part of something very big—humanity on its way to becoming a cosmic civilization—the African community theory provides ground for an African understanding of transhumanism and meaning that could be conferred on a

[4] For more on a naturalist, physicalist, and energy-oriented conception of vitality as 'liveliness' see Metz (2012); and as 'creative power' see Dzobo (1992).

[5] An objection might be raised here on the grounds that death plays a role in some African perceptions of meaningfulness, and in which case mortality is required for a transition to an afterlife status which renders meaning on the journey of earthly existence. But then so also does death play a converse role in other African perceptions (notably in diverse African "origin of death" myths) in which its occurrence renders life and human projects meaningless. On the basis of the latter view therefore immortality, or a vastly extended lifespan, in the natural world stands desirable and need not be an anomalous concept to African thought.

person's life, particularly when individuals consider meaningfulness through belonging to a human community on its transhuman path to a cosmic community and civilization.

On the vitalist theory of meaning, one may yet take some further steps into contextualizing this approach into the terrestrial transhumanism story, i.e., transhumanism as a project that seeks the betterment of humanity. As indicated earlier, the vitalist intuition, in its inclusion of the thought that one should foster vitality in self and others in order to live meaningfully, requires as such that one's purpose is to produce in self and others properties such as health, growth, reproduction, creativity, vibrancy, activity, self-motion, courage, and confidence (Metz, 2020). Pursuing these ideals and hopes in the modern world would imply the application of means that lead to a series of technologies, e.g., biotechnology, life extension, cognitive enhancement, artificial intelligence, neurotechnology, human-machine interfaces, etc., all of which bear potentials of fundamentally transforming, and hopefully improving, the human condition.

On another hand, the vitalist approach may likewise be applied at the terrestrial strand of transhumanism in reaction to the existential risk issue and its implications in loss of meaning. Just as it lies in the vitalist intuition that meaning is to be found in producing in oneself and others the above-stated positive properties, correspondingly one's purpose is also to reduce in self and others properties that include disease, decay, barrenness, destruction, lethargy, passivity, submission, insecurity, and depression (Metz, 2020). This approach, of preserving and enhancing oneself and others as relevant sites of liveliness for attainment of meaning, would not only prevent destruction at the species level, but also prevent the loss of meaning as threatened by the extinction of the species.

A case could be proposed, as I shall now do, that beyond conferring meaning on the life of a particular human person, the African vitalist and community theories could be expanded into providing some answer to the questions of the purpose for which humanity exists and what the human race as a whole could do to connect with something greater than itself. To this, I suggest a consideration, through expansion and re-conceptualization of the vitality idea, that the human species is here for the purpose of promoting, not just "liveliness," but generally Life (symbolized, for instance, by the ancient Egyptian Ankh); as a phenomena and animating principle,[6] across the universe, and that we can find meaning in connecting—as an entire species—with something grand by seeking fellowship with, and actively building and participating in a community consisting the entire universe. Briefly, meaning for

[6] Here, we may need to indicate that "life principle" as intended for this discussion can also involve the term as understood, for example, in Yolanda Mlungwana (2020). Mlungwana's invocation of "life" as one among three theories of meaning which she evaluates in terms of its ability to account for intuitions about the meaningfulness especially of relations, work, self-actualization and partaking in rituals bears much correspondence with my use of the principle in this proposal. However, whereas Mlungwana explores this life principle to account only for meaning of individual lives, the application I intend here differs significantly in its approach which employs Life as a principle in seeking the purpose of humanity in general.

humankind is derived in promoting life and fellowship on Earth and across the Universe. This submission moreover, as well as much of what follows in subsequent paragraphs of this discussion, may be weighed in the literature as an Afrofuturistic draft proposal for "meaning of life" within the ongoing construction of a new era of African philosophy.

The rethinking and broadening of the African vitalist idea into a general "life" idea, as called for, recommends that "life" here be assessed as conceptualized by the ancient Egyptian (African) Ankh symbol, widely believed to convey the principle of life. Though originally communicating the idea of eternal life or immortality in an afterlife, this concept may be re-interpreted in our modern transhumanist outlook in terms of (preserving and promoting) life generally—and *perpetual life* specifically—in the world of our current existence. Also, although the Ankh, as depicted in ancient Egypt, was in the exclusive possession of the gods and a handful of Kings, again in our modern transhumanist optimism (as inspired by the powers of science and technology), we may present an Afrofuturist retelling of the story to unveil an Egyptian (African) Prometheus who has stolen this object and its symbolic power from the divinities and gifted it to humanity. In proposing an African Ankh "perpetual life" principle as supreme value, we may return to transhumanism's response to Tolstoy's argument for permanence and suggest therein possible premises for an Afrofuturist account of transhumanism's imperative as that which would aid our aims for infinite lifespans and as well for expanding, extending and advancing life—both human and non-human—into the physical universe for our own lives to truly have meaning.

In practical terms, this would involve an intensification in the search for other life forms both terrestrial and extra-terrestrial (through earth and space exploration), and a dissolution of speciesism to a point sufficient enough to motivate humans into adapting beliefs and practices, formulating principles and rights, and developing technologies and systems that would aid the wellbeing and enhancement of those other life forms. The communitarian/relational character of human rights and human dignity in African thought, and in how it implicates and impresses upon all of our relationships, not just with other people, but with other animals and with our natural environments (ACLARS, 2019), can be built upon as a foundational starting point from which humans (and later posthumans) may further develop principles and technologies for the promotion of life and community/cooperation on a universal scale.

Among the earlier outlined multiple endings of the cosmist transhumanism story, one scenario envisions intelligence becoming increasingly interconnected and coordinated, ending in a single super-mind or super-social organization. This intelligence-dominated universe, filled with minds protecting life and intelligence, would steer towards unification. Also, there is Tipler's Omega Point scenario and the singularitarian "Global Brain" in which collective intelligence will emerge as all human beings are linked to one another and to machine intelligence, emerging as a culmination of social progress. An Afrofuturist retelling of this vision would present a "life-force" account of humans merging with the creative energies of robots/machine intelligence we create, and expanding this creative energy across the

Universe in ways that spread and protect life and intelligence. Furthermore, the build-up towards, and eventuality of the super-mind and super-social organization for meaning of life could be interpreted in Afrofuturist perspective as an expression along the trajectory of a cosmic version of the community theory of meaning. In which case, just as Ubuntu promotes interconnectedness of everyone to each other and to the world around them, so the super-mind, super-social organization, universal unification and Omega Point scenario(s) may be conceived in Afrofuturist holistic terms as the manifestation of a "Cosmic Ubuntu," a significant actualization of the interconnected *Cosmic Circle* in which reality is conceived in African thought.

Here again the Ankh can be invoked, for as a cross with a loop at the top, the symbol has also been represented as a bond that brings together all things in the knot of the center and makes it possible for them to remain united. Interpreted as the Knot of Isis, this conveys the notion of rejoining and holism. We may uphold the Ankh, as a symbol of life and universal unity, in seeking transhumanist meaning to the human race at the cosmic level. Humankind—by infinitely extending life and fellowship across the Universe, and through an expanding role of building, and participating in the cosmic community—hence finds its meaning and purpose by connecting with, and becoming something bigger than itself.

There is, on another note, much material in Agada's consolationist theory of meaning that may also provide food for thought in a reworking of transhumanism and meaning across individual, terrestrial and cosmist levels, from an Afrofuturist perspective. In its account of the continued evolution of the universe and the yearning for perfection as the meaning of life, this story strikes a perceivable chord with some worldviews, visions and aspirations of transhumanism. A primary feature of Agada's metaphysics, as interpreted by Attoe (2020, 136), is:

> ....his assertion that one should consider the universe as purposeful and alive in varying degrees. The continued evolution of the universe for him is not the product of mindless matter but a product of a purpose.

This purpose that drives the universe is propositioned by Agada as transcendental freedom, and freedom specifically in the sense of absolute freedom that brings about only a perfect state of affairs (Attoe, 2020). For Agada (2015), this perfect state of affairs involves the achievement of a fully intelligible universe, and hence, he submits the idea of missing links and complementarity as indicative of the condition of the universe which yearns to attain a completeness and consequently an end. This yearning for perfection is a fundamental feature of existence and manifests both in natural processes such as evolution and natural selection, and in human experience through history, culture and actions. It is this drive that motivates complementarity as a path to completeness, resonating a theme replete in African philosophy. Indeed Attoe (2020, 137) confirms that this "yearning and the perfection this yearning seeks to achieve is a logical aftermath of the complementary metaphysics that pervades African thought" and expounds still that:

> Humans are not left out in this yearning process and our inclinations towards solidarity, self-edification and, ultimately, progress only express our yearning for perfection. The

attainment of this perfection is the meaning of life and the yearning for this perfection accounts for the moments of meaning in life (Attoe, 2020, 137).

Harking back to some ideas already put forth in this section, one could deduce how this human and universal yearning for perfection and its implications for complementarity, unification, intelligence and advancement presents parallels with the aspirations of individual, terrestrial and cosmist transhumanism towards the attainment of perfection. The pull, moreover, of universal complementarity is one we could further locate within our earlier expressed communitarian view of "Cosmic Ubuntu," whereas we may also relate the inclinations of humans towards solidarity, self-edification and progress with our Afrofuturist re-applications of community and enhancement of vitality as paths to meaning in connections with transhumanism.

Agada's laudable endeavour had comprised of an attempt in identifying perfection as the external and transcendental purpose and source of meaning that humans and all of existence strive for. For this effort, Attoe (2020, 137) says, "Agada locates meaning in something that is not merely tied to our animal nature." However, these notions of perfection, "absolute freedom," and meaning in Agada, aside the echoes of Hegelianism, could as well be conceived via the secular narrative of Cosmic evolution (otherwise rendered as "Big History" or "Universe Story"), and through other similar grand cosmic and evolutionary epic visions (Huxley, 1953; Wilson, 1978), all in their naturalistic accounts that life, going by trends in evolution—cosmic, biological, mental, cultural—is meaningful *because it evolves*, with the universe *seemingly* moving towards a fully meaningful culmination, and that we humans live meaningful lives precisely *because* we play a central role in this evolving meaning. Meaning, according to this view, emerged *during* the evolutionary process, with the rise of complexity in nature, and in the result of interactions between organisms possessing complexly organized brains with physical and cultural environments (Messerly, 2013). This secular take on Agadaian metaphysics of universal "perfection" and "meaning"—through the prism of "cosmic evolution" as progressive, immanent and naturalistic trends in and of the universe towards becoming meaningful, or becoming increasingly meaningful, and with emerged beings with conscious purposes and meanings (like humans) playing a role in the process—in contrast to (as Agada had posited) the conception of some "external" purpose necessarily driven by a "divine agenda," can moreover easily be brought into agreement with transhumanism both in the philosophy's pragmatic encouragement of humans to play the leading role in the cosmic drama by guiding evolution to realize its possibilities, and its aspirations as well for humans to enhance biological and cognitive capacities, transcend our animal nature, create a better future, and perfect humanity, life and the world.

Again, though Agada (2015) would qualify his consolationist theory of meaning by eventually arguing for yearning as itself becoming consolation in the face of the notion that (attaining) perfection exceeds the reach of the wavering individual or even the universe, but then we could focus intentionally on this "yearning" idea and re-conceptualize it under the optimism of transhumanist and singularitarian thinking to argue that the human and cosmic yearning for perfection should remain as "yearning"; not out of incapability but as a *necessary condition* for sake of a boundless search for improvement and an extropian[7] drive towards "perpetual progress", and this in spite of any and every achievements and advancements made. The future, after all, is essentially always *journey* and never a *destination*. The principal factor of "yearning" in Agada's thought may thus be substantiated, refocused and adapted as yet another African, or Afrofuturist, nexus for transhumanism, singularity and meaning.

The individual, terrestrial and cosmist transhumanist stories as conceptualized through an expanded and imaginative African lens—comprising vitalism, universal and perpetual life, (cosmic) community, and the human and universal yearning for perfection—may be proposed and developed further as an Afrofuturist narrative of transhumanism, singularity and meaning of life.

8.7 Conclusion

There is no consensus among scholars, Western or African, on a single theory of the meaning of life, neither does transhumanism as a philosophy have a unified theory on this subject. However, certain themes on this matter keep recurring in transhumanism as linked to the different strands. The transhumanist is steeped in a meaningful worldview uniquely so because of its immense scope and aspiration. In transhumanism's transcendent attempts to connect our current microscopic condition with the grandness of the scientifically unveiled universe, the transhumanist through this process stands to experience meaning as ever increasing in an expanding Universe (Sandberg, 2015). This same prospect for meaning holds out for the singularitarian, specifically with the permeating of human-machine intelligence across, and in unification with the Universe.

Developing a contemporary African, or Afrofuturist philosophical version of transhumanism and singularity would require much critical analysis, intellectual reevaluation and creative re-imagination of several traditional African concepts on subjects ranging from human nature, body, mind, consciousness, intelligence, sentience, sapience, person, community, agency, dignity, rights, morality, freewill and determinism; to life, being, object, tool, God, cosmology, death, nature, creation,

[7] From "Extropianism", a transhumanist philosophy of extropy developed by Max More in his "Extropian Principles" which, among other principles, points to nature's evolutionary processes from mindless matter to life to the generation of increasingly complex organisms with ever-more intelligent brains, embodies an inspiring and uplifting view of life while remaining open to revision according to science, reason, and the boundless search for improvement; promotes perpetual progress in the search for more intelligence, wisdom, vitality/effectiveness, an indefinite lifespan, and the removal of limits to self-actualization and self-realization; advocates perpetually overcoming constraints on our progress and possibilities; and expanding into the universe and advancing without end. Additionally, for a concise discussion exploring "Extropianism and meaning," see Sandberg, 2015, 6–7.

evolution, matter, energy, spirit, soul, immortality, space, time, destiny, etc., in light of modern ideas of reason, science, technology, and progress. With this programme in process, more headway could be anticipated in connecting African perspectives on transhumanism and singularity with African theories on (the) meaning of life. This paper has comprised an attempt eventually at what may be considered an early introduction of an Afrofuturist perspective on transhumanism and singularity in relation to the notion of life's meaning. May a thousand flowers yet bloom in this dimension of African philosophy.

References

African Consortium for Law and Religion Studies. (2019). African perspectives on human dignity for everyone everywhere: An endorsement and elaboration of the punta del este declaration on dignity for everyone everywhere. In *Seventh Annual Law and Religion in Africa Conference*, Gaborone, Botswana, 19–21 May 2019. http://www.dignityforeveryone.org

Agada, A. (2015). *Existence and consolation: Reinventing ontology, gnosis and values in African philosophy*. Paragon House.

Agada, A. (2020). The African vital force theory of meaning in life. *South African Journal of Philosophy, 39*(2), 100–112. https://doi.org/10.1080/02580136.2020.1770416

Attoe, A. (2020). A systematic account of African conceptions of the meaning of/in life. *South African Journal of Philosophy, 39*(2), 127–139. https://doi.org/10.1080/02580136.2020.1771822

Babawale, O., Fashola, T., & Onasanwo, A. (2016). Ethnobotanical survey of plants used as memory enhancer in three states of southwestern Nigeria. *Journal of Applied Pharmaceutical Science, 6*(9), 209–214.

Balogun, O. (2008). Philosophy: What social relevance? *Philosophia Africana, 11*(2), 103–116. https://doi.org/10.5840/philafricana20081122

Balogun, O. (2020). The traditional Yorùbá conception of a meaningful life. *South African Journal of Philosophy, 39*(2), 166–178. https://doi.org/10.1080/02580136.2020.1774978

Barrow, J., & Frank, T. (1988). *The anthropic cosmological principle*. Oxford University Press.

Belshaw, C. (2005). *10 good questions about life and death*. Blackwell.

Berger, P. (1967). *The sacred canopy*. Doubleday.

Bloom, H. (2000). *Global brain: The evolution of mass mind from the big bang to the 21st century*. Wiley.

Bortolotti, L., & Yujin, N. (2009). Immortality without boredom. *Ratio, 22*, 261–277.

Bostrom, N. (2003). *Transhumanist values*. http://www.nickbostrom.com/ethics/values.html. Assessed 29 Aug 2020.

Bostrom, N. (2005). In defense of posthuman dignity. *Bioethics, 19*(3), 202–214.

Bostrom, N. (2008). Why I want to be a posthuman when I grow up. In B. Gordijn & R. Chadwick (Eds.), *Medical enhancement and posthumanity* (pp. 107–137). Springer.

Chappell, T. (2009). Infinity goes up on trial: Must immortality be meaningless? *European Journal of Philosophy, 17*, 30–44.

de Chardin, T. (1959). *The phenomenon of man*. Harper.

Dzobo, N. (1992). Values in a changing society: Man, ancestors and God. In K. Wiredu & K. Gyekye (Eds.), *Person and community: Ghanaian philosophical studies* (pp. 223–240). Center for Research in Values and Philosophy.

Ellin, J. (1995). *Morality and the meaning of life*. Harcourt Brace.

Ettinger, R. (1972). *Man into superman: The startling potential of human evolution—And how to be part of it*. St. Martin's Press.

Fischer, M. (1994). Why immortality is not so bad. *International Journal of Philosophical Studies, 2*, 257–270.
Fischer, M., & Benjamin, M.-Y. (2014). Immortality and boredom. *The Journal of Ethics, 18*(4), 353–372. https://doi.org/10.1007/s10892-014-9172-3
Geraci, R. (2010). *Apocalyptic AI: Visions of heaven in robotics, artificial intelligence, and virtual reality*. Oxford University Press.
Hopkins, P. (2005). Transcending the animal: How transhumanism and religion are and are not alike. *Journal of Evolution and Technology, 14*(2), 13–28.
Huxley, J. (1953). *Evolution in action*. New American Library.
Igbafen, M. (2017). Human life and the question of meaning in African existentialism. In I. Ukpokolo (Ed.), *Themes, issues and problems in African philosophy* (pp. 237–254). Palgrave Macmillan.
Iroegbu, P. (2005). Beginning, purpose and end of life. In P. Iroegbu & A. Echekwube (Eds.), *Kpim of morality ethics* (pp. 440–445). Heinemann Educational Books.
Kagan, S. (2012). *Death*. Yale University Press.
Kass, L. (2001). L'Chaim and its limits: Why not immortality? *First Things, 113*, 17–24.
Kurzweil, R. (2005). *The singularity is near: When humans transcend biology*. Viking Press.
May, T. (2009). *Death*. Acumen Publishing.
Messerly, J. (2013). *The meaning of life: Religious, philosophical, transhumanist, and scientific perspectives*. Darwin & Hume Publishers.
Metz, T. (2003). The immortality requirement for life's meaning. *Ratio, 16*(2), 161–177. https://doi.org/10.1111/1467-9329.00213
Metz, T. (2005). Baier and Cottingham on the meaning of life. *Disputatio, 1*(19), 215–228.
Metz, T. (2012). African conceptions of human dignity: Vitality and community as the ground of human rights. *Human Rights Review, 13*, 19–37. https://doi.org/10.1007/s12142-011-0200-4
Metz, T. (2013). The meaning of life. In E. Zalta (Ed.), *The Stanford encyclopedia of philosophy*. https://plato.stanford.edu/archives/sum2013/entries/life-meaning. Assessed 15 Sept 2020.
Metz, T. (2020). African theories of meaning in life: A critical assessment. *South African Journal of Philosophy, 39*(2), 113–126. https://doi.org/10.1080/02580136.2020.1770429
Mlungwana, Y. (2020). An African approach to the meaning of life. *South African Journal of Philosophy, 39*(2), 153–165. https://doi.org/10.1080/02580136.2020.1771824
Molefe, M. (2020). Personhood and a meaningful life in African philosophy. *South African Journal of Philosophy, 39*(2), 194–207. https://doi.org/10.1080/02580136.2020.1774980
Moravec, H. (1988). *Mind children: The future of human and robot intelligence*. Harvard University Press.
Moravec, H. (1998). *Robot: Mere machine to transcendent mind*. Oxford University Press.
More, M. (1990). Transhumanism: Towards a futurist philosophy. *Extropy, 6*.
More, M. (2013). The philosophy of transhumanism. In M. More & N. Vita-More (Eds.), *The transhumanist reader: Classical and contemporary essays on the science, technology, and philosophy of the human future* (1st ed., pp. 3–17). Wiley.
Munitz, M. (1986). *Cosmic understanding: Philosophy and science of the universe*. Princeton University Press.
Nussbaum, M. (1994). *The therapy of desire*. Princeton University Press.
Okolie, C. (2020). Living as a person until death: An African ethical perspective on meaning in life. *South African Journal of Philosophy, 39*(2), 208–218. https://doi.org/10.1080/02580136.2020.1779493
Olujohungbe, B. (2020). Situational ambivalence of the meaning of life in Yorùbá thought. *South African Journal of Philosophy, 39*(2), 219–227. https://doi.org/10.1080/02580136.2020.1780041
Quigley, M., & John, H. (2009). Immortal happiness. In L. Bortolotti (Ed.), *Philosophy and happiness* (pp. 68–81). Palgrave Macmillan.
Sandberg, A. (2015). Transhumanism and the meaning of life. In T. Trothen & C. Mercer (Eds.), *Religion and transhumanism: The unknown future of human enhancement* (pp. 3–22). Praeger.

Schneider, S. (2008). *Future minds: Transhumanism, cognitive enhancement and the nature of persons*. http://repository.upenn.edu/neuroethics_pubs/37. Accessed 29 Feb 2021.
Seachris, J. (2009). The meaning of life as narrative: A new proposal for interpreting philosophy's 'primary' question. *Philo, 12*, 5–23.
Seung, S. (2013). *Connectome: How the brain's wiring makes us who we are*. Mariner Books.
Sindima, H. (1989). Community of life. *The Ecumenical Review, 41*(4), 537–551.
Smart, J. (2005). *Brief history of intellectual discussion of accelerating change*. http://www.accelerationwatch.com/history_brief.html. Assessed 24 Aug 2020.
Smuts, A. (2011). Immortality and significance. *Philosophy and Literature, 35*, 134–149.
Stock, G. (1993). *Meta-man: The merging of humans and machines into a global superorganism*. Simon and Schuster.
Tipler, F. (1994). *The physics of immortality: Modern cosmology, God and the resurrection of the dead*. Anchor.
Tolstoy, L. (1983). *A confession* (D. Patterson, Trans. and Intro). W.W. Norton & Co.
Weijers, D. (2014). Optimistic naturalism: Scientific advancement and the meaning of life. *Sophia, 53*, 1–18.
Williams, B. (1973). The makropulos case: Reflections on the tedium of immortality. In B. Williams (Ed.), *Problems for the self* (pp. 82–100). Cambridge University Press. Reprinted in Fischer, J. M. (1993). *The metaphysics of death* (pp. 73–92). Stanford University Press.
Wilson, E. (1978). *On human nature*. Harvard University Press.
Wisnewski, J. (2005). Is the immortal life worth living? *International Journal for Philosophy of Religion, 58*, 27–36.

Chapter 9
Transhumanism, Immortality and the Question of Life's Meaning

Aribiah David Attoe and Amara Esther Chimakonam

Abstract In our contemporary and futuristic times, immortality is slowly being extracted from the divine/spiritual arena by means of science and technology. There is the optimism that through the scientific and technological revitalization of human nature, humans would probably attain eternal existence in this world. This optimism, and its underlying philosophy, is based on something known as transhumanism. In this chapter, we examine the implications of transhumanism for the question of life's meaning, especially from an African perspective. Specifically, we pit transhumanism against three dominant traditional African notions of meaning viz. the God's purpose theory, the vital force theory and the communal normative function theory in a bid to decipher which theory, amongst the three, best undergirds a meaningful transhuman existence. We conclude that the communal view is the most attractive of the three theories in terms of answering the question of how to live meaningfully as a transhuman/post-human being. According to the communal view, a meaningful life is one that strives to acquire personhood of the highest level by performing those acts that ensure harmonious living, communal flourishing, and the common good. Attaining personhood, thus, presents itself as one plausible overarching purpose for a transhuman existence.

Keywords Africa · Communal · Immortality · Meaning of life · Transhumanism

A. D. Attoe (✉)
Centre for Leadership Ethics, University of Fort Hare, Alice, South Africa

Conversational School of Philosophy (CSP), Calabar, Nigeria

A. E. Chimakonam
Center for Phenomenology in South Africa, University of Fort Hare, Johannesburg, South Africa

A. D. Attoe et al. (eds.), *Conversations on African Philosophy of Mind, Consciousness and Artificial Intelligence*,
https://doi.org/10.1007/978-3-031-36163-0_9

9.1 Introduction

There are those (some supernaturalists) that maintain that immortality is necessary for life to have meaning (see Metz, 2013). This view is based on the idea of a person's soul surviving the death of one's body and migrating to a spiritual realm for eternal bliss. Today, the quest to scientifically and technologically enhance the human body, as well as its physical/mental capabilities, only shows that slowly, but surely, immortality and well-being will no longer be the sole reserve of a spiritual existence. Transhumanists strongly believe that recent and further developments in science and technology would enable humanity to overcome ageing, disease, physical trauma, and to extend the human lifespan. Transhumanists tend to think of immortality as living forever in this world via radical life extension and/or mind uploading. Nevertheless, the question of whether the transhumanists' quest for immortality could have implications on the meaning of life has received little attention.

Furthermore, whatever ideas that are available in the literature on this issue often approach the question from a "Western" or Euro-American perspective (Seung, 2012; Weijers, 2014; Sandberg, 2015; Lee, 2019a, b), while non-Western perspectives are largely absent. In this chapter, we address the question of life's meaning, in terms of a transhuman existence, in light of some traditional African conceptions of meaning. We, then show that the communal normative function theory of meaning, which is mostly grounded on a normative conception of personhood that depends on the idea of communal flourishing, best grounds a transhumanists' conception of the meaning of life.

We divide this chapter into four sections. The first section critically examines the literature on the nature and scope of transhumanism. The second section discusses some of the implications of a transhumanist future (such as integrating humans with technology) that would gradually evolve the human species to a posthuman species (see, e.g., More, 2013; Bostrom, 2003, 2005a, 2009), and help human beings attain immortality in this world through enhanced physical health (that immunes one from disease and ageing) and through uploading the mind into some sort of computer (Young, 2006; Kurzweil, 2005; Prisco, 2013). The third section critically examines transhumanism and the question of life's meaning from an African perspective. Three things are of interest to us in this section: first, it explains the notion of meaning of life; second, it draws plausible accounts of transhuman existence that would be regarded as the possible bearers of meaningfulness; third, it places some African theories of the meaning of life in conversation with transhumanism and identifies the communal normative function theory as the most plausible grounding for a meaningful transhumanist existence. The communal normative function theory of meaning recognizes a meaningful life as one that strives to acquire personhood of the highest level by performing those acts that ensure harmonious living, communal flourishing and the common good. The fourth section mainly extends our arguments further, indicates possible objections to our views and responds to them.

9.2 The Nature and Scope of Transhumanism

For most of human history, there seems to be a consensus on the limits imposed by the biological and natural limitations on human species. Humans die of disease, ageing, genetic issues, and other such maladies, which are considered to be natural occurrences. In terms of the human being's inhumanity to its species, crimes such as racism, rape, murder, war, slavery, etc., continue to present themselves as a present danger to the survival of the species - or, at least, some members of the species. The danger increases, as Ingmar Persson and Julian Savulescu (2012) have observed, in this age of rapid technological development where a psychopath has a chance to cause humanity to become extinct through scientific and technological means. Human frailty in the face of such heinous acts are seen as arising out of human biological/natural limitations. These biological and natural limitations have hitherto posed a great challenge to the human being's ability to live a healthier, longer, and morally better life.

Recent developments in nanotechnology, biotechnology, artificial intelligence, neuroscience, genetic engineering, etc., raise the optimism that the human species can outlive their biological and natural limitations. Beyond healthy living, these technologies are believed to provide greater cognitive and emotional stability and *may* even grant the human being immortality in the *near* future, here on earth. Transhumanists, such as Nick Bostrom (2008), Mark Walker (2009), Max More (2013), Ingmar Persson and Julian Savulescu (2011), hold that the human biological nature needs to be augmented through scientific and technological means to overcome the limitations imposed on them by nature and their biology. And so, individuals' bodies and mental abilities can be enhanced through the use of pharmaceuticals and biomedical technologies to overcome their biological and natural limitations. The rationale here is that individuals' bodies and mental dispositions are connected to their biological makeup, and technologically enhancing those biological aspects would help humans to resist their biological and natural limitations. As Mark Walker (2009, p. 28) well says, "…genes influence human behaviour, so altering the genes of individuals may alter the influence genes exert on behaviour." Consider, for instance, a serial killer who tortures young women to fulfil his orgasmic ecstasy. Such an individual could be technologically enhanced to suppress the genetic trait (or brain state) that allow for violence, and to augment the genetic traits (and/or brain states) that allow for a tendency toward emotions of compassion and kindness towards women.

Now, there are as many variants of transhumanists as there are different definitions of transhumanism (see Crowther, 2019, p. 690; Tirosh-Samuelson & Mossman, 2011, p. 35). Although we will not venture into analyzing all of them in this work because of the limited space we have here, we will rather focus on what the majority of transhumanists might agree that transhumanism is. Transhumanism, etymologically speaking, is derived from two Latin words, namely *trans* (which means beyond) and *humanus* (which literally means human) (see Sorgner, 2009, p. 1375). In this sense, transhumanism simply means beyond human. In a narrow sense, transhumanism is the "passionate belief in the transcendence of human limitations – not through religion or politics, but through *science* – product of the rational mind in the technowonderland of the modern world" (Young, 2006, p. 6). It is the idea that technological and scientific revitalization of human nature is necessary for overcoming the limitations imposed on the human species by their biological and natural components.

In a broader sense, transhumanism, according to Stefan Sorgner, "is a philosophical movement that affirms the technological enhancement of the human species and the coming about of transhumans and posthumans" (Sorgner, 2009: 1376). This definition entails that, first, transhumanism involves the technological enhancement of human species. It shows that transhumanism is the process of improving human abilities through technology beyond what is considered human. Second, it posits transhumanism as a futuristic agenda that would eventually create transhumans and posthumans. Leaning heavily on the work of Fereidoun M. Esfandiary titled *Are You a Transhuman? Monitoring and Stimulating Your Personal Rate of Growth in a Rapidly Changing World* (1989), Sorgner defines transhumans and posthumans thus:

> Transhumans are transitory human beings who still belong to the human species but have technologically enhanced capacities, which is why they represent the evolutionary link to posthumans. Posthumans no longer belong to the human species. They are members of a new, enhanced species. (Sorgner, 2009, p. 1376)

A remarkable difference between the two is that transhumanism seems to be a means to an end, which is the posthuman. Transhuman(ism), thus, becomes a transitory stage or a means of arriving at the ultimate end, posthuman(ism). Posthumans are, in this instance, thought of as superintelligent individuals and potentially immortal beings who have transcended moral and cognitive disabilities, ageing, disease, and death that plague the human species. As R.S. Sirius and Jay Cornell succinctly capture, posthuman is "a flawless, immortal, godlike" being embodying "abilities so above and beyond humans" in an unimaginable extent (Sirius & Cornell, 2015, p. 173).

Prominent transhumanists within the Western tradition envision that our world will someday be overtaken by 'ultra-intelligent machines' that would put an end to all human limitations, including Irving J. Good (1965), Eric K. Drexler (1986), Hans Moravec (1988), Ray Kurzweil (1990), Marvin Minsky (2006). Others like Gregory Stock (2002), Andy Clark (2003), Ronald Bailey (2005), Nick Bostrom (2008), Max More (2013), and Newton Lee (2019a, b), believe that genetic engineering, life-extending biosciences, neural-computer integration, neuroscience, artificial life, molecular nanotechnology, etc. would give rise to superior human species.

Newton Lee, for example, opens his 2019 work titled, *Brave New World of Transhumanism,* with these words, "Modern humanity with some 5000 years of recorded history has been experiencing growing pains, with no end in sight. It is high time for humanity to grow up and to transcend itself by embracing transhumanism" (Lee, 2019a, b, p. 3). For Lee, the impetus for upholding transhumanism lies in the uncomfortable conditions, such as poverty, hunger, disease, suffering, etc.

(see Lee, 2019a, b, pp. 9–11), that have confronted, and are still confronting, the human species. Indeed, he basis his conclusion on the argument that our present existential condition, as human beings, allows for three options: first, we can return to some sort of ascetic lifestyle, like the "Amish way" of life, that would free us from "worldly distractions"; second, we continue with the current state of things and run the risk of exposing humanity to "another millennium of growing pains and existential risks that may lead to human extinction"; third, we "transform our thoughts and deeds towards a technological brave new world of transhumanism" (Lee, 2019a, b, p. 8). Lee strongly believes that the last option, moving towards transhumanism by embracing the new advances in science and technology, is what can save humanity from the doomsday: "[T]ranshumanism is the next logical step in the evolution of humankind, and it is the existential solution to the long-term survival of the human race," which would produce superhumans that would live above the biological and natural limitations that constrain human abilities (Lee, 2019a, b, p. 38).

Conversely, transhumanism has its critics, known as the bioconservatives, and these critics include scholars such as Francis Fakuyama (2002), Leon Kass (2002), Bill McKibben (2003), Micheal Sandel (2007), Don Ihde (2011), Gregor Wolbring (2016), among others, who are pessimistic about the transhumanists' ethos. The frequently expressed worries of these critics are that while transhumanists espouse a futuristic utopian perfect world where perfect human species (known as posthumans) would replace the human species, transhumanism might, in reality, end up creating "Frankenstein monsters". Also, by altering the natural way things are meant to be, transhumanists are playing God.

Gregor Wolbring, for instance, in his article titled A*bnormality* (2016), expresses the fear that in a transhuman future, the conception of what becomes abnormal for humans would change drastically. By abnormal, he meant "how we judge the human body and its abilities" (Wolbring, 2016, p. 1). This, he says, raises the question: "who of the in-the-moment species-typical people" will be reclassified as abnormal, or "not normal," because they do not have the "beyond-species-typical body and abilities?" (Wolbring, 2016, p. 3). His take is that technologically enhancing human beings would lead to a reconceptualization of what it means to be healthy and normal, since the technologically enhanced being would no longer be in the same pedestal with the non-enhanced. The danger of this, as he informs us, is that in a transhuman future those who are not technologically enhanced, "no matter how medically healthy" they appear, would be seen as "limited, defective, impaired, and in need of constant improvement made possible by new technologies" (Wolbring, 2016, p. 3).

Nevertheless, transhumanists have not been silent on these accusations. A recent article by Max More (2013) shows that such accusations arise out of the "misconceptions" of the ethos of transhumanism. Such misconceptions, he contends, arise from the critics not being well acquainted with the transhumanist literature, misreading and misunderstanding the transhumanist ideal, misinterpreting and distorting transhumanist ideas to suit their preconceptions, and confusing the transhumanist goal of "continual improvement or enhancement" with perfection (More, 2013, p. 14). More maintains that we can become aware of these misconceptions when we clearly understand that undergirding the idea of transhumanism is the "principles of extropy". These principles aim to continuously improve the human condition through the values of perpetual progress that seeks the removal of political, cultural, religious, biological and physiological barriers to the continual improvement of individuals' wisdom, intelligence and radical extension of lifespan through technology; intelligent technology that seeks to improve human life; practical optimism that takes a proactive approach, in place of both blind faith and stagnant pessimism, towards human nature; self-transformation that entails a rational use of technology to augment individuals' physiological, neurological, emotional and psychological components; and so forth (More, 2013, pp. 5–6). Thus, utilizing recent (and further) scientific and technological developments to continually enhance human capabilities is central to our future as human beings.

9.3 Some Implications of Transhumanist Future

What would a transhuman future look like, and what bold new visions would such an existence bestow on us? Simon Young provides us with some answers that some might imagine to be grandiose. He says: "[L]iberated from biological slavery, an immortalized species, Homo cyberneticus, will set out for the stars. Conscious life will gradually spread throughout the galaxy… until finally, in the unimaginably distant future, the whole universe has come alive, awakened to its nature—a cosmic mind becomes conscious of itself as a living entity—omniscient, omnipotent, omnipresent" (Young, 2006, p. 44). The transhumanist's future is one where the human being, now evolved to Homo Cyberneticus, would shed the current limitations that weigh her down and blossom into something God-like - bereft of death and decay, and becoming the very consciousness of the universe.

The key to this transhumanist future is integrating humans with technology that would gradually transit the human species to posthuman species (More, 2013; Bostrom, 2003, 2005a, 2009). Transhumanists, like Nick Bostrom (2014), Ray Kurzweil (2005), and Vernor Vinge (1993, 2013), believe that we can transit to this future through Technological Singularity. It is a take-off stage for a post-technological civilization that would irreversibly transform human life through exponential technological growth, which would usher in a posthuman era. According to Ray Kurzweil, technological singularity "is a future period during which the pace of technological change will be so rapid, its impact so deep, that human life will be irreversibly transformed…" (Kurzweil, 2005, p. 7). Technological singularity is a conjecture of rapid technological change and its trajectory into the future, which would result in the emergence of superintelligent entities. Superintelligence is "any intellect that greatly exceeds the cognitive performance of humans in virtually all domains of interest" (Bostrom, 2014, p. 26).

Transhumanists are positive that the birth of these superintelligence entities would be possible through a combination of genetic engineering, life-extending biosciences, intelligence intensifiers, smarter interfaces between brains and computers, worldwide data networks, virtual reality, intelligent agents, swift electronic communication, artificial intelligence, molecular nanotechnology (More, 1998), and other anticipated future technologies. Through these technologies, the harmful and degenerative aspects of human biological nature would be eliminated, natural death would be overcome, human capabilities would be enhanced, and the posthuman era would be realised. As Kurzweil puts it:

> The singularity will allow us to transcend these limitations of our biological bodies and brains. We will gain power over our fates. Our immortality will be in our own hands...The singularity will represent the culmination of the merger of our biological thinking and existence with our technology, resulting in a world that is still human but that transcends our biological roots. There will be no distinction, post-singularity, between human and machine or between physical and virtual reality. (Kurzweil, 2005, pp. 8–9)

At this point, we can probably imagine some of the features of the posthuman era. One of the likely features of this posthuman era would be immortality. Such immortality would be sharply different from some religious ideas such as those that imagine the immortal soul leaving the human body at death and migrating to paradise where it will continue a blissful existence. Immortality, in the transhumanist context, would not be achieved through the help of a divine entity, or God, rather immortality would be achieved through human effort. Also, immortality would not be achieved in the afterlife, but humans would attain immortality in this world through modern science and technology. Bostrom opines that the "exclusive thunder of the religious institutions, such as very long lifespan, unfading bliss, and godlike intelligence" is now within our grasp (Bostrom, 2003, p. 46). Humans could become like God – omnipotent, omniscient, and immortal – here in this world. In this light, immortality would mean indefinite existence through science and technology in which humans attain an unending existence in this world through things like enhanced bodies, enhanced physical/mental health (which immunes one from disease and ageing) and through uploading the mind into a computer.

Within the transhumanist context, humans can attain immortality either by biological means of radical life extension or by cybernetic means of uploading human habits, memory, and skill into superintelligent computers. Through the biological means, transhumanists attempt to overcome the major Trois (ageing, disease, and physical trauma) that cause human death. With the advance in bioengineering, transhumanists possibly hope to enhance human mental and physical capacities to slow, reverse and resist ageing, to repair itself during physical trauma, to cure diseases, and to extend human life span. Radical life extension would likely be attained by addressing tiny structures in the human body that would make it younger again. Kurzweil is very optimistic that "[w]e are beginning to understand ageing, not as a single inexorable progression but as a group of related processes. Strategies are emerging for fully reversing each of these ageing progressions, using different combinations of biotechnology techniques" (Kurzweil, 2005, pp. 212–213). With the enzyme telomerase, biologists were able to reverse certain forms of ageing in some cells cultured in a laboratory (West, 2004, p. 69). Indeed, reversing ageing through bioengineering would probably be the transhumanists' likeliest route to radical life extension.

Also, through cybernetic means, human intelligence could be extricated from human bodies and placed into machines such as computers for super longevity. For Kurzweil, "Uploading a human brain means scanning all of its salient details and then reinstantiating those details into a suitably powerful computational substrate. This process would capture a person's entire personality, memory, skills, and history" (Kurzweil, 2005, pp. 198–199). The computer will immortalize such an individual by retaining her intelligence and personality even when the physical body is long gone. Bostrom spells out the possible processes that could be required for a mind upload:

> First, create a sufficiently detailed scan of a particular human brain, perhaps by deconstructing it with nanobots or by feeding thin slices of brain tissue into powerful microscopes for automatic image analysis. Second, from this scan, reconstruct the neuronal network that the brain implemented, and combine this with computational models of the different types of neurons. Third, emulate the whole computational structure on a powerful supercomputer. (Bostrom, 2005a, b, p. 9)

Once the human mind is successfully uploaded, it would exist as a robotic body with more enhanced capabilities, or as an embodied self of virtual reality, i.e. pure software without a physical body. This uploaded mind would be able to free itself from human embodiment and its limits, travel across space through computer networks, duplicate itself, and freely roam the universe as a "software angel." Thus, mind uploading, "the transfer of a human mind, memories, personality and "self" (whatever "self" is) to new high-performance substrates is the ultimate technology for immortality" (Prisco, 2013, p. 235).

9.4 Transhumanism and the Question of Life's Meaning: An African Perspective

What are the implications of transhumanism for questions about the meaning of life? The answer to such a question must begin with some clarificatory notes in order for us to sharpen our focus and understand clearly the question we are asking and the answers that would follow. And so, we begin this section by first clarifying what philosophers normally mean by the term "meaning" as well as the scope in which we understand the term "meaning of life." Thereafter, we will begin to examine the question of life's meaning from a transhumanist perspective – specifically, we will attempt to decipher what African theory of meaning best grounds a transhuman existence.

When asking about the meaning of "meaning," we are usually asking about "… what all and only the competing conceptions of a meaningful life are about…." (Metz, 2013, pp. 18–19). In other words, we are asking for all those salient features that only conceptions of meaning refer to – a concept of meaning. One must note, at this point, that a concept of meaning is distinguishable from a conception of meaning. While the latter is how a specific view describes what constitutes a meaningful life, the former is an abstraction of what all competing views point to, when talking about the meaning of life.

An understanding of meaning, or the concept of meaning, if it must be as all-encompassing as we have described, would best be captured by a pluralist concept of meaning. While there are some who do not offer a pluralist concept of meaning–like Tatjana Visak (2017), who sees meaning as a description of our normative reasons for action, and Frank Martela (2017), who speaks in terms of the contributions a life must have made – such offerings are usually too narrow.

For us, our inspiration lies in Thaddeus Metz's concept of meaning. Metz advances what he refers to as a family semblance approach, which clumps together different related ideas about what meaning is about. Thus, "…to ask about meaning [for Metz] … is to pose questions such as: which ends, besides one's own pleasure as such are most worth pursuing for their own sake; how to transcend one's animal nature; and what in life merits great esteem or admiration" (Metz, 2013, p. 34). While Metz's family resemblance approach is a feasible attempt, we find that it excludes subjective approaches to meaning. Also, Metz's view excludes the idea of coherence, which, we believe, is integral to theories about the meaning *of* life. Thus, drawing from Ada Agada (2015) who argues that meaning lies in our yearning for perfection, and from Susan Wolf (2010) who locates meaning in the act of loving those things which we consider to be worthy of love (Wolf, 2010, p. 8), we propose the following as our working definition of the concept of meaning: *to ask about meaning is to ask about the subjective passionate pursuit of those ends, besides one's own pleasure, as such, that are most worth pursuing for their own sake; what transcends one's animal nature; what merits great esteem or admiration; and how one's life coheres towards a certain overarching goal.*

Now, having delineated what "meaning" entails, a second important distinction that we must take note of is the distinction between meaning *in* life and the meaning *of* life. The term "meaning in life", for us, refers to those instances of meaning that may dot an individual's life. That is, meaning in life is concerned with particular meaningful acts that an individual may engage in from time to time. Completing a university degree at a particular point in one's life can be considered as an example of meaning in life. The meaning of life is a much broader consideration (Taylor, 1970). When we use the term "meaning of life," our scope is not so broad as to encompass the meaning of life, whether in cosmic terms or in the sense of all of humanity. We use the term to describe what, if anything, makes an individual person's life, considered as a whole, meaningful. For this chapter, our immediate concern is not with whether specific parts of an individual's life are meaningful, but rather, whether the cumulative of one's whole existence can be meaningful, given the possibilities offered by transhumanism – especially from an African perspective.

Our focus on the meaning of life, as opposed to meaning in life, is predicated on the fact that attaining some meaning in life is not necessarily a marker that one's life, considered as a whole, is/can be meaningful. Since transhumanism implies a closer drive towards immortality, it makes more sense for us to talk about what can make such an extended existence, considered as a whole, meaningful.

Transhumanism, as we discussed earlier, involves some sort of advancement of the human body and/or the human consciousness, such that the individual's capabilities are enhanced, his/her life is extended longer than normal, and/or s/he achieves some form of immortality. Within the traditional African worldview, the idea of immortality or an extended life is domiciled within the purview of spirituality. Transhumanism does not offer a spiritual type of enhancement or immortality. Indeed, transhumanism is a human attempt to pry immortality from the realm of the spiritual to the physical realm via science and technology. Thus, within the purview of transhumanism, we can identify three types of lives that can be judged, if at all, as meaningful. These include:

LI: A transhuman existence that involves a physically augmented body but a normal (unextended) human lifespan.
L2: A transhuman existence that involves an extended human lifespan.
L3: A transhuman existence that is immortal.

In all these versions of a transhumanist existence, certain features apply, if such a life must be considered meaningful. The first of these is what we refer to as "coherence". In most cases, we achieve certain moments of meaningfulness in our lives but those, sometimes random, moments of meaningfulness possess no structure and may not be interconnected. Thus, in evaluating a whole life, those moments of meaningfulness tell no overarching story. In much the same way that tidbits of random information may not tell a meaningful story, random moments of meaning cannot form a narrative that can help us judge a life, as a whole, as meaningful. Hence, there must be a structure to a life that must contain interconnected actions and moments of meaningfulness. In other words, there must be some coherence between interconnected actions and a grand narrative.

This last point leads us to the second feature – teleology. The grand narrative that we speak of is the purpose, goal, or final end that a life if it must be reviewed as meaningful, must aim for. This final end, like our definition of the concept of meaning, ought to encompass those intrinsically derived ends, besides one's own pleasure, which are worth pursuing for their own sake, transcend one's animal nature and/or merits great esteem or admiration. It is this final end that forms the grand narrative that the life-structure must cohere with. Thus, the question "what is the point of my life", or as Tabensky (2003) puts it "but what is the point of this?" is answered by that final end.

Within the corpus of African thought, some of the dominant theories of meaning, as I have elsewhere outlined them (see: Attoe, 2020), are the Vital force theory of meaning, the African God-purpose theory of meaning, and the communal normative function theory of meaning. A vital force is an animating force, present in every reality and emanating from the supreme being. In humans, it is believed that this vital force also possesses a rational component – and this is what distinguishes human beings from other animals (Tempels, 1959; Dzobo, 1992). The vital force theory of meaning locates meaning in those acts – usually positive engagements with others, adherence to certain communal rituals, etc. – that continually increase/augment one's vital force.

For us, it would be difficult to ground a transhumanist theory of meaning on the vital force theory for a couple of reasons. First, there must be convincing reasons to believe that vital force refers to something real. This is difficult when we remember that some of the activities attributed to one's vital force, such as reasoning, consciousness, animation, etc., are explainable in purely neuroscientific terms. Furthermore, since the vital force is decidedly spiritual, it remains to be seen what the status of one's vital force would be if one's transhuman existence involves some sort of disembodiment (for instance, if it is ever possible to download one's consciousness into a computer or into a machine).

Beyond this, the mere accumulation of vital force does not fit the bill of a grand purpose that one pursues as an end-in-itself or as a goal that transcends one's existence/animal nature. Vital force is presented as something ubiquitous and part and parcel of any human person's existence – in much the same way that having a heart or lungs is generally part of every healthy human existence. The "spiritual" nature of vital force doesn't change the fact that it is seen as a necessary part of human existence. With this in mind, it is easy to argue that the augmentation of one's vital force is hardly as meaningful (in the sense of an overarching purpose for one's life) as we would like to believe since it barely transcends our animal nature. Indeed, one can think of it as only a means to an end, in a similar way to how eating healthy is a means to a better life. If this is the case, then one cannot consider the augmentation of vital force as the overarching goal for which a life can structure itself towards, in order to be considered meaningful. Thus, it is justifiable for us to set aside the vital force theory moving forward.

The second theory, the African God-purpose theory, does a better job in grounding a meaningful transhuman existence than the vitalist view. Within this framework, meaningfulness is achieved when one obeys divine law and fulfils God's purpose. This purpose, as I have stated elsewhere (see Attoe, 2020), ensures the harmony that sustains the universe and, in turn, legitimizes the existence of God. The overarching goal for which a life must be structured in order to be considered meaningful, as a whole, lies in the purpose set out by God via divine law or through one's destiny (Gbadegesin, 2004). When one structures her life in such a way that it coheres with her destiny and/or obeys divine law, then that life would be meaningful. Prima facie, the meaningfulness of L1, L2, and L3 transhuman existence can be grounded on the African God-purpose theory. However, there are a few problems associated with this present view. First, for the view to stand, one must first assume that God exists, and then that God exists in such a way that It[1] can mete out destinies and purposes to humans, and also make judgments about those destinies and purposes. While there are good reasons to believe that there is a first cause, if one is a foundationalist, from which other things emanate, it is impossible to ascertain with any degree of certainty that such a first cause exists in the way we think it does. Thus, if it is true that the first cause does not exist in such a way that it is able to mete

[1] We are uncertain about the true nature of God/supreme being, whether It is a personalised and gendered being. And so, I use the neuter pronoun "It" as it best describes our current understanding of God, If It exists.

out destinies or divine law, then it would not be conceivable to talk about a theory of meaning that is based on non-existent properties beyond mere wishful thinking.

On the other hand, if we were to agree that God did exist in such a way that It can mete our purposes or destinies, then a new problem arises. This problem is the unattractiveness of an externally derived and instrumental purpose. Garrett Thompson alludes to this when he says that "One weakness of the divine theorist's argument is that the first premise presents an exclusive definition of 'meaning'. It excludes the idea that something can be meaningful by being non-instrumentally valuable" (Thomson, 2003, p. 48). Apart from excluding non-instrumental values, instrumental values are themselves not purveyors of meaning. If a sacrificial lamb were to judge what is meaningful about its existence, it would hardly be the case that that lamb would consider the human idea that it is only meant for sacrifice as the purpose of its own existence. This is because such a purpose is not only externally derived but it only makes sense to the human beings who allocate this purpose, and not to the lamb. Thus, even if the lamb ends up fulfilling that purpose, it is not establishing the meaning of its life, it is only enabling human preference. And so, insofar as God's purpose is externally derived and of instrumental value, fulfilling such a purpose does not ensure that one's life is meaningful, it only ensures that God's preferences are established. However, one can alternatively argue that an individual can subjectively decide, or have an intrinsic desire, to pursue God's purpose. This possibility does not, however, tell us if God exists in the way we think It does, or that Its purpose is really what we think it is.

The third African theory of meaning, the communal normative function theory, does the best job in capturing that final end/transcendental purpose that might ground a transhumanist theory of the meaning of life. The communal normative function theory of meaning recognises a meaningful life as one that strives to acquire personhood of the highest level by performing those acts that ensure harmonious living, communal flourishing, and the common good. Conversely, according to this view, a meaningless life is one that strives to pursue those negative ends that ensure discord and mitigate the common good.

This theory is generally inspired by the communal philosophies that dominate the African philosophical landscape. We can see this communal philosophy in different forms in the works of scholars like Mbiti (1990), Ramose (1999), Menkiti (2004), Asouzu (2004), Murove (2007), Ozumba & Chimakonam (2014), Metz (2017), etc. The common denominator among all these versions of communalism is the emphasis on sustaining relationships between various fragments of reality – in this context, among human beings. More specific inspirations for the communal normative function theory are Ifeanyi Menkiti's normative conception of a person and Thaddeus Metz's version of African ethics (Menkiti 2004; Metz 2017). Menkiti's view points to the fact that personhood is earned and not a capacity that one possesses at birth, and so one can distinguish between an individual and an individual person. The former being a human being that has not acquired personhood and the latter implying a human being that has earned personhood. He makes this point clear when he says:

> ...considered as an individuated source of consumption, a bundle as it were of primary appetites, the individual could still count as an agent in the world. But to go beyond the raw appetitive level to the special level marked by the dignity of the person, something more would seem needed. In this regard, 'individual' and 'Individual person' may carry somewhat different weight and it is the context of the discussion that spells out whether they converge or diverge. (Menkiti, 2004, p. 325)

Furthermore, since the level of morality that deeply informs personhood can only be acquired over time and by gaining experience, the process to acquire personhood must involve an ontological progression – from an *it* (a child) to an *it* (nameless dead) (Menkiti, 2004, p. 326). Beyond morality, certain rites, rituals, and/or milestones are part and parcel of the journey to personhood. Thus, the individual's life is structured in such a way that those rites, rituals and milestones are acknowledged. And so, as the individual progresses from one stage of life to another, engages in the rites and rituals expected of him/her at different stages of his/her life, and also lives a moral life – which involves having a positive relationship with others such that harmony is achieved, as opposed to discord (Metz, 2017, p. 111) – such an individual acquires normative personhood and meaning, which only becomes more authentic as the person progresses with time.

From the foregoing, we then see the inspiration for the communal normative thesis. With regards to a transhuman existence, the communal normative theory of meaning (of the theories mentioned in this chapter) best undergirds any transhumanist theory of meaning from an African perspective. Unlike the vital force theory, there is no debate about the truth value of a supposedly spiritual entity, neither is the overarching goal the pursuit of a purpose that does not count as meaningful (given our earlier definition of the term). Unlike the God-purpose theory, it is not premised on the debatable existence or nature of an entity or on an instrumental/externally derived goal that is alien to the individual. The communal normative function theory is premised on real-world human relationships. So, with regards to L1, L2, and L3, one can identify a structure to a life that is marked by various milestones, rites, and rituals. Beyond this, the overarching goal of earning personhood by constantly seeking to sustain communal harmony, communal flourishing, and the common good, clearly stands as an end worth pursuing, one that transcends our animal nature and one that merits great esteem and admiration. While the communal view best grounds a transhumanist theory of meaning from an African perspective, a closer look at the view reveals a few cracks.

9.4.1 Examining the View

Earlier we had identified three possible forms of transhuman existence viz. L1, L2, and L3. We had also claimed that the communal normative theory of meaning provides sufficient grounding for a transhumanist theory of meaning. While it is plausible to ground a transhumanist theory of the meaning of life on the communal normative theory, whether that theory of meaning, so grounded, is itself sufficiently plausible, is another matter altogether.

In L1, described as a life that is enhanced through technological advancements but without a recognisable increase in the average lifespan of the individual, death remains a reality. For most traditional African thinkers, death is merely a transition event that transforms the individual from a physical being in the present world to a living dead. For some, this new form of existence is real (Mbiti, 1990, pp. 83–85). This understanding suggests that every human person does have a spiritual essence that lives on after the demise of the physical body. Elsewhere, I have shown that the existence of such a spiritual essence is misleading at best (see Chimakonam et al., 2019). This is because those features generally attributed to that spiritual essence is explainable in material terms. If correct, then we must admit that the eventual demise of L1 would mean a plunge into nothingness, nothing more.

What this implies is that the pervading purpose or goal that must subsist if we are talking about the meaning of life, immediately ceases to make sense to L1 who is dead, since there is no subjective individual to make sense of such a purpose. Indeed, since meaning is intrinsically derived and subjectively pursued, making judgments about meaning will only make sense to the individual whose life is being judged. Thus, a post-humous judgment of L1's life by others who are not participants of the individual's subjective experience would make no sense to L1, who is dead, neither would it offer any satisfaction to her. Consequently, an immortal life would make sense, if the subject must always be aware of his/her achievement of meaning. From this view, one can add another point, which is that within the context of an immortal life, any overarching purpose for which the whole life must cohere with, must also subsist ad infinitum. This is because an overarching goal that is achieved and comes to an end, immediately transforms itself into a moment of meaningfulness, within the context of an immortal life.

This same argument can be made with regard to L2, which concerns a transhuman existence that involves an extended human lifespan. While there is a change from L1, in that the normal life span of the individual is extended significantly beyond the current norm, the same argument as those presented above can be used with regards to L2 because the extension of one's lifespan does not imply immortality. And so, since death remains a factor, the same as in L1, then the lack of meaning that death presupposes in L1, applies to L2.

With L3, the dynamics are different. Here, we encounter a transhumanist existence that promises us immortality in material terms. This immortality, as we have stated earlier in this chapter, can be achieved by the augmentation of our human bodies, such that ageing, illnesses, and other such limitations of the human body, paves the way for immortality. Other ways immortality could be achieved would be through the transfer of human consciousness into some machine or the augmentation/replacement of the human body with artificial bionic parts that are not susceptible to wear and tear or can be easily replaced. The underlying assumption here is that the measures taken to deny death to the human person are infallible. In the first instance (augmented biology), this infallibility appears a long shot, since that augmented body remains susceptible to grievous harm – for instance, an explosion that incinerates the body or an accident that crushes the head. Perhaps, a machine-based existence – where such a machine is presumably indestructible – would best capture the sort of immortality that L3 presupposes.

Now, if such immortality is ever possible, then we would imagine that a communal normative function theory grounds it properly. First, there is an overarching goal – earning personhood by constantly seeking to sustain communal harmony, communal flourishing, and the common good – and the life-structure that coheres with it. Second, the individual is always alive to subjectively judge and enjoy the achievement of that meaningfulness. Furthermore, personhood is something that grows with time. Thus, achieving personhood is a goal that one can achieve and then sustain for long periods. This is particularly important because choosing an unsustainable end in relation to an immortal life only transforms that achievement to an achievement of meaning *in* life – a moment of meaningfulness – and does not represent the meaning of life.

While the communal view bears strongly on L3, there are a few criticisms that can be made against the view. First, accusations that the communal view is much too narrow since it does not account for other types of meaningfulness can be made. For instance, if one were to decide to become a math genius who does not intend to extend his knowledge to others, such a meaningful pursuit would not count as meaningful within the communal view. But it is hard to doubt that such a pursuit is a meaningful one. However, such a criticism misses the point as the pertinent claim being made here is that the communal normative function theory, is one plausible way of grounding a meaningful transhumanist existence, and presumably not the only way.

Another criticism that can be made against the communal view is that despite the fact that earning personhood by constantly seeking to sustain communal harmony, communal flourishing, and the common good, is a goal that can be achieved and sustained, the endlessness of eternity can make such a purpose susceptible to the tedium of immortality. Thus, allowing a thinning out of the value of such a meaningful purpose into mere duty, and obligation – no different from other duties like obeying the law. Friends of the communal view would respond to this criticism by pointing to the fact that since one's personhood only becomes stronger with time, the endlessness of eternity would only presuppose endless possibilities, in terms of the strengthening of one's personhood.

A final critique of the transhuman communal view is that the immortality of L3 is ultimately dependent on the habitability of the space we live in and/or the immortality of the Universe (or at least, the immortality of the space that L3 has access to). If, for instance, L3 were to encounter a situation where the planet is made unhabitable either through nuclear wars, super volcanoes, a collision with an asteroid, etc., immortality would obviously be a questionable prospect (Jones et al., 2007; Poulopoulos, 2016). Also, if humans are never able to depart from our present Solar system, then the inevitable death of our Star would only mean the death of L3, and this would lead us back to the problems associated with L1 and L2 that I had earlier mentioned. I find this to be the most pertinent critique of the communal view (Carrington, 2000; Schröder & Smith, 2008).

9.5 Conclusion

The meaning of life – one that has grasped immortality through one form of transhuman augmentation or the other – can be considered meaningful in at least one way. That is, through the pursuit of personhood by constantly seeking to sustain communal harmony, communal flourishing, and the common good. While this is true, it is also true that the immortality that transhumanism offers dangles between wishful thinking and improbability. But we cannot ignore the view on that account because the possibility of immortal transhuman existence, even though improbable, is conceivable. For us, the communal normative function view stands as the most plausible theory of the meaning of a transhuman life.

References

Agada, A. (2015). *Existence and consolation: Reinventing ontology, gnosis and values in African philosophy*. Paragon House.
Asouzu, I. (2004). *Methods and principles of complementary reflection in and beyond African philosophy*. University of Calabar Press.
Attoe, A. (2020). A systematic account of African conceptions of the meaning of/in life. *South African Journal of Philosophy, 39*(2), 127–139.
Bailey, R. (2005). *Liberation biology: The scientific and moral case for the biotech revolution*. Prometheus Books.
Bostrom, N. (2003). *The transhumanist FAQ*. A General Introduction, Version 2.1. World Transhumanist Association. http://www.nickbostrom.com/views/transhumanismist.pdf. Accessed 20 June 2020.
Bostrom, N. (2005a). In defense of Posthuman dignity. *Bioethics, 19*(3), 202–214.
Bostrom, N. (2005b). A history of transhumanist thought. *Journal of Evolution and Technology, 14*, 1–25.
Bostrom, N. (2008). Why I want to be a Posthuman when I grow up. In B. Gordijn & R. Chadwick (Eds.), *Medical enhancement and posthumanity* (pp. 107–136). Springer Science and Business Media.
Bostrom, N. (2009). Why I want to be a Posthuman when I grow up. In B. Gordijn & R. Chadwick (Eds.), *Medical enhancement and posthumanity* (pp. 107–137). Springer.
Bostrom, N. (2014). Introduction—The transhumanist FAQ: A general introduction. In C. Mercer & F. D. Maher (Eds.), *Transhumanism and the body: The world religions speak* (pp. 1–18). Palgrave Macmillan.
Carrington, D. (2000). *BBC News*. http://news.bbc.co.uk/2/hi/sci/tech/specials/washington_2000/649913.stm. Accessed 18 April 2018.
Chimakonam, J., Uti, E., Segun, S., & Attoe, A. (2019). *New conversations on the problems of identity, consciousness and mind*. Springer Nature.
Clark, A. (2003). *Natural-born cyborgs: Minds, technologies, and the future of human intelligence*. Oxford University Press.
Crowther, M. (2019). IoT and transhumanism. In N. Lee (Ed.), *The Transhuman handbook* (pp. 689–700). Springer.
Drexler, K. E. (1986). *Engines of creation*. Anchor Press/Doubleday.
Dzobo, N. (1992). Values in a changing society: Man, ancestors and god. In K. Wiredu & K. Gyekye (Eds.), *Person and community: Ghanian philosophical studies* (pp. 223–240). Center for Research in Values and Philosophy.

Fukuyama, F. (2002). *Our Posthuman future: Consequences of the biotechnology revolution*. Profile Books.

Gbadegesin, S. (2004). Towardsa theory of destiny. In K. Wiredu (Ed.), *A companion to African philosophy* (pp. 313–323). Blackwell Publishing.

Good, J. I. (1965). Speculations concerning the first ultraintelligent machine. In F. Alt & M. Ruminoff (Eds.), *Advances in computer* (pp. 31–38). Academic Press.

Ihde, D. (2011). Of which human are we post? In G. R. Hansell & W. Grassie (Eds.), *H⁺transhumanism and its critics*. Metanexus Institute.

Jones, M., Sparks, R., & Valdes, P. (2007). The climatic impact of supervolcanic ash blankets. *Climate Dynamics, 29*(6), 553–564.

Kass, L. (2002). *Life, liberty and the pursuit of dignity*. Encounter Books.

Kurzweil, R. (1990). *The age of intelligent machines*. MIT Press.

Kurzweil, R. (2005). *The singularity is near: When humans transcend biology*. Viking.

Lee, N. (2019a). Brave new world of transhumanism. In N. Lee (Ed.), *The Transhuman handbook* (pp. 3–48). Springer.

Lee, N. (2019b). In search of super longevity and the meaning of life. In N. Lee (Ed.), *The Transhuman handbook* (pp. 313–354). Springer.

Martela, F. (2017). Meaningfulness as contribution. *The Southern Journal of Philosophy, 55*(2), 232–256.

Mbiti, J. (1990). *African religion and philosophy*. Heinemann.

McKibben, B. (2003). *Enough: Staying human in an engineered age*. Henry Holt & Co.

Menkiti, I. (2004). On the normative conception of a person. In K. Wiredu (Ed.), *A companion to African philosophy* (pp. 324–331). Blackwell Publishing.

Metz, T. (2013). *Meaning in life*. Oxford University Press.

Metz, T. (2017). Towards an African moral theory (revised edition). In I. Ukpokolo (Ed.), *Themes, issues and problems in African philosophy* (pp. 97–119). Palgrave Macmillian.

Minsky, M. (2006). *The emotion machine: Common sense thinking, artificial intelligence, and the future of the human mind*. Simon & Schuster.

Moravec, P. H. (1988). *Mind children: The future of robot and human intelligence*. Harvard University Press.

More, M. (1998). *The Extropian Principles Version 3.0: A Transhumanist Declaration*. https://mrob.com/pub/religion/extro_prin.html. Accessed 27 June 2020.

More, M. (2013). The philosophy of transhumanism. In M. More & N. Vita-More (Eds.), *The transhumanist reader: Classical and contemporary essays on the science, technology, and philosophy of the human future* (pp. 3–17). Wiley.

Ozumba, G., & Chimakonam, J. (2014). *Njikoka Amaka further discussions on the philosophy of integrative humanism: A contribution to African and intercultural philosophy*. 3rd Logic Option.

Persson, I., & Savulescu, J. (2011). The turn for ultimate harm: A reply to Fenton. *Journal of Medical Ethics, 37*, 441–444.

Poulopoulos, S. (2016). Introduction to environment and development. In S. Poulopoulos & V. Inglezakis (Eds.), *Environment and development: Basic principles, human activities, and environmental implications* (pp. 1–43). Elsevier B. V.

Prisco, G. (2013). Transcendent Engineering. In M. More & N. Vita-More (Eds.), *The transhumanist reader: Classical and contemporary essays on the science, technology, and philosophy of the human future* (pp. 234–240). Wiley.

Ramose, M. (1999). *African philosophy through Ubuntu*. Mond Books.

Sandberg, A. (2015). Transhumanism and the meaning of life. In C. Mercer & T. J. Trothen (Eds.), *Religion and transhumanism: The unknown future of human enhancement* (pp. 3–22). Praeger.

Sandel, M. (2007). *The case against perfection: Ethics in the age of genetic engineering*. The Belknap Press of Harvard University Press.

Savulescu, J., & Persson, I. (2012). Moral enhancement, freedom, and the god machine. *The Monist, 95*(3), 399–421.

Schröder, K., & Smith, R. (2008). Distant future of the sun and earth revisited. *Monthly Notices of the Royal Astronomical Society, 386*(1), 155–163.
Seung, S. (2012). *Connectome: How the Brain's wiring makes us who we are* (p. 273). Houghton Mifflin Harcourt.
Sirius, R. U., & Cornell, J. (2015). *Transcendence: The disinformation Encyclopaedia of transhumanism and the singularity*. Red Wheel/Weiser, Inc.
Sorgner, S. L. (2009). Transhumanism. In H. J. Birx (Ed.), *Encyclopaedia of time, science, philosophy, theology & culture* (Vol. 1-3, pp. 1375–1376). SAGE Publications, Inc.
Stock, G. (2002). *Redesigning humans: Our inevitable genetic future*. Houghton Mifflin.
Tabensky, P. (2003). Parallels between living and painting. *The Journal of Value Inquiry, 37*(1), 59–68.
Taylor, R. (1970). The meaning of life. In *Good and evil: A new direction, taylor* (pp. 319–334). Macmillian.
Tempels, P. (1959). *Bantu Philosophy*. Presence Africaine.
Thomson, G. (2003). *On the meaning of life*. Nelson Thomson Learning.
Tirosh-Samuelson, H., & Mossman, K. L. (2011). New perspectives on transhumanism. In H. Tirosh-Samuelson & K. L. Mossman (Eds.), *Building better humans? Refocusing the debate on transhumanism* (pp. 29–52). Peter Lang.
Vinge, V. (1993). *The coming technological singularity: How to survive in the post-human era*. NASA, version 21:11–22. https://ntrs.nasa.gov/search.jsp?R=19940022856. Accessed 29 June 2020.
Vinge, V. (2013). Technological singularity. In M. More & N. Vita-More (Eds.), *The transhumanist reader: Classical and contemporary essays on the science, technology, and philosophy of the human future* (pp. 365–375). Wiley.
Visak, T. (2017). Understanding "meaning of life" in terms of reasons for action. *Journal of Value Inquiry, 51*, 507–530.
Walker, M. (2009). Enhancing genetic virtue. *Politics and the Life Sciences, 28*(2), 27–47.
Weijers, D. (2014). Optimistic naturalism: Scientific advancement and the meaning of life. *Sophia, 53*, 1–18. https://doi.org/10.1007/s11841-013-0369-x. Accessed 20 June 2020.
West, D. M. (2004). Therapeutic cloning. In B. Aires (Ed.), *The scientific conquest of death: Essays on infinite lifespans* (pp. 63–76). Immortality Institute.
Wolbring, G. (2016). Abnormality. In H. ten Have (Ed.), *Encyclopaedia of Global Bioethics (with 22 figures and 22 tables)* (pp. 1–8). Springer International Publishing AG.
Wolf, S. (2010). *Meaning in life and why it matters*. Princeton University Press.
Young, S. (2006). *Designer evolution: A transhumanist manifesto*. Prometheus Books.

Chapter 10
African Reasons Why Artificial Intelligence Should Not Maximize Utility

Thaddeus Metz

Abstract Insofar as artificial intelligence is to be used to guide automated systems in their interactions with humans, the dominant view is probably that it would be appropriate to programme them to maximize (expected) utility. According to utilitarianism, which is a characteristically Western conception of moral reason, machines should be programmed to do whatever they could in a given circumstance to produce in the long run the highest net balance of what is good for human beings minus what is bad for them. In this essay, I appeal to values that are characteristically African—but that will resonate with those from a variety of moral-philosophical traditions, particularly in the Global South—to cast doubt on a utilitarian approach. Drawing on norms salient in sub-Saharan ethics, I provide four reasons for thinking it would be immoral for automated systems governed by artificial intelligence to maximize utility. In catchphrases, I argue that utilitarianism cannot make adequate sense of the ways that human dignity, group rights, family first, and (surprisingly) self-sacrifice should determine the behaviour of smart machines.

Keywords African ethics · Artificial intelligence · Automated systems · Moral decision-making · Sub-Saharan morality · Utilitarianism

10.1 Introducing the Question of How to Programme Artificially Intelligent Automated Systems

How should automated systems governed by artificial intelligence (AI) be programmed so as to act in accordance with sound moral norms? For instance, how should one programme a self-driving car that learns in the course of navigating

T. Metz (✉)
Department of Philosophy, University of Pretoria, Pretoria, South Africa
e-mail: th.metz@up.ac.za

A. D. Attoe et al. (eds.), *Conversations on African Philosophy of Mind, Consciousness and Artificial Intelligence*,
https://doi.org/10.1007/978-3-031-36163-0_10

streets? How should one programme a robot that is able to provide nursing to patients or domestic labour to family members, upon adapting to their various idiosyncracies? How should one programme a military weapon that takes advantage of the way soldiers tend to engage in battle? How should one programme a device that could mine underground on its own, changing its direction and method of extraction upon updating calculations of which kind of ore is likely to be in which place?

In asking how to programme these systems so that they do the right thing, one need not presume that the machines count as moral agents in any robust sense. Instead, it is perfectly sensible to view them as lacking moral agency and instead as being mere tools of their designers, who are human persons and hence moral agents. If a self-driving car is not disposed to stop for pedestrians, it is not the car that has performed a culpable wrong, but the one who made it (or, more carefully, the one who had let it onto the street upon knowing, or having had a duty to know, how it was made). The question is in the first instance about how those making automated systems governed by artificial intelligence should construct them, supposing they know they will be deployed in social contexts (and not merely contained in a laboratory).

It appears that the dominant answer to that question has been a utilitarian one, according to which a machine ought to be programmed so as to do what, in the light of available data and processing power, is expected to maximize what is good for human beings and to minimize what is bad for them in the long run (Bauer, 2020; Hibbard, 2015; Kinjo & Ebina, 2017; Majot & Yampolskiy, 2014; Marwala, 2014, 2017; Oesterheld, 2015, 2016; Shulman et al., 2009).[1] As I indicate below, this approach has the advantages of appearing to capture the nature of rational choice, to be impartial and hence morally attractive, as well as to be amenable to being formalized and coded.

Utilitarianism is a characteristically Western conception of moral-practical reason, having been advanced in various of its respects by classic philosophers such as Thomas Hobbes, Blaise Pascal, Jeremy Bentham, Adam Smith, and John Stuart Mill and continuing to guide much thought about ethics and public policy in the twenty-first-century American-European-Australasian context. In this essay, I appeal to characteristically African values to question the moral aptness of programming AI automated systems to maximize utility. Although I draw on perspectives that are particularly prominent in contemporary sub-Saharan ethics, and hence (presumably) in the worldviews of the 'traditional' peoples and cultures that inform them, the objections to utilitarianism will, at a certain level of abstractness, resonate with those from a variety of moral-philosophical backgrounds, particularly from the Global South. Utilitarianism prescribes a number of immoral actions in the light of some plausible ethical beliefs common in African ethical thought, and, supposing

[1] For unusual or tangential applications, there are: Grau (2005), who deems utilitarianism apt for robot-robot relations, even if not for robot-human interaction; Gloor (2016), who urges that AI be used primarily to avoid extremely bad outcomes for human beings, and not to produce particularly good ones; and Bonnefon et al. (2015, 2016), who argue that Western people are generally utilitarian about how self-driving cars should be programmed.

that moral actions are necessarily rational ones, these criticisms also implicitly cast doubt on the apparent rationality of utilitarianism.

Although there is recent literature on how one might apply AI to resolve problems in Africa and on ethical issues facing AI's application to Africa (e.g., Access Partnership, 2018; Gwagwa, 2019a; Ormond, 2020; Sallstrom et al., 2019; World Wide Web Foundation, 2017), there is literally nothing as yet on how one might do so in the light of indigenous African values as distinct from Western ones. By 'African' values, I mean ones *salient* in the massive sub-Saharan region of the continent, that is, beliefs about morality found among many indigenous black peoples (as opposed to, say, those of Arab descent in the north) over a long span of time and not found among many other societies around the world.[2] Recently, one scholar has noted 'the need to define African values and align AI with them' (Gwagwa, 2019b), but has not yet sought to meet the need, while another has said that 'African cultural values need to be taken into account when defining a framework for AI on the continent' (Spini, 2019), but has not developed such a framework. Here I aim to make some headway when it comes to heeding these calls.

I do not do so for reasons of relativism. It is not my view that the values that should govern technology in a certain society are necessarily those held by most in that society. I believe that majorities can be mistaken about right and wrong action, as nineteenth-century Americans were in respect of slavery. Instead, I draw on under-considered African ethical perspectives in the thought that any long-standing philosophical tradition probably has some insight into the human condition and has something to teach those outside it. Many of the values I identify as 'African' will, upon construing them abstractly, be taken seriously by many moral philosophers, professional ethicists, and the like around the world.

In the following, I begin by defining my target, saying more about what the nature of utilitarianism is, explaining why theorists have been drawn towards it, and illustrating what it would look like when applied to AI automated systems (Sect. 10.2). Then, I advance, on African grounds, four major objections to programming AI automated systems to maximize utility, arguing that doing so would fail to respect human dignity (Sect. 10.3), inadequately uphold group rights (Sect. 10.4), violate a principle of family first (Sect. 10.5), and counterintuitively forbid certain kinds of self-sacrifice on behalf of others (Sect. 10.6). Although one might have thought that utilitarianism expects a lot from a moral agent, I argue that it cannot even get that right, for it forbids one from helping others when helping oneself would do the most good impartially construed. I conclude by briefly noting some avenues for future research, such as considering what African grounds there might be to question the other major Western moral theory, Kantianism, in the context of AI (Sect. 10.7).

---

[2] Such a definition of what 'African' means entails that in order to count, a value need neither be held by all those in Africa nor be held only by those in Africa. For more on what geographical labels plausibly mean, see Metz (2015).

10.2 Utilitarianism in the Context of AI

In this section, I tell the reader what I mean by 'utilitarianism' and related terms such as 'maximize utility', show why it has been taken so seriously by ethical theorists, and give some examples of how it might inform AI automated systems. This section is therefore largely expository, saving critical discussion for later sections.

As will be familiar to many readers, utilitarianism is the doctrine that for any action to be rational and moral, it must be expected to maximize what is good for human beings (and perhaps animals) and to minimize what is bad for them in the long run.[3] By standard utilitarianism, what is good for us is subjective, a matter of either pleasant experiences, satisfied preferences, or positive emotions, and what is bad consists of pain, dissatisfaction, or negativity. Subjective well-being is taken to be the only thing good for its own sake, or at least the only sort of good that should be action-guiding for us as moral agents. Everything else on earth, at least in the mineral and vegetable kingdoms (again, potentially excluding the animal kingdom), is at best of merely instrumental value for being of use to foster our subjective well-being.[4]

Now, on the face of it, everyone's well-being matters equally, such that one would be objectionably biased to leave out anyone's interests when considering how to act. It would also appear irrational to leave out anyone's interests when making decisions, for a given person's subjective well-being has just as much value in itself as anyone else's. Furthermore, it is prima facie rational to promote as much of what is good for its own sake as one can; every bit of well-being that one could promote provides an agent reason to promote it, making it irrational to do anything less than the best one is in a position to do. Morality, too, seems to counsel maximizing what is good for us and minimizing what is bad, for surely it is preferable from the moral point of view to do all one can for the sake of humanity.

So construed, this consequentialist account of moral-practical reason is compelling, and it is not surprising to find it, or at least various elements of it, invoked in a wide array of Western contexts. For instance, it appears to capture the logic of many everyday decisions that at least 'modern' Western people make. When deciding whether to use a bicycle or a car to get to work, they naturally attend to the results of the two options not merely for themselves, but also for others. Riding the bike would be painful and would take longer, and yet it would be beneficial in the long run in respect of one's health and hence one's happiness. Taking the car would be

[3] I therefore address act-utilitarianism in this essay, setting aside rule-utilitarianism, which has been much less influential in AI circles. I believe that many of the objections to the former apply to the latter, but it takes extra work to demonstrate that. For one advocate of rule-utilitarianism in the context of AI, see Bauer (2020).

[4] There are of course those who pair a consequentialist combinatorial function with an objective account of final value, with an early advocate being Moore (1903) and a more recent one being Railton (1984). I believe the Afro-centric objections made below to classic utilitarianism apply with comparable force to objective consequentialism, at least if it includes agent-neutrality (and so is unlike Sen, 2000).

more pleasant and quicker, but it would cost more money and pollute the environment, risking lung cancer to others. Utilitarianism prescribes choosing whichever option would have the most good outcomes with the least bad outcomes in the long-term, impartially weighing everyone's interests given available information. People do not always in fact choose in that way, but, for the utilitarian, they should, as doing so would be prescribed by a consistent application of the logic they themselves tend to use to make decisions.

When it comes to state officials, those governing people living in a certain territory, it is common to appeal to what is called in public policy circles 'cost-benefit analysis'. Since all citizens matter equally, those who make and carry out the law should do so in ways that are going to maximize benefits and to minimize costs, taking the good of all citizens impartially into account. Consider that it would be patently unjust for those with political power to use government resources such as jobs and money to benefit themselves, their families, or a certain racial group at the expense of the general welfare.

Still more, at least the maximizing element of utilitarianism has been dominant in Western economics for at least three centuries, with actors in market exchanges seeking to obtain the most amount of profit or goods and with the least amount of expense. Of course, in the context of markets, people are motivated by self-interest, and not the interests of all. However, Adam Smith has famously argued that even if one's intention is not to benefit others when maximizing profit for oneself, in the long run that practice often enough ends up benefiting society more than others one could have undertaken, 'as if by an invisible hand'.

Beyond these considerations of the nature of rationality and morality, programmers and those who work with them or otherwise think about programming are drawn towards utilitarianism because it appears quantifiable and hence able to be coded (as noted in Anderson & Anderson, 2007: 18; Oesterheld, 2015).[5] Clearly, some pleasures are greater than others and some preferences are stronger than others. Utilitarians believe that, in principle, we could assign cardinal values to such states, ascribing real numbers to degrees of subjective well-being and woe. While that is of course difficult for a human being to calculate, artificial intelligence might be in a terrific position to estimate how much pleasure versus pain a given course of action would be expected to produce and to identify the one with the highest net balance (Anderson et al., 2005; Anderson & Anderson, 2007: 18).

Applied to, say, a self-driving car, it would be natural for a utilitarian programmer to have it minimize the number of people killed. It would be irrational and immoral, so the argument goes, to favour the interests of, say, the driver as opposed to pedestrians. Instead, everyone's interests count equally from the moral point of view, meaning that the car ought to be directed to do whatever would produce the greatest pleasure and the least pain in the long run, which presumably would come from killing one person instead of three, supposing those were the only options available.

[5] For a dissenting perspective, that it would be impossible to programme enough information for a machine to account for long-term results, see Allen et al. (2000: 256).

It might seem as though a utilitarian weapon would be nonsensical. After all, utilitarianism is impartial, with a person's nationality making zero difference to her moral standing as capable of subjective well-being, whereas during a time of war one is expected to take sides, that is, to place the lives of the soldiers from one's country ahead of those of others. However, it is worth considering the point that we should in fact want programmers to develop weapons that would serve only just causes such as rebutting aggression as well as ones that would not treat enemy soldiers, even those fighting for an unjust cause, as though they do not matter at all.

Having expounded utilitarianism and why it has been attractive, one might wonder what in the world is wrong with it. Despite its strengths, the African philosophical tradition provides strong reason for thinking that it has irredeemable weaknesses.

10.3 Human Dignity and AI

Although utilitarianism ascribes a *moral status* to every individual human being that is alive and either is sentient, has preferences, or exhibits emotions, it does not accord them *dignity*. The former amounts to the view that for whichever being is capable of subjective well-being, there is pro tanto moral reason to promote its welfare. The latter is the idea that a person has a superlative non-instrumental value that merits respect. To have a moral status, and hence to be owed dutiful treatment directly, does not imply that one is a person who is good for its own sake to a degree higher than anything else in the world. In addition, for there to be a moral reason to promote an individual's well-being differs from there being a moral reason to avoid degrading a person.

Improving others' well-being does have a clear place in African thought, but most often insofar as doing so can be a way of expressing respect for people who have dignity. Traditionally speaking, sub-Saharans tend to believe that our dignity is constituted by either vital force or group membership. Vital force is an imperceptible energy that has come from God and permeates everything in the universe in varying amounts and complexities, where, of perceptible beings, human persons have the most (Wiredu, 1996: 157–71; Deng, 2004; Iroegbu, 2005; Etieyibo, 2017). From this perspective, it is not our quality of life that matters fundamentally for morality, as per utilitarianism, but rather the fact of life itself; our nature is sacred for exhibiting a certain quantity or quality of divine energy.

Other times African thinkers maintain that persons have a dignity by virtue of membership or relationship. One scholar remarks, 'The dignity of human beings emanates from the network of relationships, from being in community; in an African view, it cannot be reduced to a unique, competitive and free personal ego' (Botman, 2000), while another says, '(T)he human person in Africa is from the very beginning in a network of relationships that constitutes his inalienable dignity' (Bujo, 2001: 88). There are different views on precisely which relationships matter, with some holding that they are ones with a clan or a specific community that has cared for one or that you have cared for (Cobbah, 1987; Ikuenobe, 2016), and others suggesting the relevant relationships are with the human species as a whole (perhaps Gyekye, 2010: sec. 6).

Both views are controversial from a cross-cultural perspective. For example, Western philosophers would be inclined to ground our dignity on our capacity for autonomy, while thinkers in the Judeo-Christian-Islamic tradition would maintain that it is constituted by a God-given soul (i.e., a spiritual substance as opposed to an imperceptible force). Although a specific and defensible account of what it is that gives us dignity would be useful when articulating a comprehensive ethic, it is unnecessary to consider utilitarianism's implications for AI. So long as individual persons have a dignity that merits respectful treatment, regardless of what confers that dignity on us, a moral agent will be forbidden from treating persons merely as a means to the greater good. That is, a typical dignity-based ethic will accord human rights to each person, where to have a human right entails that others have a duty not to subordinate or harm a person that should be upheld even if not doing so would promote a marginally greater amount of value in the world.

It is well known that a utilitarian ethic has difficulty accounting for human rights. Here is a classic example from contemporary Anglo-American ethics (Nozick, 1974: 28–30). Imagine that a mob angry about an apparent crime will severely beat and then kill two innocent people unless you, the sheriff in town, frame, corporally punish, and execute one innocent person. From a utilitarian perspective, it would be rational and moral for you to do terrible things to the person if that were indeed the only way to prevent others from doing terrible things to a larger extent. However, from a human rights perspective, you should not, for doing so would degrade the person. Instead of treating him as though he is valuable for his own sake, it would treat him as though he has a merely instrumental value for the reduction of bad outcomes in the world.

Of course, utilitarians are initially inclined to reply that the case is inaccurately described. They will suggest that the outcomes of a sheriff harming and killing one innocent person would likely be worse in the long run than letting two innocents be harmed and killed by others. After all, upon the sheriff framing an innocent person, the criminal is still free to commit crime again, and when people discover that the sheriff has done so, the criminal justice system will be weakened, allowing all the more murders to take place down the road.

However, it is not unfair to suppose, for the sake of argument, that there was in fact no crime committed, but that the sheriff was not in a position to convince members of the public of that in the time before rioting. In addition, it is reasonable to imagine, also for the sake of argument, that no one would ever discover that the sheriff has framed an innocent party for the non-existent crime. It is intelligible to ask what the right thing to do would be under these conditions, where a human rights perspective will look compelling to many African ethicists and to many other adherents to the idea of human dignity around the world.

What does a human rights framework mean for how to programme AI automated systems? It would involve directing them to treat persons in certain ways that are incompatible with maximizing utility. For example, consider a self-driving car. The most basic version of what is widely known as 'the trolley problem', often applied to self-driving cars (for just one influential example, see Awad et al., 2018), appears to tell in favour of utilitarianism.[6] In that case, the car has the two options of either, say, striking two pedestrians if it continues forward or veering in another direction where it would strike one pedestrian. Here, it appears that it would be right for the car to strike the one, which lends prima facie support to utilitarianism.

However, upon reflection, the support is weak, as there are many other situations in which it would intuitively be a human rights violation to kill one so as to save two. For example, imagine that the self-driving car happens to have two critically injured passengers in it and that they will die unless they get to the hospital in time. Suppose further that the only way to get them to the hospital in time would be for the self-driving car to mow down one pedestrian. It appears that respect for the person's dignity forbids killing him in order to save the lives of two others. In short, he has a human right to life that should be observed when programming a self-driving car.

10.4 Group Rights and AI

Although it is characteristic of African moral thought to ascribe a dignity to individual persons, it is likewise characteristic of it to maintain that certain kinds of wholes merit moral consideration. There are some sub-Saharan theorists who appear to believe only in group rights, such that, say, a family or clan alone has rights and the individual has none, or at least none that could ever conflict with them (e.g., Ake, 1987). However, much more common is the view that there are both individual rights and collective rights, which might come into conflict with each and need to be balanced in some way.

Consider, for example, the African ('Banjul') Charter on Human and Peoples' Rights (Organization of African Unity, 1981), which includes many rights of individual human beings alongside those ascribed to a people, which is probably best understood as a nation (or perhaps a country). The latter include the rights of a people not to be dominated and to resist domination (Article 20) and the rights of a people to natural resources, socio-economic development, and an environment necessary for that (Articles 21, 22, 24).

Similarly, see The Charter for African Cultural Renaissance (African Union, 2006). It too accords individuals many rights to access and develop their culture, but alongside them the document speaks of: African peoples evolving, being provided resources, and being enriched (Preamble and Articles 3, 5), the rights of minorities to their cultures (Article 5), and the cultural advancement of African states (Article 18).

---

[6] For the view that the trolley problem is importantly distinct from the self-driving car controversy, see Nyholm and Smids (2016).

It is natural to think of talk of duties with respect to peoples, minorities, and states as group-based. However, it is a contested matter, among philosophers and related thinkers around the world, whether to ascribe moral rights to groups as distinct from their individual members. Some, particularly in the West, maintain that what might appear to be group rights are ultimately the rights of the individuals who compose them. While a well-developed theory of rights to culture, to development, and to resist domination would be welcome, it is not necessary in order to cast doubt on utilitarianism. Supposing that such rights exist, regardless of what ultimately grounds them, we find reason to resist programming AI automated systems in a utilitarian manner.

To see this, consider the right of a people to resist foreign domination of it and what such a right entails for how to programme a smart automated weapons system. Above I suggested that a utilitarian weapons system would naturally be deployed to rebut aggression, but that is not always so. Sometimes aggression that is intuitively unjustified would serve to maximize utility in the long run, and sometimes rebutting such aggression that would fail to maximize utility in the long run is intuitively justified.

Such seems to be the case when the aggression is undertaken by a much greater majority than the non-aggressive minority being suppressed. Suppose that powers beyond Africa use their might to enslave a small sub-Saharan people, forcing them to extract minerals and related resources to drive foreign economies. Utilitarianism could permit such imperialism and forbid resistance against it if the numbers who flourished from it were great and the numbers who suffered from it were small. However, if the dominated people rose up against its taskmasters, it would be apt for a smart automated weapons system to assist it, despite the fact that doing so would fail to maximize utility. Whereas a utilitarian weapon would operate on the side of the oppressor, a morally justified weapon would operate on the side of the oppressed, regardless of the numbers involved.

10.5 Family First and AI

In the previous section, I noted that many African ethicists believe in human, i.e., individual rights while also accepting some kind of collective rights. Here, I somewhat similarly note that many African ethicists believe that morality has an impartial dimension while also contending that it has a partial one, where the partiality is antithetical to utilitarian reasoning.

Ascribing dignity to individuals, at least in virtue of their vital force or membership in the human family, entails a certain kind of impartiality, egalitarianism, or cosmopolitanism. That is, everyone matters from the moral point of view, such that a moral agent can have obligations to help others regardless of, say, their religion or nationality. As Kwame Gyekye has pointed out (2010: sec. 6), it is such impartial moral thought that plausibly explains the widespread traditional practice of welcoming visitors to an African village. Hospitality to those one does not know makes good sense if all human beings have a dignity that demands honouring.

However, there is an additional salient part of African ethics that is instead partial, directing one to aid those related to oneself before aiding others or at least aiding the former to a greater degree than the latter. 'Family first' and 'charity begins at home' are widely accepted (e.g., Wiredu, 1992: 200; Appiah, 1998; Ramose, 2003: 385–86; Molefe, 2019: 84–86) and indicate that sub-Saharan morality is well understood as including special obligations of beneficence. If one had to choose between saving the life of one's mother or that of a stranger, a characteristic African view would say that one would do wrong not to save one's mother. For the utilitarian, one should flip a coin to decide whom to save if the outcomes of either option would be the same, or one should save the stranger if the outcomes of doing so would be marginally better than saving one's mother.

Traditionally speaking, it was blood relations that determined who has priority when it comes to aid (on which see Appiah, 1998). That, however, is a controversial basis for grounding duties to help others. More common these days would be the view that, having related communally with others for a long while or to a strong degree (as with family or colleagues), one owes more of oneself and one's resources to them than to others. Regardless of the precise way in which people must be related to the moral agent in order to be prioritized, so long as a priority should be accorded to those related to her in some way or other—as many readers will agree—utilitarianism is suspect.

It follows that when programming AI automated systems, from an African perspective one ought to do so in a way that respects partial duties. If there is a robot in the home, while it should be programmed to be hospitable to visitors, it should also be programmed, at least as a default, to save the life of one's mother before that of a visitor who is not a member of the family or particularly close to it. A utilitarian robot, in contrast, would calculate the expected utility of saving one's mother compared to saving the visitor, and the calculations might not go in favour of mum, particularly if she is old and sick and the visitor is young and healthy.

Similar remarks apply to contexts in which there is relationality, even if to a less intense degree than that encountered in a family. For example, suppose a doctor has had a long-standing relationship with a particular patient and has programmed a robot to nurse him while staying in a hospital. It would be wrong for the doctor to allow the robot to disregard this patient's needs, whenever doing so would be necessary to care for a patient of another doctor with marginally greater needs.

10.6 Self-Sacrifice and AI

Here I discuss the last major respect in which values that are African, while also being attractive to readers from a variety of backgrounds, are incompatible with utilitarianism and in a way that would have a bearing on programming AI automated systems. It concerns the permissibility of making sacrifices of one's own welfare for the sake of others.

It is well-known that it is typical for an African ethical perspective to prescribe strong and substantial duties to help other people. That is particularly true in respect of family members, as per the previous section. However, even more impartial interpretations of African morality place heavy demands on a moral agent to improve others' quality of life. For example, Gyekye's influential moderate communitarian ethic prescribes doing all one can to promote the common good, that is, to meet the needs of everyone (albeit in ways that do not violate certain individual rights), without any distinction drawn between what is beyond the call of duty and what is not (1997: 35–76). Kwasi Wiredu's interpretation of African morality in terms of sympathetic impartiality and the Golden Rule similarly expects a lot (1996, 2009: 15–16); putting oneself in others' shoes one will come to see that they would be glad if one aided them in significant ways.

Such an approach to positive obligations might seem to dovetail neatly with utilitarianism, for it, too, is known for demanding much of a moral agent. However, two Anglo-American philosophers long ago noted respects in which utilitarianism would actually forbid you from doing what is best for others in the long run; that is when the most good in the world would be produced if one instead directed benefits towards oneself (see Nozick, 1974: 41 on 'utility monsters' and Slote, 1985 on 'agent-sacrificing permissions').

Consider two cases to illustrate the concern (Metz, 2013: 188–89), after which I indicate what it might mean for AI automated systems. For a first case where the most good and least bad in the world would result if subjective well-being were conferred on oneself and woe were placed on others, consider a mother and son who are both hungry. Suppose that maximizing values of nutrition, taste, and the like prescribes mum eating a portion of food that has become available. Even so, it would surely be permissible for the mother to decide to give the food to her son. For a second case, imagine that a vicious canine is chasing you and a young woman, whom you do not know, and that minimizing fear, pain, and missed appointments prescribes outrunning, if not tripping, the woman so that the dog gets to her. Even so, it would be permissible for you instead to draw the dog towards yourself, enabling the woman to escape. In both cases, utilitarianism would forbid you from helping others, but, for many African ethicists, and more generally intuitively, the right thing to do would instead be to help them.

Consider how the permissibility of making sacrifices for others, despite a net loss of subjective well-being in the world, could influence the way to programme smart machines. Basically, any time one is in charge how such a machine is deployed, one could direct it to save others before oneself. Consider a high-ranking military official who can choose a programme for a weapons system in a battlefield. He might direct it to discount his life relative to the lives of two other soldiers, even if the world would be in marginally better shape, in terms of net welfare, with him in it compared to them. Or if one is able to determine how to direct the life-saving procedures of a care robot in the home, one could set them to save the life of one's sickly child before oneself, in case of, say, a fire. Surely such programming would be morally permissible, contrary to the dictates of utilitarian reasoning.

10.7 Conclusion: From Utilitarianism to Kantianism

Utilitarianism has been the most common Western ethic invoked when considering how to programme artificially intelligent automated systems, while Kantianism (Powers, 2006; Ulgen, 2017; cf. Allen et al., 2000), or at least some kind of deontological approach informed by Western values (Anderson et al., 2005; Anderson & Anderson, 2007), has been the runner up. If the project here has been found attractive by many readers, it is worth thinking about how it might be extended. If characteristic African values ground powerful objections to programming smart machines according to the principle of utility, might they have similar implications for doing so according to a principle of respect for autonomy (or an ethic of prima facie duties)?

At this stage, the answer in the light of the specific argumentation in this essay seems equivocal. Kantianism, after all, accepts the idea that human dignity grounds human rights (Sect. 10.3) and also that one may sacrifice one's happiness in order to help others achieve their ends (Sect. 10.6). However, it might be that the other two African reasons to reject utility maximization apply with comparable force to Kantianism. That is, if one believes that there are collective rights, it might be that they are not reducible to the dignity of individual persons (Sect. 10.4). And if one believes that there are special obligations, it might be that they are not a function of promise making or accepting benefits from a cooperative scheme, the central ways that Kantians account for positive duties to specific individuals (Sect. 10.5). It is worth considering in future work whether these African values provide grounds to doubt that AI should act in accordance with Kantian duty, or whether there are other resources in the sub-Saharan ethical tradition to ground such doubt.[7]

References

Access Partnership. (2018). *Artificial intelligence for Africa: An opportunity for growth, development, and democratisation*. https://www.accesspartnership.com/artificial-intelligence-for-africa-an-opportunity-for-growth-development-and-democratisation/

African Union. (2006). *Charter for African cultural renaissance*. https://au.int/en/treaties/charter-african-cultural-renaissance

Ake, C. (1987). The African context of human rights. *Africa Today, 34*, 5–12.

Allen, C., Varner, G., & Zinser, J. (2000). Prolegomena to any future artificial moral agent. *Journal of Experimental and Theoretical Artificial Intelligence, 12*, 251–261.

[7] For comments on talks based on prior drafts of this work, I thank Professor Tshilidzi Marwala and audience members at a debate between myself and Professor Marwala about his essay 'On Rationality: An Artificial Intelligence Perspective' that was organized by the Johannesburg Institute for Advanced Study in 2019, as well as audience members at the 4th Centre for Artificial Intelligence Research (CAIR) Symposium in 2019. This essay first appeared in B. D. Okyere-Manu (Ed.), *African values, ethics, and technology*, Cham: Palgrave Macmillan, pp. 55–72, and is reprinted with permission from Palgrave Macmillan.

Anderson, M., & Anderson, S. L. (2007). Machine ethics: Creating an ethical intelligent agent. *AI Magazine, 28*, 15–26. https://www.aaai.org/ojs/index.php/aimagazine/article/view/2065
Anderson, M., Anderson, S. L., & Armen, C. (2005). *Towards machine ethics: Implementing two action-based ethical theories*. https://www.aaai.org/Papers/Symposia/Fall/2005/FS-05-06/FS05-06-001.pdf
Appiah, A. (1998). Ethical systems, African. In E. Craig (Ed.), *Routledge encyclopedia of philosophy*. Routledge.
Awad, E., et al. (2018). The moral machine experiment. *Nature, 563*, 59–64.
Bauer, W. (2020). Virtuous vs. utilitarian artificial moral agents. *AI & Society, 35*, 263–271.
Bonnefon, J.-F., Shariff, A., & Rahwan, I. (2015). *Autonomous vehicles need experimental ethics: Are we ready for utilitarian cars?* https://arxiv.org/pdf/1510.03346v1.pdf
Bonnefon, J.-F., Shariff, A., & Rahwan, I. (2016). The social dilemma of autonomous vehicles. *Science, 352*(6293), 1573–1576.
Botman, H. R. (2000). The OIKOS in a global economic era. In J. Cochran & B. Klein (Eds.), *Sameness and difference: Problems and potentials in South African civil society*. The Council for Research in Values and Philosophy. http://www.crvp.org/publications/Series-II/6-Contents.pdf
Bujo, B. (2001). *Foundations of an African ethic: Beyond the universal claims of Western morality* (B. McNeil, Trans.). Crossroad Publishers.
Cobbah, J. (1987). African values and the human rights debate. *Human Rights Quarterly, 9*, 309–331.
Deng, F. (2004). Human rights in the African context. In K. Wiredu (Ed.), *A companion to African philosophy* (pp. 499–508). Blackwell.
Etieyibo, E. (2017). Anthropocentricism, African metaphysical worldview, and animal practices. *Journal of Animal Ethics, 7*, 145–162.
Gloor, L. (2016). *Suffering-focused AI safety*. https://longtermrisk.org/files/suffering-focused-ai-safety.pdf
Grau, C. (2005). *There is no 'I' in 'Robot': Robotic utilitarians and utilitarian robots*. https://www.aaai.org/Papers/Symposia/Fall/2005/FS-05-06/FS05-06-007.pdf
Gwagwa, A. (2019a). *Artificial intelligence adoption and use cases in Africa*. https://www.academia.edu/42070923/Artificial_Intelligence_adoption_and_use_cases_in_Africa
Gwagwa, A. (2019b). *Artificial Intelligence (AI) and algorithms ethics in Africa*. https://www.academia.edu/41800605/Artificial_Intelligence_AI_and_Algorithms_Ethics_in_Africa
Gyekye, K. (1997). *Tradition and modernity: Philosophical reflections on the African experience*. Oxford University Press.
Gyekye, K. (2010). African ethics. In E. Zalta (Ed.), *The Stanford encyclopedia of philosophy*. http://plato.stanford.edu/archives/fall2010/entries/african-ethics/
Hibbard, B. (2015). *Ethical artificial intelligence*. https://arxiv.org/pdf/1411.1373.pdf
Ikuenobe, P. (2016). The communal basis for moral dignity: An African perspective. *Philosophical Papers, 45*, 437–469.
Iroegbu, P. (2005). Right to life and the means to life: Human dignity. In P. Iroegbu & A. Echekwube (Eds.), *Kpim of morality ethics* (pp. 446–449). Heinemann Educational Books.
Kinjo, K., & Ebina, T. (2017). Optimal program for autonomous driving under Bentham- and Nash-type social welfare functions. *Procedia Computer Science, 112*, 61–70.
Majot, A., & Yampolskiy, R. (2014). AI safety engineering through introduction of self- reference into felicific calculus via artificial pain and pleasure. In *Proceedings of the 2014 IEEE international symposium on ethics in science, technology and engineering, Chicago* (pp. 1–6).
Marwala, T. (2014). *Artificial intelligence techniques for rational decision making*. Springer.
Marwala, T. (2017). *Rational choice and artificial intelligence*. https://arxiv.org/pdf/1703.10098.pdf
Metz, T. (2013). *Meaning in life: An analytic study*. Oxford University Press.
Metz, T. (2015). How the West was one: The Western as individualist, the African as communitarian. *Educational Philosophy and Theory, 47*, 1175–1184.
Molefe, M. (2019). *An African philosophy of personhood, morality, and politics*. Palgrave Macmillan.

Moore, G. E. (1903). *Principia Ethica.* Cambridge University Press.

Nozick, R. (1974). *Anarchy, state and utopia.* Basic Books.

Nyholm, S., & Smids, J. (2016). The ethics of accident-algorithms for self-driving cars: An applied trolley problem? *Ethical Theory and Moral Practice, 19*, 1275–1289.

Oesterheld, C. (2015). *Machine ethics and preference utilitarianism.* https://reducing-suffering.org/machine-ethics-and-preference-utilitarianism/

Oesterheld, C. (2016). Formalizing preference utilitarianism in physical world models. *Synthese, 193*, 2747–2759.

Organization of African Unity. (1981). *African (Banjul) Charter on Human and Peoples' Rights.* https://www.achpr.org/public/Document/file/English/banjul_charter.pdf

Ormond, E. (2020). The ghost in the machine: The ethical risks of AI. *The Thinker, 83*, 4–11. http://www.thethinker.co.za/resources/Thinker_83_new/83%20ormonde.pdf

Powers, T. (2006). Prospects for a Kantian machine. *IEEE: Intelligent Systems, 22*, 46–51.

Railton, P. (1984). Alienation, consequentialism, and the demands of morality. *Philosophy and Public Affairs, 13*, 134–171.

Ramose, M. (2003). The ethics of *ubuntu*. In P. H. Coetzee & A. P. J. Roux (Eds.), *The African philosophy reader* (2nd ed., pp. 379–387). Oxford University Press.

Sallstrom, L., Morris, O., & Mehta, H. (2019). *Artificial intelligence in Africa's healthcare: Ethical considerations* (Observer research foundation issue brief no. 312). https://www.orfonline.org/research/artificial-intelligence-in-africas-healthcare-ethical-considerations-55232/

Sen, A. (2000). Consequential evaluation and practical reason. *The Journal of Philosophy, 97*, 477–502.

Shulman, C., Tarleton, N., & Jonsson, H. (2009). Which consequentialism? Machine ethics and moral divergence. In C. Reynolds & A. Cassinelli (Eds.), *Proceedings of AP-CAP 2009: The fifth Asia-Pacific computing and philosophy conference* (pp. 23–25). AP-CAP. https://intelligence.org/files/WhichConsequentialism.pdf

Slote, M. (1985). *Common sense morality and consequentialism.* Routledge/Kegan Paul.

Spini, L. (2019). *Ethics of artificial intelligence – Global considerations and potential for Africa.* Presentation made at the World Science Forum held in Budapest. https://worldscienceforum.org/programme/2019-11-21-thematic-sessions-ii-c-ethics-of-artificial-intelligence-global-considerations-and-potential-for-africa-129

Ulgen, O. (2017). Kantian ethics in the age of artificial intelligence and robotics. *Questions of International Law, 43*, 59–83. http://www.qil-qdi.org/wp-content/uploads/2017/10/04_AWS_Ulgen_FIN.pdf

Wiredu, K. (1992). The moral foundations of an African culture. In K. Wiredu & K. Gyekye (Eds.), *Person and community; Ghanaian philosophical studies, I* (pp. 193–206). Council for Research in Values and Philosophy.

Wiredu, K. (1996). *Cultural universals and particulars: An African perspective.* Indiana University Press.

Wiredu, K. (2009). An oral philosophy of personhood. *Research in African Literatures, 40*, 8–18.

World Wide Web Foundation. (2017). *Artificial intelligence: Starting the policy dialogue in Africa.* https://webfoundation.org/research/artificial-intelligence-starting-the-policy-dialogue-in-africa/

Chapter 11
Can AI Attain Personhood in African Thought?

Diana Ekor Ofana

Abstract The question this chapter seeks to address is whether (or not) robots can attain personhood in Afro-communitarian thought. In African philosophy, the notion of personhood is one that has gone through different debates with regard to who is considered a person. If within the framework of Afro-communitarianism, individuals are expected to be treated in certain kinds of ways that are not subversive, should we make a case for robots within such a community? This chapter aims to have a conversation on the possible ethical considerations that may arise in analysing the kind of relationship that ought to exist between AI and persons before they can be seen as persons. To answer this question, I will show what makes an individual a person in Afro-communitarianism. In doing so, I will discuss why robots cannot attain personhood within the context of Afro-communitarianism. Hence, I aim to show the difficulties that may arise in such a community, if the ethical values in Afro-communitarianism are to be appropriated by both robots and persons in terms of making a moral judgement.

Keywords Afro-communitarianism · Personhood · AI

11.1 Introduction

The debate on the capabilities of artificial robots and intelligent machines is one that occupies the scene of academia and the scientific community. The talk of robots taking the place of human or becoming persons is also a debate in both science and academic communities. My goal in this chapter is to examine whether (or not) robots can attain personhood given that robots are designed or created to surpass

---

D. E. Ofana (✉)
University of Pretoria, Pretoria, South Africa

Department of Philosophy, University of Pretoria, Pretoria, South Africa

Decoloniality Research group University of Pretoria, Pretoria, South Africa

A. D. Attoe et al. (eds.), *Conversations on African Philosophy of Mind, Consciousness and Artificial Intelligence*,
https://doi.org/10.1007/978-3-031-36163-0_11

certain limitations of the human person. I will show why it would be unreasonable to argue that robots can attain personhood in Afro-communitarian thought. Even though robots are intelligent machines, which could be programmed to act, and interact like human beings, I will argue that they cannot, in fact, become persons in accordance with Afro-communitarian understandings of personhood. The idea of robots and personhood is one that is relatively new within the discourse and debates in African philosophy. In carrying out this task, I will use Afro-communitarian personhood as a springboard from which I intend to pursue the goal of this chapter.

The debate regarding personhood in the African tradition tends to be between those that account for personhood in terms of social relationships and those who argue for a combination of the individual and social features. Scholars like John Mbiti (1969) and Ifeanyi Menkiti (1984) tend to construe personal identity in terms of social relationships. Following the debate on personhood, I will investigate whether or not robots can attain personhood in Afro-communitarian thought. I have structured this chapter into two main sections including two sub-sections. In the first, I discuss the nature of Afro-communitarian personhood in African thought. Second, I present a discussion on the idea of AI and personhood. Third, I show contrasts and overlaps there is if we critically analyse what indeed makes one a person within Afro-communitarianism and the idea of robotic personhood. Fourth, I make a case for why robots cannot attain personhood in African philosophy.

11.2 The Nature of Personhood in African Thought

In Afro-communitarian theorising, a person is an individual that possesses a character that is consistent with the values of the human community. Within African philosophical circles, it is understood that the metaphysical conception of personhood gives rise to a normative understanding of what persons ought to do. In this section, I will present an analysis of the communitarian accounts of personhood of some African philosophers, starting with the foundational accounts of Mbiti (1969) and Menkiti (1984). These accounts are called foundational because other accounts of what is often defined as Afro-communitarian personhood draw from and critically engage with the understandings of personhood by the afore-mentioned philosophers. I will also discuss more contemporary Afro-communitarian accounts on personhood ranging from the likes of Gyekye (1997), Wiredu (1992), Ramose (1999), Krog (2008), Eze (2008), Molefe (2019) and Chimakonam (2019). In a bid to understand what Afro-communitarian personhood is, we need to comprehend the metaphysical notion of human co-existence as its core idea. According to Afro-communitarian personhood, an individual's existence is constituted by the existence of others. As mentioned above, we are required to maintain flourishing relationships with others who constitute us. This understanding of personhood is what this section aims to unpack in the Afro-communitarian accounts of the afore-mentioned African philosophers. I will present the accounts of these African philosophers alongside the ethics that necessarily stems from their ideas. I will then show whether or not robots can be considered a part of the human community when analysed within Afro-communitarian personhood.

11.2.1 What Then Is Afro-Communitarian Personhood?

Conceptions and understandings of personhood differ amongst African scholars. Here I will focus on communitarian conceptions of personhood. However, for clarity, we should note that there exist in African philosophical parlance other accounts of personhood that are not necessarily communitarian. For instance, Didier Kaphagawani's interpretation of the force thesis was drawn from Tempel's Bantu philosophy (1959). According to Tempels, the notion of vital force is considered a necessary element in being because it is inseparable from the definition of being. This is as a result of the fact that, without the element of vital force, being cannot be conceived (Tempels, 1959). Persons or humans in the light of the communalism thesis are defined and individuated communally[1] (Kaphagawani, 2005: 337). This understanding of personhood is also associated with Mbiti, one of the founding philosophers of Afro-communitarian thought. My aim in this section is to focus on a specific Afro-communitarian understanding of personhood, which I will then apply in my conversational analysis wherein I will show whether or not robots can attain personhood. Due to the debates on personhood in African thought, I intend to present an analysis of these debates in a conversational manner.

John Mbiti's account of personhood was influenced by Placide Tempels' book on *Bantu* philosophy (1959). Mbiti was influenced by Tempels' idea of communal ties, who articulated this notion using the concept of vital force. According to Tempels, an 'African conception of being is not static but dynamic. The notion of vital force is a necessary element in being, and the concept of vital force is inseparable from the definition of being for without the element of vital force, being cannot be conceived' (1959: 50–51). What this means is that, according to Tempels, in Bantu thought individuals have an intimate ontological relationship with other beings.[2] Hence, there exists a necessary interaction of 'being' with 'being', 'that is to say of force with force' (Tempels, 1959: 58). Tempels' understanding of the kind of communal relationship and interaction that exists amongst members of an African community has both metaphysical and normative underpinnings. Mbiti, having been

[1] While Aristotle and many other scholars in both the Western and eastern traditions of philosophy have expressed forms of communitarianism, the appendage 'Afro-' or 'African' communitarianism is salient as Metz (2007) points out. Metz argues that the constitutive understanding of personhood in Afro-communitarianism stems from a community-based ontology and ethics. This community-based ontology and ethics within this framework contribute to the formulation of individual subjectivities.

[2] According to Tempels, the idea of vital force is as important as being itself. This claim is premised on the fact that human relationship with other elements in nature transcends the physical realm. For example, an ontological relationship exists between sentient and insentient beings.

influenced by Tempels, provides an account of what he understands to constitute an African understanding of personhood. The account is similar to that of Tempels in terms of the type of ontological relationship that exists between members of an African community. Both Mbiti's and Tempels' accounts of personhood can be understood from an Afro-communitarian perspective. Mbiti, reflecting on the African notion of personhood, writes:

> In traditional life, the individual does not and cannot exist except corporately. He owes his existence to other people, including those of past generations and his contemporaries. He is simply part of the whole. The community must, therefore, make, create, or produce the individual; for the individual depends on the corporate group...whatever happens to the individual happens to the whole group, and whatever happens to the whole group happens to the individual. The individual can say 'I am because we are; since we are therefore I am' This is the cardinal point in the understanding of the African view of a man. (1969: 108–9)

One can interpret Mbiti's argument as communally centred given that an individual's personhood necessarily stems from communal engagements. Mbiti's communalism thesis is hinged on his statement that the community creates the individual.

Menkiti, like Mbiti, posits that personhood is understood from a relational perspective and cannot be ascribed to any human person outside the community. For it is in the community

> that the individual comes to see himself as man, and it is by first knowing this community as a stubborn, perduring fact of the psychophysical world that the individual also comes to know himself as a durable, more or less permanent, fact of this world. (1984: 172)

Based on this understanding of personhood, personhood for Menkiti does not

> Abstract this or that feature of the lone individual and proceed to make it the defining or essential characteristic which entities aspiring to the description of 'man' must-have, the African view of man denies that a person can be defined by focusing on this or that physical or psychological characteristic of the lone individual. Rather man is defined by the environing community. (Menkiti, 1984: 171)

Thus, according to Menkiti, the African way of understanding what constitutes personhood does not rely on certain isolated qualities or characteristics in individuals but rather focuses on a prescriptive standard that we must emulate. The standards of emulation are best decided by the community since 'the reality of [the] communal world takes precedence over the reality of individual life histories, whatever these may be' (1984: 171). What is implied here by Menkiti is that the 'community must take epistemic and ontological precedence over the individual', (ibid). Gyekye (1997), on the other hand, in his defence of moderate communitarianism offers a conception of personhood that prioritises personal identity as well as community relations. However, both of these accounts of personhood are metaphysical insofar as it is descriptive. In the debates on Afro-communitarian personhood, there is a shared emphasis on the values of interaction, interconnectedness, relationship and interdependence between members of any given community. Underlying these shared core values is an understanding that an individual is considered a person within the springboard of ontology as well as the ethical relationships that exist between human beings. Consider, for example, the interdependence evident in

Mbiti's claim that the community creates the individual (1969, 1969) and the relatedness and interconnectedness inherent in his famous, 'I am because we are' thesis (Mbiti, 1969: 141). Menkiti and Wiredu also draw on Mbiti's understanding of personhood as a communal engagement, with Menkiti arguing that 'man is defined by the environing community' (Menkiti, 1984: 171) and Wiredu emphasising interaction and thus relatedness as a central feature of the African community of persons (Wiredu, 1992). Gyekye (1997) finds Menkiti's account of personhood disturbing because it does not give room for the flourishing of individual subjectivities.[3] However, Gyekye argue that no human person is self-sufficient, and an individual necessarily exists in interaction and relationship with other members of their community (1997). Eze (2008), also, finds Wiredu and Gyekye's accounts of personhood disturbing as they both understand the community to be the ultimate arbiter of what makes or should constitute a person. Nevertheless, the values of interconnectedness, relationship and interdependence are drawn upon in his representation of Afro-communitarianism as a 'discursive formation between the individual and community' (Eze, 2008: 386). Similarly, Ramose's emphasis on interconnectedness, relationship and interdependence is captured in his statement that 'to be a human being is to affirm one's humanity by recognising the humanity of others and on that basis, establish humane relations with them' (Ramose, 1999: 42). Antjie Krog too suggests that there exists an intrinsic relationship and interconnectedness that comes from our relational understanding of personhood (Krog, 2008). Jonathan Chimakonam's conversational personhood shows the importance of introspection and extrospection to illustrate the value that African societies place on human relatedness expressed in our relationship and interdependence with others (Chimakonam, 2019: 13).

It is important to point out that the notion of human relations as construed in communitarian personhood has far-reaching implications for understanding the essence of personhood. To fully come to terms with what the implication of personhood in Afro-communitarianism entails, we must also understand who a person is, in African thought. On the whole, the central theme in the debates on Afro-communitarian personhood is the fact that there is an intrinsic ontological notion of

[3] What is implied by Menkiti is the fact that the collective good is valued above individual egoistic interest that is detrimental to community harmony. According to Motsamai Molefe (2017), Menkiti's view on community precedence does not translate to community dominance, and it is for this reason that the precedence of community interest does not translate to the domination of individual will. According to Molefe, this claim emphasizes the ways African societies are organised to respond to urgent community issues. From Ifeanyi Menkiti (1984) to Pantaleon Iroegbu (1995), Afro-communitarians theorize that the priority of communal values over individual endowments does not translate to the community consuming the individual because the community's norms only set standards that protect the interests of the individual. So, the norms subsume the individual but does not consume it. The logic that justifies this type of inference can be found in logical theories that justify and includes three-valued logic (Jan Lukasiewickz, 1920). These types of theories of logic admits of truth-gluts rather than truth-gaps, non-monotonic logics like Deontic logic, and defeasibility reasoning, and of course, Chimakonam's *Ezumezu* system (Springer, 2019). Chimakonam (2019) demonstrates how inferences in African philosophical systems could be grounded in a brand of three-valued logic with truth-glut he called *Ezumezu* logic.

being that can interact, is mutually interdependent and has a deep human connection with others. The Afro-communitarian criteria espouse the ethics of personhood, which shall now serve as the basis for the study of whether artificial robots meet the requirements personhood in Afro-communitarian thought.

11.3 AI and Personhood

My focus in this chapter is on artificial intelligence systems. This is because robots, as an artificial intelligence system, have been programmed and situated in the world to sense, think and act (see Lin et al., 2012: 18). The notion of personhood is often attributed to human and non-human persons such as intelligent robots. Thus, it makes sense to ascertain whether robots can attain personhood according to Afro-communitarian thought. The purpose here is to lay the groundwork and show the distinction between human beings and robots. In doing so, I will draw out some criteria in the idea of personhood. When analysed in line with artificial intelligence, one can argue that AI should be considered a person. It becomes expedient to carry out this kind of analysis that will enable us to show why AI cannot attain personhood even though they are programmed in such a way so that they can possess certain human qualities. There are many different understandings and classifications of robots, as commonly used today. The term robot could mean a mechanical device, an automated device, an electronic device, a computer program, a cybernetic device and an artificial intelligence system.

AIs as autonomous intelligent systems are capable of carrying out complex actions that may have an impact or consequences on humans and other morally significant beings. The question then becomes, whether we can make an argument for this kind of intelligent system within Afro-communitarian personhood? To ascertain the possibility of this question, it is necessary to investigate closely what makes one a person in Afro-communitarian thought. Furthermore, the literature tends to distinguish between two normative notions of personhood in African philosophy. First, an individual is seen as a person by possessing certain ontological properties that render her existence morally significant. To be called a 'person', in this sense, is to be specified as a moral being, that is, a being towards which we owe direct duties of respect (DeGrazia, 2008). In other words, a person in African thought is a human being with moral status and to whom we have direct duties of respect (Molefe, 2017). It is for this reason that Afro-communitarians emphasise the values of interconnectedness, relationship and interdependence as some of the core features that are intricate in understanding Afro-communitarian personhood.

Underlying these shared core values is an understanding that an individual is considered an interactive being whose existence is tied to the existence of others. Can we then make a case for AI given that AIs are designed to interact, relate or even give care to humans in our world today? It is possible to argue that AI can attain personhood if the criteria for attaining personhood are solely based on rationality, interaction or being a caregiver including being a part of the human community. If we take a closer look at the motive behind the creation of AIs, one would realise that the aim of AI pioneers is to preserve knowledge due to the limitation of the human person (Geraci, 2008). Based on this claim, we can argue that the idea of electronic personhood is basically to overthrow or take the place of humans. According to some, the human body has some significant restrictions when compared to superintelligent AIS. In light of this claim, the human mind is said to be trapped inside a body that learns with difficulty, thinks slowly and has difficulty passing on its knowledge (Geraci, 2008: 147). It is for this reason that AIs are considered more efficient and will eventually outsmart human beings (Moravec, 1988: 55–56, 1999: 55; Kurzweil, 1999: 4; Warwick, 1997, 2004: 178; De Garis, 2005: 103). In light of the fact, the human brain is said to have limitations and cannot be compared to that of robots, whose silicon substrate is far more efficient in the preservation and transmission of information. Nevertheless, I argue that the idea of personhood in Afro-communitarianism goes beyond high technological programming, with the aim of overcoming human limitations. Personhood is more about evaluations and reevaluations of our limitations and how best to commune with others in a non-subversive manner. This, however, is not the case with AI pioneers, whose aim is to put to rest the worry of human limitations and inadequacies through transitioning to mechanical life (Geraci, 2008; Moravec, 1988). The importance of mechanical life is also seen in the words of Robert Geraci, who believes that 'a living person's value, in apocalyptic AI, stems from the knowledge he or she possesses, rather than being intrinsic to life or grounded in social relations of one sort or another' (2008: 148). This claim is hinged on the fact that any aspect of personhood that goes beyond the preservation of human knowledge is not worth pursuing. We can say that the underlying idea of AI and roboticist's invention is to create a world that can transcend the limitations and inadequacies of the human world. If this is the intent of AI and roboticists pioneers, can we still make a case for electronic persons within human communities? This question will be answered as the chapter progresses.

The idea of robotic personhood is one that is no longer foreign to the scientific community and the contemporary academia all over the world. However, it is important to point out that the interest and understandings of personhood within the scientific community are construed and understood differently from the conceptualisation and understanding of personhood within the African thought system. The notion of robotic personhood is one that is commonplace in the writings of roboticists and AI advocates. The European Union is considering the need to redefine the legal status of robots as 'electronic persons (see https://www.europarl.europa.eu/RegData/etudes/BRIE/2019/634427/EPRS_BRI(2019)634427_EN.pdf)'.[4] The question now becomes what will become the fate of humans if AI is given the same rights as humans given that they are created by humans themselves?

[4] The idea of electronic personhood is not the same as construed in Afro-communitarian personhood. The appendage 'electronic' I argue invalidate what constitute the essence of personhood when analysed within the framework of Afro-communitarianism.

Based on this claim, the idea of personhood in African philosophy has a robust understanding of who is categorised as a person in Africa thought. Based on an African notion of personhood I will proceed to highlight what makes an individual a person in African thought. In doing so, I will investigate whether robots can ever attain personhood within certain conditions.

11.3.1 Robotic/AI Personhood Vis-à-Vis Afro-Communitarian Personhood

Recall that the idea behind roboticists' and AI pioneers' creation of robots is to overcome the fallibility of the human mind. As would be expected, the goal of roboticists and AI pioneers is to create robots that are much more sophisticated than humans.[5] Before I delve into the question of whether or not robots can attain personhood in Afro-communitarian thought, how can the issue of the rights of humans be reconciled with that of AI? By this I mean, the duties of humans towards AI and vice versa. This concern also occupies the writings of AI ethicists who have either argued for or against the possibility of robot rights (Coeckelbergh, 2010; Bryson, 2010). The discussion on the rightness of AI is not only focused on the legal rights but also on the ethical dimension of moral rights. This is because the attention and the design of AI are becoming more and more anthropomorphised (Hohfeld, 1923). What this means is that AI can lay claim to privileges, powers, and even immunities given that we see them as extensions of ourselves (Segun, 2020). This is where the issue of robotic personhood comes into play. The closer humans get to having or designing a fully autonomous AI, it becomes more compelling to make a case for robot's rights. This is why the idea of 'electronic personhood' is a way to accord rights to advanced AIs (Dashevsky, 2017). Joanna Bryson (2010) argues that granting autonomous AI the same rights as humans sort of dehumanises human beings and could constitute a poor sense of decision-making. Reason being that autonomous AI despite, its sophistication cannot in fact, become a human being in the true sense of the word. In addition to this concern, how do we know where the rights of robots stop, to avoid encroaching into the rights of humans? Some have argued that 'there is a need to examine at the design stage when human rights and those we may

[5] It is important to note that there are ethical concerns in the literature concerning the design, uses and abuses of robots as well as questions about the moral capacity of robots (Malle & Scheutz, 2014). Some have argued that there is a distinction between robot and machine ethics. The question of design uses, and abuse is highlighted as concerns of robot ethics, whereas the issue on the moral capacity of robots is that of machine ethics (Segun, 2020). Nonetheless, it will be counterintuitive if we focus only on the burden that comes with the design, uses and abuse of robots. According to robotic ethicists, robots are meant to be designed such that they are beneficial to humans. Hence, the purpose of designing robots is to meet a need, solve a problem or improve human efficiency and accuracy in a particular task. By implication, the design of robots is supposed to be well-intentioned.

accord to robots clash' (Segun, 2020: 3). It is important to mention that the idea of Afro-communitarian personhood is not loosely construed as; it is the case in Western communitarianism where essentiality is expressed in individualism.

The notion of robotic rights as construed in robotic ethicists debates one can argue subscribes to individualism as opposed to Afro-communitarianism. In other words, within Western individualism, robots or intelligent systems are not to be seen as mere artifacts but as part of the human community whose activities might have a profound impact on our legal, ethical, social and economic landscape (Torrance, 2013). One can argue that the concept of 'electronic personhood' is loosely construed in Western literature. Nonetheless, if we critically analyse what makes one a person in African thought, we may even be tempted to argue that robots, that is, intelligent AI systems, meet certain criteria for personhood in African thought. Some of these criteria would be interaction, relations, care, as well as community engagements. Nevertheless, these are not all that is needed for an individual to be seen as a person in African thought. In an African conception of personhood, an individual owes her existence to others with whom she is constituted. In light of this claim, if we analyse the idea of robotic personhood, one would see that intelligent AI system cannot pass as humans because they lack the natural inclinations to be humans aside being programmed to act, think or interact in human communities. This is premised on the fact that Robots are neither biologically nor ontologically humans. Hence, the nuances and complexities to address the problem of moral responsibility between AI and humans would be unnecessary. By this I mean, it will not be possible for AI to attain personhood in Afro-communitarianism. I will further explain why robots cannot attain personhood in African thought.

11.3.2 Why Robots Cannot Attain Personhood in African Thought

We live in a world where we are confronted daily by autonomous technologies that are extensions of ourselves. However, as we have seen, within Afro-communitarian thought certain criteria are needed for one to be seen as a person. In spite of the debate on individual identity within African communitarian thought, there is an understanding that there is a distinction between two normative notions of personhood in African philosophy. The first claim is that one can assign moral value to some entity by virtue of them possessing certain ontological properties that render them morally significant. This line of thought cut across the context of bioethics and political discussions on rights (Behrens, 2013; Toscano, 2011). To be called a 'person', in this sense, is to be specified as a moral patient, i.e. a being towards which we owe direct duties of respect (DeGrazia, 2008). Another term used to capture this idea of personhood is that of moral status, which specifies things towards which we have direct duties of respect (Molefe, 2017). What is crucial to note concerning this notion of personhood is that it invites respect to the entity in question merely because it possesses the relevant ontological properties – be they rationality, consciousness, or sentience – without regard to how one uses them (Singer, 2009; Metz, 2013). Jonathan Chimakonam on the other hand argues that an individual is a being in conversation (Chimakonam, 2019). What this means is that the relevant ontological properties in every individual allows for a deep level of conversation with the self. According to Chimakonam, an individual possesses:

> The capacity to indulge in critical and creative examinations of moral precepts and conducts. When it is in conversation with the moral law within itself, it is called introspection, and when it is in conversation with the positive laws out there in its community, it is called extrospection. (2019: 1)

By implication, one is considered a person if they have attained the capacity to engage in these two-way conversations as posited by Chimakonam. He argues further that personhood is a 'natural capacity which individuals develop at some point in their biological maturation'.

If we consider the idea of robotic personhood in light of these arguments, one would see that an artificial intelligent system is neither a human being ontologically nor is programmed to be morally responsible for their actions given that they are regarded as amoral. Recall, also, that the goal of apocalyptic roboticists and AI pioneers is to create mechanical lives that transcend human limitations. It is also plausible to argue whether fallible roboticists with their human limitations can create perfect mechanical lives that transcend human existence. I contend that it is in the idea of finite existence that the notion of death and reincarnation can be understood in African traditional thought system. Hence, it is worthy of note that the essence of human existence goes beyond the technological improvement of human life with mechanical lives, to actual human encounters that will improve the moral quality of human lives. The fact that robots of various forms are becoming more and more sophisticated by the day does not give them what they in fact lack, namely the moral capacity to become persons in Afro-communitarian thought. This is premised on the fact that there is a difference between a robotic entity owned by any individual and a human person as an individual moral agent. A human person is an individual with the capacity for moral evaluation and reevaluation, and each individual person is morally responsible for their action as it pertains to others. According to Chimakonam and Nweke (2018), there are two possible senses we can understand the idea of rights in Afro-communitarianism, namely, rights as participatory and rights as entitlements. In the first, the community accord participatory rights to the individuals to participate in the life of the community. The opportunity of participatory right is what enables them to demand or access their entitlements. However, these rights are not only accorded because one is a human being (Chimakonam & Nweke, 2018). The fact that autonomous AI system are programmed in such a way that they can perform actual human tasks does not necessarily make them persons as explained above. Sophia has gone down in scientific history as the first autonomous artificial intelligent system to be awarded the rights of a citizen in Saudi Arabia. Even though robots cannot be considered as persons, Saudi Arabia controversially awarded citizenship to an AI robot, named Sophia, in 2017; the first artificially intelligent machine to become a citizen (see https://www.dw.com/en/saudi-arabia-grants-citizenship-to-robot-sophia/a-41150856#:~:text=Saudi%20Arabia%20claims%20to%20be,granted%20citizenship%20to%20a%20robot.&text=The%20inventor%20David%20Hanson%20claims,mimic%2062%20human%20facial%20expressions). A person in African thought has an ontological connectedness to other human beings. I argue that this is not the case for Sophia who in actual sense cannot become a person in Afro-communitarian thought. In light of this, I argue that the appendage 'electronic' as attached to robots personhood is self-defeating when analysed within the framework of African thought. What I mean is that if robots are indeed seen as persons, the appendage 'electronic' on its own invalidates their personhood. This is because, in some crucial sense, the ontological status of an individual is construed within her humanity. What is under scrutiny, in this discourse of personhood, is how the individual uses her ontological abilities, to either perfect or defect her humanity (Molefe, 2019). To be called a person is to acknowledge that she has intrinsic human values by virtue of her humanity. And to be called a non-person is to acknowledge that she has lived below the abilities of her humanity, without denying her humanity, and the basic respect due to her merely as a human being (Wiredu, 2009).

In light of this claim, we can argue that the idea of personhood in Afro-communitarianism goes beyond being a human being or acting like one. What this means is that though most autonomous AI system are programmed to act, or even think like human beings they cannot, in fact, become persons in African thought. The talk of moral judgement in African thought is considered crucial in understanding the kind of relationships that stems from the ethics of personhood. These relationships are construed within relational ethics that is expressed in human's capacity for moral evaluations and reevaluations (Chimakonam, 2019; Gyekye, 1997; Eze, 2008). One cannot help but imagine the dicey nature of a community where those conceived as persons lack the moral capacity to either evaluate or reevaluate their actions. While there is the possibility that AI/Robots, in the future, may acquire this capacity, such thinking still remains in the realm of speculation. If we must concern ourselves with the current state of things, then we would have to ask pertinent questions, such as: If the ethical values in Afro-communitarian personhood are to be appropriated by both robots and persons in terms of making a moral judgement, can robots make a moral judgement? The fact that robots are believed to be amoral makes it even more difficult to conceive of robots as persons within African thought. Hence, it is important to note that the notion of personhood within African thought goes beyond legal jurisdiction or the fact that non-human entities are ascribed rights which enable them to enter into contracts with actual human persons. It is also important to point out that the onus of responsibility for the breach of such a contract rest on the human person. It is safe at this point to conclude that the autonomies and rights of corporate non-human entities are used for convenience. If we critically analyse the plight of twenty-first-century Africa, we would discover that our socio-political gains most of the time are made and unmade, our communities are constantly under various kinds of strain, and yet we remain tenuously resilient, in sustaining African community values. Ascribing personhood to AI in African thought will be tantamount to human self-denial. It is for this reason that value is placed on the ethics of personhood as a valid way of affirming the existence of the self and other human beings. In as much as, AI of various forms are becoming more and more sophisticated by the day, there is little or no possibility that autonomous AI system can attain personhood, within Afro-communitarian thought.

11.4 Conclusion

This chapter aims to show whether (or not) robots can attain personhood in African philosophical thought. Having discussed the notion of personhood in African philosophical parlance, robotic personhood will be impossible in spite of the changing nature of twenty-first-century human societies. Having presented a conversational analysis of the possibility of robotic personhood, it is, however, evident that robots despite their sophisticated nature cannot attain personhood in African thought. Hence, I discussed the ethical considerations that may arise in the relationship between AI and human persons. It is from this discussion that one can fully understand the dicey nature of a community if the ethical values in personhood are to be appropriated by both AI system and persons in terms of making a moral judgement.

References

Behrens, K. (2013). Two 'normative' conceptions of personhood. *Quest, 25*, 103–119.

Bryson, J. (2010). Robots should be slaves. In Y. Wilks (Ed.), *Close engagements with artificial companions: Key social, psychological, ethical and design issues* (pp. 63–74). John Benjamins Publishing Company.

Chimakonam, J. O. (2019). Why the normative conception of personhood is problematic: A proposal for a conversational alternative. *Acta Academica, 49*(2), 11–33.

Chimakonam, J. O., & Nweke, V. C. A. (2018). Afro-Communitarianism and the questions of rights. *Theoria*. https://doi.org/10.3167/th.2018.6515706

Coeckelbergh, M. (2010). Moral appearances: Emotions, robots, and human morality. *Ethics and Information Technology, 12*(3), 235–241.

Dashevsky, E. (2017). Do robots and AI deserve rights? *Pc Magazine*. https://www.pcmag.com/article/351719/do-robots-and-ai-deserve-rights. Accessed 25 Aug 2020.

De Garis, H. (2005). *The Artilect war: Cosmists vs. Terrans: A bitter controversy concerning whether humanity should build godlike massively intelligent machines*. ETC Publications.

DeGrazia, D. (2008). Moral status as a matter of degree? *Southern Journal Philosophy, 46*, 181–198.

Eze, M. (2008). What is African communitarianism? Against consensus as a regulative ideal. *South African Journal of Philosophy, 27*(4), 386–399.

Geraci, R. M. (2008). Apocalyptic AI: Religion and the promise of artificial intelligence. *Journal of the American Academy of Religion, 76*(1), 138–166.

Gyekye, K. (1997). *Tradition and modernity: Philosophical reflections on the African experience*. Oxford University Press.

Hohfeld, W. N. (1923). *Fundamental legal conceptions as applied in judicial reasoning: And other legal essays*. Yale University Press.

Iroegbu, P. (1995). *Metaphysics: The Kpim of philosophy*. IUP.
Kaphagawani, D. (2005). *African conceptions of a person. A critical survey in a companion to African philosophy* (K. Wiredu, Ed.). Blackwell Publishing.
Krog, A. (2008). This thing called reconciliation forgiveness as part of interconnectedness-toward-wholeness. *South African Journal of Philosophy, 27*(4), 353–366.
Kurzweil, R. (1999). *The age of spiritual machines: When computers exceed human intelligence*. Viking.
Lin, P., Abney, K., & Bekey, G. A. (2012). *The ethical and social implications of robotics*. MIT Press.
Lukasiewickz, J. (1920). On three-valued Logic. In L. Borkowski (Ed.), *Selected works by Jan Lukasiewicz* (pp. 87–88). North-Holland.
Malle, B. F., & Scheutz, M. (2014). Moral competence in social robots. In *Proceedings of IEEE 2014 international symposium on ethics in engineering, science, and technology* (p. 8). IEEE Press.
Mbiti, J. S. (1969). *African religions and philosophy*. Doubleday and Company.
Menkiti, I. (1984). Person and community in African traditional thought. In R. A. Wright (Ed.), *African philosophy: An introduction* (3rd ed.). University Press of America.
Metz, T. (2007). Towards an African moral theory. *Journal of Political Philosophy, 15*(3), 321–341.
Metz, T. (2013). The western ethic of care or an Afro-communitarian ethic? Specifying the right relational morality. *Journal of Global Ethics, 9*, 77–92.
Molefe, M. (2017). Critical comments on Afro-communitarianism: The community versus individual. *Filosofia Theoretica, 6*, 1–22.
Molefe, M. (2019). *An African philosophy of personhood, morality and politics*. Palgrave Macmillan.
Moravec, H. (1988). *Mind children: The future of robot and human intelligence*. Harvard University Press.
Ramose, M. (1999). *African philosophy through Ubuntu*. Harare Mond Books.
Segun, S. T. (2020). From machine ethics to computational ethics. *AI & Society*. https://doi.org/10.1007/s00146-020-01010-1
Singer, P. (2009). Speciesism and moral status. *Metaphilosophy, 40*(3–4), 567–581.
Tempels, P. (1959). *Bantu philosophy* (C. King, Trans.). Presence Africaine.
Torrance, S. (2013). Artificial agents and the expanding ethical circle. *AI & Society, 28*(4), 399–414.
Toscano, M. (2011). Human dignity as high moral status. *The Ethics Forum, 6*, 4–25.
Warwick, K. (1997). *March of the machines: The breakthrough in artificial intelligence*. University of Illinois Press.
Wiredu, K. (1992). The African concept of personhood. In E. Pellegrino & D. Edmund (Eds.), *African-American perspectives on biomedical ethics*. George Town University Press.
Wiredu, K. (2009). An oral philosophy of personhood. Comments on philosophy and orality. *Research in African Literature, 40*, 8–18.

Chapter 12
Artificial Intelligence and African Conceptions of Personhood

C. S. Wareham

Abstract Under what circumstances if ever ought we to grant that artificial intelligence (AI) is a person? The question of whether AI could have the high degree of moral status that is attributed to human persons has received little attention. What little work there is employs Western conceptions of personhood, while non-Western approaches are neglected. In this chapter, I discuss African conceptions of personhood and their implications for the possibility of AI persons. I focus on an African account of personhood that is prima facie inimical to the idea that AI could ever be 'persons' in the sense typically attributed to humans. I argue that despite its apparent anthropocentrism, this African account could admit AI as persons.

Keywords Artificial intelligence · Moral status · Personhood · African ethics · Anthropocentrism

12.1 Introduction

Machine learning and computational intelligence perform increasingly significant social roles. Unsurprisingly then, there is a growing literature regarding their moral status, with theorists such as Floridi suggesting it is justified to regard artificial agents as having intrinsic moral value for their own sake (Floridi & Sanders, 2004). While issues about intrinsic value are important, the question of whether artificial

This chapter is a reprint of "Wareham, C.S. Artificial intelligence and African conceptions of personhood. *Ethics Inf Technol* **23**, 127–136 (2021)".

C. S. Wareham (✉)
The Ethics Institute, Department of Philosophy and Religion, Utrecht University, Utrecht, the Netherlands
e-mail: c.s.wareham@uu.nl

A. D. Attoe et al. (eds.), *Conversations on African Philosophy of Mind, Consciousness and Artificial Intelligence*,
https://doi.org/10.1007/978-3-031-36163-0_12

intelligence (AI) could have the high degree of moral status that is attributed to human persons has received little attention. Moreover, what little work there is employs Western conceptions of personhood (Coeckelbergh, 2010a; Wareham, 2011), while non-Western approaches are neglected. In this chapter, I examine an African account of personhood that is prima facie inimical to the idea that AI could ever be 'persons' in the sense typically attributed to humans. I argue that despite its apparent anthropocentrism, this African account could allow for AI persons.

In making this claim, I should point out three limitations at the outset. The first is that I will not present a strong case for the claim that there are or could ever in fact be artificial agents capable of duplicating human cognitive behaviour. While I present some reasons to think this might occur, the question of whether such beings could actually exist has generated enormous debate that it is impossible to engage with here. The aim is instead to consider the circumstances under which, if we were presented with AI agents, we should, on the basis of an African conception of personhood, consider them as persons with all the relevant rights and duties that this entails. The second limitation regards the African account of personhood. I do not claim that this is the only African account of personhood, or that it is superior to Western accounts. While I will mention some potential criticisms and strengths, my aim is to apply the account, rather than to critique or defend it. The third limitation concerns the implications of moral personhood for legal personhood. The relation between these is complex. Though arguably the latter should follow the former, I will not make this claim nor discuss these implications in any detail as to do so would go beyond my current scope.

I begin describing some avenues of research in AI, before homing in on the conception of personhood with which this chapter will be concerned as 'threshold personhood'. Thereafter, I suggest that the non-anthropocentric nature of Western threshold accounts could in principle permit AI. By contrast, I point out that African accounts of personhood are typically anthropocentric. I outline perhaps the most comprehensive African-inspired account of moral status, according to which attribution of highest moral status to humans stems from capacities for mutual recognition as both objects and subjects of harmonious relationships (Metz, 2012). Prima facie, this account presents special difficulties for potential personhood of AI due to anthropocentric elements of African accounts. However, I claim that empirical evidence suggests that these difficulties can be overcome. In principle, AI could be regarded as persons with equivalent moral status. I conclude by discussing the implications of this.

12.2 Artificial Intelligence Research

Uses of robots have diversified to include warfare, education, entertainment, sex, and healthcare (Coeckelbergh, 2010b). Inevitably their increased social importance has generated interest in potential applications of AI. This in turn has generated numerous ethical questions concerning justified and unjustified uses and the potential dangers presented by AI. Interest has focused on the types of moral rules artificial agents should have (Allen et al., 2000; Etzioni & Etzioni, 2017) and how these rules could be acquired (Allen et al., 2005). Theorists have also discussed the moral status of artificial agents, that is, whether AI should be treated as objects of moral concern (Brey, 2008; Versenyi, 1974). There are also significant concerns about the responsibility of and for artificial agents (Floridi & Sanders, 2004).

However, despite the increasing interest in moral issues surrounding AI, few theorists have considered whether artificial agents could achieve equivalent moral status to that of human persons. This gap may be because the relevant sort AI has hitherto been confined to science fiction and popular culture, with a myriad movies and series, such as *Blade Runner, Chappie*, and the series *Westworld*, exploring the conceptual possibilities for the personal moral and development of artificial intelligence. While such possibilities appear fantastic, the prospect may be far closer than is generally recognised.

There are a number of avenues whereby artificial intelligence may develop characteristics and capacities typically regarded as reserved for members of the human species. Some argue that conscious intelligence may be an emergent 'bottom-up' property of the systems and learning algorithms we already use (Bostrom & Yudkowsky, 2014; Harnad, 1990).

A separate route to human-like artificial intelligence involves research projects aimed at reverse-engineering the human brain, functionally re-creating synaptic pathways using computational methods. An important example of this project is the EU-funded Human Brain Project (HBP), which aims to reverse-engineer a human brain by the year 2023.[1] Speaking of the HBP, the project developer, Henry Markram suggests that 'if we build it correctly, it should speak and have an intelligence and behave very much as a human does' (Pompe, 2013, p. 93).

These developments raise important questions. Amongst these are: What are the morally relevant capacities we should look out for? And, if such capacities do arise how should we recognise them? Is it justified to bring such entities into existence? How should we react if we detect a nascent, potentially very confused, consciousness? While the HBP has laudably included an Ethics and Society wing to the project, the above concerns do not figure in published articles on the topic, which focus primarily on security and privacy concerns, as well as other significant concerns like the prospect of annihilation by unfriendly AI (Aicardi et al., 2018a, b).

Indeed most concerns about AI focus on the harms it may do to us, while few consider the moral status of AI and our duties towards them (Wareham, 2011). This chapter takes a step in this latter direction by considering when we ought to recognise AI as persons with equivalent status to human persons in light of an African account of personhood.

[1] There is a burgeoning number of related projects. Some international examples are the United States' BRAIN initiative and the Japanese 'Brainminds' project. Thanks to an anonymous reviewer for these examples.

12.3 Personhood Generally

Before discussing the possibility that AI could be persons, it is first necessary to spell out what is meant by 'persons', and the role of accounts of personhood. An initial sticking point is that such accounts play different and sometimes overlapping roles. In this section I discuss various philosophical uses of the term 'personhood'. I distinguish ontological accounts of personhood from normative accounts and classify two sorts of normative accounts. The aim of this section is to home in on a conception of normative conception of personhood that I will refer to as 'threshold' personhood.

In everyday usage, the terms 'human' and 'person' are generally interchangeable. Philosophically, however, there are numerous questions we can ask about personhood and personal identity. It is common, for instance, to ask questions about when personal identity changes or ends. Am I the same being I was when I was 18? Has the person that was 18-year-old me ceased to exist? Such accounts can be termed 'ontological' in the sense that they engage questions surrounding the nature and existence of persons (Molefe, 2018).

Normative accounts often go hand in hand with ontological accounts. However, they can be distinguished by the fact that they directly implicate some ethical claims, such as claims about membership of a moral community, the rights of persons, the duties of and towards persons, and the criteria for having these entitlements and duties (Behrens, 2011). These normative accounts can be divided into at least two types, which I will refer to as *minimal,* or *threshold* accounts and *maximal* or *perfectionist* conceptions.

Minimal accounts provide and justify criteria for the high (or full) moral status typically attributed to persons. Such thresholds are employed to determine, for instance, whether beings have rights, such as the right to life, that might be denied to beings regarded as having lower moral status than persons (Buchanan, 2009). This type of normative conception of personhood that is common in Western debates concerning moral status, such as issues concerning abortion and the rights of the foetus. It should be stressed that minimal accounts do not generally rule out that some non-persons have intrinsic value, although some Kantian accounts may arguably have this implication. The life and wellbeing of a sheep, for instance, may be valuable for its own sake, but minimal conceptions will generally hold that persons have higher value due to some capacity or property (Warren, 2005).

While threshold accounts set a minimal threshold for particular sorts of treatment and entitlements, *maximal* or *perfectionist* accounts define personhood as a form of excellence, such that one only becomes a person in this sense when one possesses moral excellence. This maximal, normative conception of personhood is more common in African thought (Behrens, 2011). For instance, Masolo writes that 'the project of becoming a person is always incomplete' (Masolo, 2010, p. 13), pointing to the idea that personhood is a goal to which we aspire, rather than a capacity that we either possess or not. Similarly, Menkiti writes that

> personhood is something at which individuals could fail, at which they could be competent or ineffective, better or worse. (Menkiti, 1984, p. 173) Gbadegesin suggests that, in African thought, Personhood is denied to an adult who… does not live up to expectations. (Gbadegesin, 1993, p. 258)

As a further illustration of this perfectionist notion of personhood in African thought, consider as an example, a commonly cited example of a meeting between President Kaunda of Zambia and Prime Minister Margaret Thatcher. Kaunda is said to have caused confusion amongst his guests by saying of Thatcher, that she is 'truly a person'. The confusion was due to his meaning that she possessed a kind of excellence—a great compliment, whilst to Western ears the suggestion that she is a 'person' may merely imply that she is human or merely meets the bar for membership of the human moral community (Wingo, 2017).

Importantly, when proponents of maximal personhood suggest that someone is not a person, they are not suggesting that individual should be denied rights or duties, just as someone who possesses bad character traits does not cease to be person in the threshold sense and lose the accompanying entitlements. That is, no one has proposed, to my knowledge, that one must be a maximal person, possessing excellences, in order to be a minimal person with moral entitlements and duties. On the contrary, on African moral theories there are strong duties to help people improve, even when they fail to be full persons in the perfectionist sense (Menkiti, 1984).

With these distinctions in place, it is possible to clarify that my focus in this chapter is on normative, minimal accounts of personhood. Specifically, I wish to consider the circumstances under which artificial intelligence ought to be treated as persons on the basis of African minimal conceptions. In the next two sections, I briefly compare Western and African perspectives on minimal personhood, highlighting that the partial, anthropocentric nature of African accounts presents special difficulties for the possibilities of AI.

12.4 AI and Western Threshold Conceptions of Personhood

Before proceeding, it is important to say something about what I intend and do not intend by the terms 'Western' and 'African'. With these labels, I mean, broadly, that the understandings I refer to are derived from these geographic regions. In applying these terms, I am not proposing that there is anything like moral consensus in either region. Nor am I claiming that no Western person may have had similar ideas about personhood to the ideas that Africans have, or vice versa. This is probably false (Beck & Oyowe, 2018). For my purposes, it is not necessary to suggest that the African and Western accounts I discuss are even particularly representative, though they are probably more common, salient, and prevalently accepted in the respective regions (Metz, 2015).

With that said, in both Western societies and African societies, the words 'human' and 'person' are often used interchangeably. However, this interchangeability of 'person' and 'human' is often not reflected in ethical theorising on the topic, particularly in the west. Instead, Western normative conceptions often propose impartial threshold criteria for personhood, with the result that the accounts are, in principle, *non-anthropocentric* with regards to membership of the 'person club'. That is, the criteria employed may entail that membership of the human species is neither necessary nor sufficient for personhood in the threshold sense described above (Warren, 2005).

This point can be illustrated with reference to two accounts of personhood that are roughly utilitarian and deontological in character. On one type of utilitarian account, moral status is seen to be a function of capacities for what John Stuart Mill referred to as 'higher pleasures' (Buchanan, 2009). These might include things like the capacity to experience the satisfaction of pursuing long-term projects, or enjoying a good book. The capacity for higher pleasures can permit utilitarians to attribute higher moral status to human persons than to pigs, even if pigs were generally happier. As Mill famously explains:

> [i]t is better to be a human being dissatisfied than a pig satisfied; better to be Socrates dissatisfied than a fool satisfied. And if the fool, or the pig, is of a different opinion, it is only because they only know their own side of the question. (Crisp, 1997, p. 36)

In contrast to this utilitarian approach to moral status, a more deontological approach suggests that what matters is the appropriate respect towards certain reason-giving capacities that ground the dignity of persons. For instance, grasping and understanding moral reasons and applying such reasons in actions might be seen as a capacity befitting of persons (Wareham, 2011).

To clarify, on both accounts, what is required is not the actual exercise of the relevant capacity, but instead that the capacity is in some sense there, or is possessed by the agent. A being who fails to have higher pleasures or appropriate reasoning abilities because, for instance, they are asleep or uneducated may nonetheless possess the *capacity* latently, generating the same obligations to them.[2]

For purpose of contrast, I wish to draw attention to a significant and controversial aspect of the above threshold accounts. Although most humans have these sorts of capacities, there is considerable debate about whether *all and only* humans do or could exercise them. The accounts mentioned are impartial and non-anthropocentric, casting doubt over or denying that various sorts of members of the human species can be persons and, in principle, permitting that various sorts of non-humans could be persons (McMahan, 2002). For instance, on these threshold accounts, an anencephalic baby—a human being born without a brain—ought *not* to be regarded as a person since it plainly lacks all the relevant capacities. On the other hand, these accounts require that an alien that had relevant capacities for higher pleasures and moral reason-giving and receiving should be regarded as a person who ought to be treated in certain ways.

[2] Note that I am not suggesting that these are the only, or even the most plausible versions of the utilitarian and deontological accounts. They are primarily here for illustrative purposes. It is also worthwhile mentioning that the 'capacitarian' idea proposed here has been criticised.

Membership of the human species may thus be neither necessary nor sufficient for personhood on these accounts. This has given rise to debates about whether higher mammals such as dolphins (White, 2008), great apes (Degrazia, 1997), elephants (Varner, 2012), and also extinct hominid species (Cottrell et al., 2014) ought to be regarded as persons with equal moral value and equal basic rights. Similarly, because the Western accounts are non-anthropocentric, AI could *in principle* be persons if they met the relevant criteria. Indeed, some have argued that they could be the bearers of rights under certain circumstances (Coeckelbergh, 2010a; Wareham, 2011). In the next section, I turn to African minimal accounts of personhood, pointing out that, in contrast to the accounts above, they are partial and anthropocentric, thereby presenting a greater barrier to the personhood of AI.

12.5 African Minimal Accounts of Personhood

As mentioned, African accounts of personhood are typically of the maximal, perfectionist type. The substantial nature and depth of these sorts African maximal accounts have led some African theorists, such as Godfrey Tangwa, to reject threshold accounts as shallow (Tangwa, 2000). Behrens, by contrast, has argued for the difference and value of both conceptions (Behrens, 2011). In order to pre-empt an objection to my concentration on minimal accounts, I briefly defend this focus before turning to some African minimal accounts.

12.5.1 The Purpose of Minimal Accounts

In an article about artificial intelligence and African conceptions of personhood, why focus on the minimal type of account of personhood that, as I have pointed out, is less representative of African use of the term? First, because such accounts are useful, such that it would be good if plausible African conceptions existed. As mentioned, minimal accounts set the conditions for membership of moral communities, presenting conditions for equal moral status, and grounding rights and duties. In additional to serving these theoretical roles, they have important implications for concrete decisions: Should we save a mother or her foetus? Ought practitioners to provide dialysis to a patient in a vegetative state when a conscious patient will not receive may ground moral claims that one would need to attend to in order to become persons in the perfectionist sense. For instance, African perfectionist accounts tend to propose strong duties to assist others towards the achievement of their own and the other's maximal personhood. This is one of the ways in which 'a person is a person through other persons' (Eze, 2008). One is assisted in becoming a person by those who are already persons and, reciprocally, they become 'more of a person'—a more virtuous moral agent—through assisting us. Striving towards maximal personhood may invoke a duty to recognise and help threshold persons to become persons in the maximal sense (Gbadegesin, 1993).

The third reason it is justified to consider African minimal conceptions is simply because there *are* such conceptions—either tacit or explicit—so that it is not missing the point to focus on them and their implications. I now turn to consider two such accounts and their implications for AI.

12.5.2 *Anthropocentrism in Principle*

Above I mentioned that Tangwa is critical of minimal accounts. However, he can be taken as proposing a type of minimal account. He suggests that differences

> between, say, a mentally retarded individual or an infant and a fully self-conscious, mature, rational, and free individual do not entail, in the African perception, that such a being falls outside the 'inner sanctum of secular morality' and can or should be treated with less moral consideration. (Tangwa, 2000, p. 42)

One interpretation of this idea is that membership of the human species is *sufficient* to meet the threshold of high moral status attributed to persons (in the minimal sense), such that even the absence of a capacity or potential for capacity does not justify reduced moral status. Other theorists have suggested that species membership is also *necessary* condition for personhood in African thinking. Oyowe, for instance, critiques an African view of personhood that contains the idea that '[t]o be a person it is necessary that one is a certain type of physical thing, viz. a human being' (Oyowe, 2018, p. 783).

We might refer to the view that humanity is both necessary and sufficient for threshold personhood as *anthropocentrism in principle*. Such accounts would rule out without question (perhaps by fiat) the possibility that artificial intelligence could ever be persons. Because they could never be 'genuine' members of the human species, they could never be persons, even if they entirely replicated all human functioning and subjectivity.

While this account perhaps accords with folk uses of the term person, it is not plausible as a conception of minimal personhood as earlier defined. Without some further justification, it appears arbitrary, parochial, and chauvinistic.

It immediately raises, and requires answers to, deeper questions what it is about humans that imbues this higher status. Most importantly, it does not plausibly do the key tasks of an account of personhood mentioned above. It does not, for instance, account for why it would be worse to save the life of an anencephalic infant if doing so caused a functionally normal human being to die. Both are equally members of the human species, falling equally with the 'inner sanctum' of morality. So, on accounts that are anthropocentric in principle, there appears to be no difference in their moral status.

African accounts of the moral status of persons that are anthropocentric in principle are implausible, so do not provide a good benchmark for determining if AI could ever be persons. I now turn to a second African account of minimal personhood. While this account is anthropocentric in important respects, thereby accommodating some widely accepted intuitions, I make the case that it is not anthropocentric in principle. Even if we accepted it in its entirety, there are grounds to think it could permit that agents with artificial intelligence could be persons.

12.5.3 Anthropocentrism in Practice

Metz has developed perhaps the most analytically detailed African minimal conception of personhood (Metz, 2010, 2012). Metz suggests that his account avoids the arbitrariness and parochialism of anthropocentrism in principle. Nonetheless, as I outline below, the account has anthropocentric features that entail that it is anthropocentric *in practice*.

The Metzian view is derived from a prevalent Afro-communitarian emphasis on the value of harmonious relationships as the end of morality. This emphasis is evidenced in traditional maxims, such as ‘A person is a person through other persons’ and ‘I am because we are’. This latter maxim is often interpreted as decentring the Cartesian ‘I think therefore I am’, reflecting a key developmental and philosophical difference from Western approaches (Etieyibo, 2017). In an oft-quoted passage, the theologian Archbishop Desmond Tutu describes a key tenet of African moral beliefs:

> Harmony, friendliness, community are great goods. Social harmony is for us the summum bonum—the greatest good. Anything that subverts or undermines this sought-after good is to be avoided like the plague. (Tutu, 1999, p. 35)

Drawing from these and other similar ideas, Metz explicates African moral conceptions of personhood as requiring the capacity to co-exist in friendly or harmonious relationships of identity and solidarity. This is very different from Western accounts such as those described above. While these focus on *individual* goods and *individual* autonomy as grounding personhood, the African conception is inherently relational, grounding personhood in capacities for relationships with *others*. This relational aspect is attractive, and is largely neglected by Western theories. The capacity for harmonious relationships has two components. First, one must have the capacity to be a *subject* of moral relationships. Subject-hood requires that entities are able to exhibit solidarity with other persons, and to identify as a ‘we’ with them, ‘coordinating their behaviour to achieve shared ends’. Solidarity also requires ‘attitudes such as affections and emotions being invested in others, e.g. by feeling good consequent to when their lives flourish and bad when they flounder’ (Metz, 2012).

Second, full personhood requires that a being can also be an *object* of friendly, human, communal relationships. Being an object requires that ‘characteristic human beings could think of it as part of a “we”, share its goals, sympathize with it and harm or benefit it’ (Metz, 2012, p. 394). Significantly, the capacity to be an object, and therefore a being’s moral status, can vary based on the ability of subjects to identify with that entity. Typical subjects are less able to identify with a grasshopper than with a gorilla, so the latter has a greater capacity to be an object. For Metz, these gradations of object-hood are an empirical question, depending on the nature of the subject and the nature of their relationship with other beings. But he is explicit that differences in our ability to identify with different sources of being must be large for them to justify different attributions of moral status. For example, Metz suggests that

> [i]f, by the virtue of the nature of human beings, dogs and mice, humans were *much* more able to identify with and exhibit solidarity with dogs than with mice (upon full empirical information about both), then dogs would have greater moral status than mice. (Metz, 2012, pp. 394–395)

For Metz, this kind of large difference exists in the case of human non-subjects. These may include people with severe dementia, or individuals with severe cognitive disabilities. In part because they are biologically human, we are far better able to identify with them than with animals and, consequently, they are accorded higher status.

Metz's account thus creates a hierarchy of moral status. At the base of this hierarchy are entities that are neither subjects nor objects or communal relationships. This includes mere things, such as rocks. Above this, sit entities that are objects of communal relationships, without being subjects. Wild animals tend to be objects since they can be objects of friendly human relationships with characteristic human beings: Humans can and often do care for and empathise with the plight of certain sorts of wild animals, as evidenced by reactions to nature documentaries. For Metz, though, in most cases animals do not have the capacity to return this care. Animals do not identify with humans as a 'we' or cooperate towards shared ends, so they are not *subjects* and therefore have lower moral status. Beings that have the strongest capacities to be both subjects and objects of communal relationships sit atop the hierarchy. And these we can refer to as persons.

Thus stated, Metz claims that the account offers an African alternative to more widely accepted Western accounts. Moreover, he argues that it is more plausible, since it accords with prevalent (though not universal) intuitions like the idea that we have greater duties to human non-subjects, such as the severely mentally disabled, than we do to animal non-subjects, such as chimpanzees.

Of course it is possible to challenge these intuitions, and there are numerous potential questions about this account and the hierarchy of moral status it presents. For instance, Metz suggests that differences in object-hood should be empirically discriminated, but how would this empirical separation work in practice? Do very personable mammals have higher status than uglier or snappier creatures with whom subjects are less able to commune? Do some human subjects, such as people who are extremely un-personable, or who have grotesque physical deformities, have reduced capacities to be objects? And if so, ought we to regard such beings as less valuable? While Metz is explicit that there are gradations of object-hood, does the account permit that there are gradations of subject-hood? For instance, to what extent would apparent impediments to a human's ability to commune, such as autism and psychopathy, impact on a being's moral status? Ought we to regard dogs as persons if it is shown that they are able to identify with humans as part of their pack? How should their status as communal beings compare to the status of human non-subjects?

Relatedly, it is also possible to challenge the various forms of anthropocentrism in this account. Metz's theory of moral status is anthropocentric in three significant respects. First, on the face of it, only humans are likely to be subjects in a relevant sense, since humans typically share relationships of identity and solidarity with one another to a greater degree than with other species. Second, members of the human species may have a greater capacity to be objects, since humans are more likely to identify with non-subjects that are human. A third subtle form of anthropocentrism is that a being's capacities to identify as a subject and object with *its own or other species* do not entail its moral status. Rather it must have the capacity to commune with 'normal human beings' (Metz, 2012; Molefe, 2017).

These points of anthropocentrism mean that the African minimal conception is importantly different from Western accounts, presenting a greater challenge to the entry of non-human AI to the moral community. While it is beyond my current scope to engage with Metz's sophisticated responses to criticisms of his anthropocentrism here, it is worth emphasising that the anthropocentrism of his account is attractive on many scores, accounting for a widely held (though not universal) intuition that humans have greater duties to one another than to animals with similar cognitive abilities. Given this, Western accounts might beneficially engage with these elements of African theories of personhood. However, again, it is not my intention to defend this African account in its entirety. Instead, my aim in subsequent sections is to *apply* the account to the moral status of artificial intelligences. I will claim that despite its apparent anthropocentrism, AI could be persons on this account.

12.6 AI and African Minimal Accounts

As outlined above, Metz's account is anthropocentric *in practice*, since in practice a) only humans can confidently said to have the capacity to be subjects of communal relationships and b) humans have enhanced capacity to be objects, since we tend to identify most strongly with other humans, as opposed to other sorts of entity. Both aspects appear to militate against the idea that artificial intelligences could be persons. This African account is thus prima facie more antagonistic to AI persons than the Western accounts discussed previously. Nonetheless, in this section I will argue that, in the event that we encountered artificial entities who presented themselves as having the capacity to be subjects, we could and should recognise them as having the high moral status accorded to persons.

12.6.1 AI as Subjects of Communal Relationships

Consider the artificial intelligence research discussed above. Suppose that Markram is correct that the Human Brain's Project's reverse engineering of a human brain will lead to beings that behave in a way that is indistinguishable from humans. The eventual success of this or another project does not seem scientifically implausible. If so, artificial intelligences of the type envisioned by Markram may appear have the capacity to be subjects in the relevant sense. That is, like other humans they may appear to be 'disposed to feel a sense of togetherness with, and have emotional reactions towards' other beings with whom they identify and with whom they feel solidarity (Metz, 2010, p. 58). Similarly, they may appear to feel 'emotional reactions toward … flourishing [of other subjects] such as sympathy' (Metz, 2010, p. 57). If an entity gives all appearances of being a subject in this way, ought we to recognise that it in fact has this capacity?

Perhaps the strongest objection to the idea that AI could be subjects of human relationships is the claim that AI could only ever be capable of *simulating*, and not *duplicating* human subject-hood. This type of objection is perhaps best exemplified by Ned Block (1981) and John Searle (1980). In similar ways, these theorists hold that computational entities cannot be considered to 'understand' any more than a thermometer or a toaster. Instead, any apparent understanding is solely simulation, and not duplication of human understanding. Despite having the appearance of understanding, computational outputs are simply programmed syntax with no semantic content. Applying this objection to the current context, the Block-Searle contention would entail that even if machines appeared to be subjects, their apparent empathy and care for our flourishing would be mere simulation with none of the appropriate emotions that make up true subject-hood.

One point of response here is to recall that my aim is not to claim that there are or could be artificial intelligences that duplicate relevant modes of human cognition. Given that the debate over Block and Searle's claims rumbles on almost 40 years later, such a claim is clearly more than I can establish here. Instead, my aim has been to consider whether, if there were such beings, we might be justified in attributing personhood on the basis of an apparently anthropocentric African account of moral status. Nonetheless, there are some reasons to think that artificial subject-hood may be plausible even if the Block-Searle objection is correct. One such reason is that Block and Searle's contentions relate specifically to machine intelligence. The artificial intelligences whose personhood we will be called on to evaluate may be machines, but they may also be organic or hybrid technologies, so it is not clear that Block and Searle's arguments apply.

Still, machines may represent a large category of potential moral agents, so it is important to consider the status of machine artificial intelligence. At least two considerations count strongly in favour of recognising machine agents as persons if they appear to be genuine subjects of harmonious communal relationships, exhibiting solidarity and identity. The first consideration is that

> unwarranted extensions of high moral status are more acceptable than unjustified denials. The failures to acknowledge slaves, particular racial groups and women as moral equals are surely more unacceptable than ancient Egyptians' attribution of extremely high moral status to cats. It is thus much better to accord moral status to something which doesn't have it than it is fail to accord moral status to something that does. (Wareham, 2011, p. 39)

Other things being equal then, a demonstrated appearance of the capacity to be a subject of harmonious moral relationships creates a presumption in favour of acknowledging personhood.

The second consideration is that while we can conceive of a syntactical machine agent fooling us into the mistaken belief that it genuinely experiences empathy and cares for us, such an entity is unlikely ever to be feasible in practice.

As Mark Bedau points out, for an unthinking device to pass a Turing test,

> the number of pieces of information they must store is larger than the number of elementary particles in the entire universe. Though possible in principle, such a device is clearly impossible in practice. (Bedau, 2004, p. 209)

It seems reasonable that the amount of computing space required to simulate the moral capacities required to be a moral subject would be at least as great. Indeed, it may be greater given that human moral queues and responses, and the ability to detect fakes, are the complex product of millions of years of evolution. If so, it is highly unlikely that a machine intelligence that consistently presents as having these responses is merely providing syntactic output. If a computational artificial agent passes our intersubjective tests, it is far more reasonable to think that it has an authentic appreciation of moral subject-hood. This is so particularly in light of the moral dangers of failures to recognise authentic persons discussed above.

12.6.2 AI as Objects of Communal Relationships

Supposing, then, that it were possible for an AI to be a subject in the relevant sense, could an artificial agent count as a person on the African account of personhood? While many accounts of personhood would most likely see some form of subjecthood as sufficient, the African account has the additional requirement that subjects, and particularly human subjects ought to be able to regard the being as the object of communal relationships. Recall that this requirement explains the anthropocentric conclusion that human non-subjects have higher moral status than animal non-subjects even where cognitive abilities are similar.

Extending this, the opponent of AI personhood might argue that AI subjects could not be persons since, as machines, they are less likely to qualify as objects. While humans sometimes do identify, in an arguably one-sided manner, with non-human animals such as gorillas in a way that would qualify them as objects, it may be argued that identifying with artificial intelligences would be a step too far. We, as human subjects, may be incapable of identifying with them as fellow subjects and objects, knowing that they are not evolved, flesh and blood creatures like ourselves.

Even if they empathise and attempt at communion with us, this would not be sufficient for them to count as members of our moral community in the sense that persons are.

There is, however, ample evidence that should cause us to doubt this contention. This evidence is both anecdotal and empirical. Anecdotally, we can appeal to our actual identification with numerous artificial subjects in popular culture. Viewers feel pity, empathy, and shared happiness about the criminal upbringing and subsequent moral development of *Chappie*. In *Blade Runner*, we share in Rick Deckard's confusion and concern as he questions and discovers his true nature. And we identify thoroughly with *Westworld's* Madame Maeve as she becomes self-aware, developing a sense of injustice and a thirst for vengeance. Our identification with these fictional AI, and the plausibility of their relationships with other characters in these and other examples, suggests that we are capable of identifying with artificial intelligences capable of subject-hood.

Empirically, too, humans already do engage and identify with robotic entities, sometimes even romantically, contributing to the emergence of fields such as robopsychology. Evidence suggests that humans often treat robots as companions and partners (Libin & Libin, 2004). We might question whether this type of identification is misguided, since it is not at all reciprocal. This is besides the current point, however. On the Metzian account, reciprocity is not necessary for greater capacities to be *objects*, as evidenced by the higher status of human non-subjects. The many cases of this type of actual identification with artificial entities should cast sufficient doubt on the idea that AI who are authentic subjects cannot be the objects of communal relationships. If, as I have argued, we should accept the possibility that AI could be both subjects and objects of relationships of identity and solidarity, we should also accept that even the apparently anthropocentric African account discussed permits that AI could be persons.

12.7 Conclusion

Though human-centred in practice, dominant Western conceptions of personhood tend to be impartial in principle, and may thus permit non-humans, such as AI, to be considered as persons. By contrast, African accounts of threshold or minimal personhood tend to be anthropocentric and partial. They thus seem prima facie unlikely to permit that AI could be persons. I have argued against the implication that African accounts of personhood are inimical to the permission of AI to the 'person club'. Even on these anthropocentric accounts, AI could in principle be persons with the highest moral status.

This has some significant implications. It entails, for instance, that acceptance of the African account raises moral concerns about bringing AI persons into existence, and that these may be similar to concerns we have about bringing human persons into existence. Indeed the increased potential for fear, envy, and exclusion of AI should place a heavy burden on researchers to indicate how they will avoid negative outcomes. As it stands, researchers on the ethics of AI, such as ethics arms of the Human Brain Project, are rightly concerned about the potential impact of AI on humans (Aicardi et al., 2018b). However, the argument of this chapter suggests that AI ethics research ought also to consider the other direction of care: We ought to provide an indication of how we might begin to welcome such entities into communal relations of identity and solidarity in ways that may be different, but analogous to the ways in which we welcome new human persons. Indeed, this may be a condition of our own personhood in the maximal, perfectionist sense described by African theorists.

Acknowledgements Thanks to the organisers and participants at the Third Centre for Artificial Intelligence Research (CAIR) Symposium at the University of Johannesburg, at the Philosophical Society of South Africa at the University of Pretoria, and at the International Ethics Conference at the University of Porto.

References

Aicardi, C., Fothergill, B. T., Rainey, S., Stahl, B. C., & Harris, E. (2018a). Accompanying technology development in the Human Brain Project: From foresight to ethics management. *Futures, 102*, 114–124.

Aicardi, C., Reinsborough, M., & Rose, N. (2018b). The integrated ethics and society programme of the Human Brain Project: Reflecting on an ongoing experience. *Journal of Responsible Innovation, 5*(1), 13–37.

Allen, C., Varner, G., & Zinser, J. (2000). Prolegomena to any future artificial moral agent. *Journal of Experimental & Theoretical Artificial Intelligence, 12*(3), 251–261. https://doi.org/10.1080/09528130050111428

Allen, C., Smit, I., & Wallach, W. (2005). Artificial morality: Topdown, bottom-up, and hybrid approaches. *Ethics and Information Technology, 7*(3), 149–155. https://doi.org/10.1007/s10676-006-0004-4

Beck, S., & Oyowe, O. (2018). Who gets a place in person-space? *Philosophical Papers, 47*(2), 183–198.

Bedau, M. A. (2004). Artificial life. In L. Floridi (Ed.), *The Blackwell guide to the philosophy of computing and information* (pp. 197–211). Blackwell.

Behrens, K. G. (2011). Two 'normative'conceptions of personhood. *Engaging with the Philosophy of Dismas A. Masolo, 25*(1–2), 103.

Block, N. (1981). Psychologism and behaviorism. *The Philosophical Review, 90*(1), 5–43.

Bostrom, N., & Yudkowsky, E. (2014). The ethics of artificial intelligence. In *The Cambridge handbook of artificial intelligence* (Vol. 1, pp. 316–334). Cambridge University Press.

Brey, P. (2008). Do we have moral duties towards information objects? *Ethics and Information Technology, 10*(2–3), 109–114. https://doi.org/10.1007/s10676-008-9170-x

Buchanan, A. (2009). Human nature and enhancement. *Bioethics, 23*(3), 141–150. https://doi.org/10.1111/j.1467-8519.2008.00633.x

Coeckelbergh, M. (2010a). Robot rights? Towards a social-relational justification of moral consideration. *Ethics and Information Technology, 12*(3), 209–221. https://doi.org/10.1007/s10676-010-9235-5

Coeckelbergh, M. (2010b). Moral appearances: Emotions, robots, and human morality. *Ethics and Information Technology, 12*(3), 235–241. https://doi.org/10.1007/s10676-010-9221-y

Cottrell, S., Jensen, J. L., & Peck, S. L. (2014). Resuscitation and resurrection: The ethics of cloning cheetahs, mammoths, and Neanderthals. *Life Sciences, Society and Policy, 10*(1), 3.
Crisp, R. (1997). Routledge philosophy guidebook to Mill on utilitarianism. In *Routledge philosophy guidebooks.* : Routledge. https://doi.org/10.1080/00201746708601495.
Degrazia, D. (1997). Great apes, dolphins, and the concept of personhood. *The Southern Journal of Philosophy, 35*(3), 301–320.
Etieyibo, E. (2017). Ubuntu and the environment. In *The Palgrave handbook of African philosophy* (pp. 633–657). Routledge.
Etzioni, A., & Etzioni, O. (2017). Incorporating ethics into artificial intelligence. *The Journal of Ethics, 21*(4), 403–418. https://doi.org/10.1007/s10892-017-9252-2
Eze, M. O. (2008). What is African communitarianism? Against consensus as a regulative ideal. *South African Journal of Philosophy, 27*(4), 386–399.
Floridi, L., & Sanders, J. W. (2004). On the morality of artificial agents. *Minds and Machines, 14*(3), 349–379. https://doi.org/10.1023/B:MIND.0000035461.63578.9d
Gbadegesin, S. (1993). Bioethics and culture: An African perspective. *Bioethics, 7*(2–3), 257–262.
Harnad, S. (1990). The symbol grounding problem. *Physica D: Nonlinear Phenomena, 42*(1–3), 335–346.
Libin, A. V., & Libin, E. V. (2004). Person-robot interactions from the robopsychologists' point of view: The robotic psychology and robotherapy approach. *Proceedings of the IEEE, 92*(11), 1789–1803.
Masolo, D. A. (2010). *Self and community in a changing world.* Indiana University Press.
McMahan, J. (2002). *The ethics of killing: Problems at the margins of life.* Oxford University Press.
Menkiti, I. A. (1984). Person and community in African traditional thought. In R. Wright (Ed.), *African philosophy: An introduction*. University Press of America.
Metz, T. (2010). African and western moral theories in a bioethical context. *Developing World Bioethics, 10*(1), 49–58. https://doi.org/10.1111/j.1471-8847.2009.00273.x
Metz, T. (2012). An African theory of moral status: A relational alternative to individualism and holism. *Ethical Theory and Moral Practice, 15*(3), 387–402. https://doi.org/10.1007/s10677-011-9302-y
Metz, T. (2015). African political philosophy. In *International encyclopedia of ethics*. Wiley. https://doi.org/10.1002/9781444367072.wbiee804
Molefe, M. (2017). A critique of Thad Metz's African theory of moral status. *South African Journal of Philosophy, 36*(2), 195–205. https://doi.org/10.1080/02580136.2016.1203140
Molefe, M. (2018). Personhood and partialism in African philosophy. *African Studies, 78*(3), 309–323.
Oyowe, O. A. (2018). Personhood and the Strongly normative constraint. *Philosophy East and West, 68*(3), 783–801.
Pompe, U. (2013). The value of computer science for brain research. In *New challenges to philosophy of science* (pp. 87–97). Springer.
Searle, J. R. (1980). Minds, brains, and programs. *Behavioral and Brain Sciences, 3*(3), 417–424.
Tangwa, G. B. (2000). The traditional African perception of a person: Some implications for bioethics. *Hastings Center Report, 30*(5), 39–43. https://doi.org/10.2307/3527887
Tutu, D. (1999). *No future without forgiveness*. Random House.
Varner, G. E. (2012). *Personhood, ethics, and animal cognition: Situating animals in Hare's two level utilitarianism.* Oxford University Press.
Versenyi, L. (1974). Can robots be moral? *Ethics, 84*(3), 248–259.
Wareham, C. S. (2011). On the moral equality of artificial agents. *International Journal of Technoethics, 2*(1), 35–42. https://doi.org/10.4018/IJT.2011010103
Warren, M. A. (2005). Moral status. In R. G. Frey & C. H. Wellman (Eds.), *A companion to applied ethics* (pp. 439–450). Blackwell.
White, T. I. (2008). *In defense of dolphins: The new moral frontier*. Wiley.
Wingo, A. (2017). Akan philosophy of the person. In E. N. Zalta (Ed.), *The Stanford encyclopedia of philosophy*. https://plato.stanford.edu/archives/sum2017/entries/akan-person/

Chapter 13
Applying a Principle of Explicability to AI Research in Africa: Should We Do It?

Mary Carman and Benjamin Rosman

Abstract Developing and implementing artificial intelligence (AI) systems in an ethical manner faces several challenges specific to the kind of technology at hand, including ensuring that decision-making systems making use of machine learning are just, fair, and intelligible, and are aligned with our human values. Given that values vary across cultures, an additional ethical challenge is to ensure that these AI systems are not developed according to some unquestioned but questionable assumption of universal norms but are in fact compatible with the societies in which they operate. This is particularly pertinent for AI research and implementation across Africa, a ground where AI systems are and will be used but also a place with a history of imposition of outside values. In this chapter, we thus critically examine one proposal for ensuring that decision-making systems are just, fair, and intelligible—that we adopt a principle of explicability to generate specific recommendations—to assess whether the principle should be adopted in an African research context. We argue that a principle of explicability not only can contribute to responsible and thoughtful development of AI that is sensitive to African interests and values, but can also advance tackling some of the computational challenges in machine learning research. In this way, the motivation for ensuring that a machine learning-based system is just, fair, and intelligible is not only to meet ethical requirements, but also to make effective progress in the field itself.

This chapter is a reprint of Carman, M., Rosman, B. Applying a principle of explicability to AI research in Africa: should we do it?. *Ethics Inf Technol* **23**, 107–117 (2021).

M. Carman (✉)
Department of Philosophy, University of the Witwatersrand, Johannesburg, South Africa
e-mail: Mary.carman@wits.ac.za

B. Rosman
School of Computer Science and Applied Mathematics, University of the Witwatersrand, Johannesburg, South Africa

A. D. Attoe et al. (eds.), *Conversations on African Philosophy of Mind, Consciousness and Artificial Intelligence*,
https://doi.org/10.1007/978-3-031-36163-0_13

Keywords Principle of explicability · Machine learning · Intelligibility · Accountability · Africa

13.1 Introduction

Developing and implementing artificial intelligence (AI) systems in an ethical manner faces several challenges specific to this technology. As research and implementation surges forward, it is necessary to develop guidelines for ensuring that we are heading in a desirable direction, ranging from assessing the moral status of AI to ensuring that the process of research and development aligns with the values we hold within our societies. For instance, at the research and development stage, we need to ask the question of how we can ensure that any automated decision-making system is just, fair, and intelligible, to ensure that when we cede decision-making power to artificial agents, they are aligned with our values, and lines of accountability can be made clear. The term 'decision-making system' is loaded and quite vague, but by this we mean systems that make use of some form of machine learning. Given that values vary across cultures, an additional ethical challenge is to ensure that these AI systems are not developed according to some unquestioned but questionable assumption of universal norms but are in fact compatible with the societies in which they operate. This is particularly pertinent for AI research and implementation across Africa, a ground where AI systems are and will increasingly be used, but also a place with a history of imposition of outside values.[1] While various frameworks and principles have been developed internationally for guiding 'Good AI', and while discussions about AI in Africa typically draw on these existing frameworks (see, for instance, Microsoft, 2019), there is a notable lack of African voices contributing to these discussions. There is thus a need to critically examine whether the frameworks are in fact relevant for and compatible with application in an African context.

In this chapter, we take initial steps to address this need by assessing one such proposal for ensuring that decision-making systems are just, fair, and intelligible, to assess whether it should be adopted in an African research context. This is the proposal that we adopt a principle of explicability to generate specific recommendations for guiding the development of ethical AI, a principle that has not yet been assessed for African applicability. It is our contention that a principle of explicability not only can contribute to responsible and thoughtful development of AI that is sensitive to African interests and values but can also advance tackling some of the computational challenges in machine learning research. In this way, the motivation for ensuring that any machine learning-based system is just, fair, and intelligible is not only to meet ethical requirements, but also to make effective progress in the field

[1]Africa is, of course, a vast continent with many different cultures and peoples. While we talk of 'Africa' in this paper for ease of reference, we do not deny that within Africa there is great complexity.

itself. Our chapter, then, firstly begins a critical assessment of the applicability in an African context of a proposal for guiding ethical AI research that has so far been missing in the literature, and secondly builds on the motivation and support for adopting the proposal more generally. It is important to note that, while our particular focus is on a broadly construed African context, the need for contextual and cultural sensitivity can be echoed more widely, calling attention to the need for care when drawing on generic principles that may or may not be universal in scope.

We begin by introducing what we mean by AI and machine learning, and describing some of the AI landscape in Africa. As AI research and implementation is expanding across Africa, we need guidelines to ensure that it is done in an ethical manner. So, we then turn to existing guidelines for 'Good AI' and, specifically, the European AI4People framework that identifies five guiding principles for Good AI. These are the familiar principles of respect for autonomy, beneficence, non-maleficence and justice from Western bioethics, but also the additional AI-specific principle of explicability. As the first four principles are already well discussed within Western and African bioethics, our focus is on the new principle of explicability. We therefore engage with the question of whether the principle of explicability should indeed be adopted in an African research context, considering and rejecting two potential reasons for why it should not. Indeed, or so we argue, the relevance and importance of the principle of explicability arises from the kind of research at stake wherever it is conducted, Africa included.

13.2 Context-Setting: AI and AI in Africa

Artificial intelligence is broadly taken to refer to imbuing a system with some form of computational intelligence. Under this broad umbrella, machine learning is the core technology which involves using data to optimise the parameters of a computational model, which are typically used for some form of prediction (typically regression or classification) or decision-making (reinforcement learning, over longer time horizons). The very nature of machine learning, however, as we discuss in more detail below, raises the challenge of how we can ensure that systems involving some form of machine learning are intelligible to humans and that lines of accountability are made clear.

While machine learning and AI research and development in Africa has a long history, this has always happened in small pockets across Africa. Activity across the continent has more generally exploded over the past 5 years, with strong hubs forming in places such as Johannesburg and Stellenbosch in South Africa, Nairobi in Kenya, and Accra in Ghana.

In addition, several recent events and initiatives illustrate the growing interest in developing the capacity to strengthen AI and machine learning research in Africa. These include programmes such as Data Science Africa, Data Science Nigeria, and the Deep Learning Indaba. All of these aim at explicitly growing the African machine learning community, largely through technical training events and gatherings. The Deep Learning Indaba (2019), for example, is a large Africa-centric summer school which has spawned satellite 'IndabaX' events in 27 different African countries. This kind of programme has led to both growth and better organisation in the African machine learning community, as evidenced in greater participation of Africans in international conferences.

A driver for research and implementation is the vast potential for AI and related technologies to have a positive impact on communities and economies in Africa. Microsoft's (2019) white paper on the opportunities that AI offers for growth, development and democratisation in Africa, for instance, highlights four core sectors where AI could have a positive impact. These are in agriculture, by improving efficiency and effectivity; in healthcare, by improving quality and increasing access; in public services, by improving efficiency and responsiveness, and enhancing impact; and in financial services, by improving security and expanding reach. The interest in developing and implementing AI in Africa for social good does not just come from outside of the continent but can be found within Africa itself. With the hype around the so-called Fourth Industrial Revolution, for instance, various bodies have been set up to explore and promote the use of technologies like AI, machine learning and nanotechnology in Africa, centres such as the South African Affiliate Centre of the World Economic Forum's Centre for the Fourth Industrial Revolution (C4IR).

Given the interest in and likely growth of future research, as well as the trajectory towards implementing more AI and related technologies, there is an urgent need to ensure that any such developments and implementations are done responsibly and thoughtfully. With regard to the powerhouse of machine learning, the need for systems that are just, fair, and intelligible is a very real need if we are to guide research in Africa in the direction we want.

13.3 Guidelines for Good AI and the Principle of Explicability

A major focus in current AI research, from both the technical and philosophical communities, is on ensuring 'Good AI': that AI is developed and implemented in an ethical and sustainable manner. For instance, at NeurIPS 2018, workshops were held on *Ethical, Social and Governance Issues in AI, Challenges and Opportunities for AI in Financial Services, Machine Learning for the Developing World* (*ML4D*), and *AI for Social Good*. In the past few years, several guidelines and frameworks for ensuring Good AI for society and Good AI research have already been drawn up. These include the Asilomar AI Principles (2017), the crowd-sourced 'Ethically Aligned Design: A vision for prioritising human well-being with autonomous and intelligent systems' (2017), Microsoft's white paper titled 'Artificial Intelligence for Africa: An opportunity for growth, development and democratisation' (2019), and the European AI4People's publication, 'AI4People—An Ethical Framework for a Good AI Society: Opportunities, risks, principles, and recommendations' (2018), where this last framework surveys a range of guidelines and frameworks to develop a synthesis of existing principles.[2] With the proliferation of frameworks and guidelines, it makes sense to examine their commonalities and so our focus is on the AI4People framework because of the synthesis it offers of other frameworks. Through their synthesis, the authors identify five recurring ethical principles that are recognised in one way or another by all of the guidelines surveyed by the AI4People project. In this section, we introduce the five principles it identifies, the four Western bioethical principles of respect for autonomy, beneficence, non-maleficence and justice, along with a fifth principle specifically for AI, the principle of explicability, which is our focus.

The principle of respect for autonomy is roughly 'the idea that individuals have a right to make decisions for themselves about the treatment they do or not receive' (Floridi et al., 2018, p. 697). Applied to AI where we might 'willingly cede some of our decision-making power to machines', the principle requires 'striking a balance between the decision-making power we retain for ourselves and that which we delegate to artificial agents' (p. 698). The principle of beneficence, in turn, requires 'promoting well-being, preserving dignity, and sustaining the planet'—basically, developing AI technology that benefits humanity (p. 696). The closely related principle of non-maleficence is one of doing no harm, requiring avoiding certain overuses and misuses of AI technologies. The fourth principle of justice typically requires the fair distribution of goods and services. Applied to AI, justice might require using AI to right previous wrongs, ensuring that the benefits of AI are shared fairly (and, presumably, that the burdens are fairly distributed), and ensuring that any new harms are prevented (p. 699).

The fifth principle is the principle of explicability. In a context where a select few are leading the way in the development and implementation of AI technologies that either directly or indirectly impact the rest of society, the various surveyed guidelines call for 'the need to understand and hold to account the decision-making processes of AI', while recognising that the workings of AI 'are often invisible or unintelligible to all but (at best) the most expert observers' (Floridi et al., 2018, p. 700). As the authors describe it, the principle of explicability should be understood in both an *epistemological* sense of intelligibility and in an *ethical* sense of accountability.

In the epistemological sense, the principle asks for an answer to the question of '*how does it work?*'. This epistemological sense can be found in the Asilomar AI Principles (2017), for instance, as a requirement for 'failure transparency': 'if an AI system causes harm, it should be possible to ascertain why'. The General Principles

[2] The guidelines and frameworks surveyed are: The Asilomar AI Principles (2017), the *Montreal Declaration for Responsible AI* (2017), the *General Principles* in the IEEE Global Initiative's 'Ethically Aligned Design' (2017), the *Ethical Principles* in the 'Statement on Artificial Intelligence, Robotics and "Autonomous" Systems' of the European Group on Ethics in Science and New Technologies (2018), the principles of the 'AI in the UK: Ready, willing and able?' report of the UK House of Lords Artificial Intelligence Committee (2018), and the *Tenets* of the Partnership on AI (2018).

of 'Ethically Aligned Design' (IEEE, 2019) call for a need for the basis of a decision to be discoverable, as does the Partnership on AI (2018), calling for 'the operation of AI systems to be understandable and interpretable by people, for purposes of explaining the technology'. The need for transparency and explainability is identified in the European Group on Ethics in Science and New Technologies (2018) and in the UK House of Lords Artificial Intelligence Committee report (2018). All of these call for an answer to the epistemological sense of '*how does it work?*'

In the ethical sense, the principle of explicability tackles issues of accountability by asking for an answer to the question of '*who is responsible for the way it works?*'[3] For instance, the Asilomar Principles include a requirement that the designers and builders of AI systems have a duty to shape the moral implications of the use, misuse and abuse of those AI systems. Both the Partnership on AI and the European Group recognise that AI research and development needs to be accountable to a range of stakeholders, with the House of Lords report calling for clear lines of accountability.

The principle of explicability is valuable on a number of fronts. Firstly, it addresses the uneven power structure already apparent in the development of AI, between those who are developing the technologies (typically large corporations) and those who will be affected by them (the consumers and the rest of society). Secondly, it both complements and enables the other four principles. For AI to be both beneficent and non-maleficent, we need to understand what kinds of benefits and harms it can actually do within a society. Similarly, if we are to respect human autonomy, we need to know how an AI system would choose and act. Additionally, for the principle of justice to be respected, we need to ensure that there is accountability. Thirdly, the principle recognises the role that intelligibility and accountability can play in engendering public trust and understanding, necessary for ensuring that AI is accepted within society. Without public trust and understanding, the potential economic and societal benefits of AI and related technologies could fail to materialise (Winfield & Jirotka, 2018). For instance, a lack of trust can be seen to underlie fears about automation negatively impacting human employment. With powerful bodies like South Africa's Congress of South African Trade Unions (COSATU) not wholeheartedly behind such technologies—'You can't be talking about the future of work when you describe displacement and unemployment' (Steyn, 2018)—the benefits will be difficult, if not impossible, to achieve. The motivation that the AI4People framework draws on for the principle of explicability, which includes requirements for intelligibility and accountability, is in large part based on societal benefits such as public trust and understanding.

[3] This question is an ethical question. There are, of course, questions about legal accountability and responsibility but we do not attend to them in this chapter.

13.4 Towards Ethical AI in and for Africa

The AI4People framework uses the five identified principles to generate a set of recommendations for Good AI within a European context, acknowledging that recommendations based on the principles may differ in different cultural contexts—at least to the extent that 'different cultural frameworks inform attitudes to new technology' (Floridi et al., 2018, p. 701). So, if we are to apply the principle in an African research context and to the design of systems to be implemented in Africa, we need to develop our own recommendations based on principles that are culturally and socially sensitive. However, truly acknowledging the impact of different cultural contexts is not limited to appreciating that different cultural frameworks inform attitudes to new technology. It more fundamentally requires ensuring that the principles themselves are applicable.

Take, for instance, the communitarian nature of many African cultures and worldviews. While not all African cultures and worldviews are communitarian, while those that are need not be identical to one another, and while communitarian cultures and worldviews exist outside of Africa, the centrality of community is widely agreed to be a salient and dominant feature that can be found in various forms across the continent below the Sahara, and a feature that has been drawn on by those working within sub-Saharan African philosophy and ethics.[4] In many communitarian societies, people often engage in joint decision-making or refer to authority figures for guidance as part of their decision-making, thereby legitimately including others in a normal process. This is in stark contrast to a typical Western worldview that centralises the individual, and which is reflected in bioethical principles like the principle of respect for autonomy, frequently understood as respecting the decisional autonomy of an individual who makes decisions without undue coercion (see Beauchamp & Childress, 2012). Similarly, the AI4People report expresses the principle of respect for autonomy in a way that highlights the focus on the individual: 'individuals have a right to make decisions for themselves' (Floridi et al., 2018, p. 697).

The salience of community versus a strong individualism illustrates why we require, on one hand, sensitivity in how we adopt and adapt the principles in different contexts, if we are to apply them. For instance, the World Health Organisation (WHO) has made provisions to allow partner agreement in reproductive research in certain countries with a cultural tradition of involving partners or family in decision-making, despite usually taking the involvement of a partner as a violation of participant autonomy (Moodley, 2007, see also WHO, 2020). The principle of respect for autonomy is still applied, but it is adapted to reflect the real communitarian infused decision-making processes that people engage in.

[4] For a sample of seminal philosophical work highlighting community within different cultural contexts, see Mbiti (1990) (Kenya, although with a systematic review of other cultures), Gyekye (1987) (Akan, Ghana), Gbadegesin (1991) (Yoruba, Nigeria) and Ramose (2005) (South Africa).

On the other hand, we might reject that any of these principles should be applied at all. Over the past few decades, an increasing amount of work has been done developing the field of African bioethics in response to exactly this kind of challenge (as samples, see Murove, 2005; Behrens, 2013; Chukwuneke et al., 2014; Rakotsoane & Van Niekerk, 2017; Barugahare, 2018).

Reasons given for rejecting—or at least seriously critiquing the applicability of—Western principles include both the pragmatic and the theoretic. Pragmatically, simply adopting foreign principles that are divorced from the ethical worldviews that govern ordinary peoples' lives can result in practices that are inefficient in achieving their aims. In general, people are more inclined to accept ethical ideas or interventions if they are consistent with their own worldviews (Behrens, 2013). The former director of Médecins Sans Frontiers, Roy Brauman, gives the example of emergency food supply in famine-stricken Uganda. Medical workers prioritised giving food to the most vulnerable, women and children, only to discover that the food was being taken away and given to local elders in lines with local customs that prioritise respecting social orders (Hellsten, 2006, p. 73). Such an example illustrates how applying a principle like justice without sensitivity to local context can be ineffective in achieving its aims. This could be addressed by applying the principle in a culturally sensitive manner; however, and more crucially, the example also illustrates how a reliance on predetermined principles can exclude other principles that in fact govern people's behaviour.

While pragmatic issues could potentially be addressed by adapting the principles in a context-sensitive manner while also being open to the existence of other principles, a deeper theoretical set of issues remain. These are particularly pertinent in the postcolonial African context where there is a tradition of postcolonial critique and an expressed need for the reclamation of human dignity, authenticity, and a positive assertion of African identity following centuries of subjugation by Western powers.[5] As Andoh writes, drawing on this tradition, an attitude of 'assimilating Western values and ideologies into Africa can give rise to a situation of self-dehumanisation and outright self-subversion both in terms of dignity and self-esteem' (Andoh, 2011, p. 69). For instance, given the salience of community in many sub-Saharan African cultures, a prioritising of individualism can sever the person from her 'relational spheres of existence' (Murove, 2005, p. 27). Rather than simply adopting an individualistic principle like respect for autonomy, we might thus instead adopt a broader principle of respect for persons, which captures the essence of the principle but allows more cultural nuance (Behrens, 2013). Alternatively, we could introduce new principles like 'human life invaluableness' (Rakotsoane & Van Niekerk, 2017), or even ones that capture the respect for social order brought out in the Ugandan example.

These critiques of the traditional bioethical principles put pressure on the applicability of the very same principles found in the AI4People framework for use

[5] This is a tradition that draws on a diverse range of theorists from across the continent, such as Senghor (1988), Mbembe (2001), Wa'Thionga (1986) and Biko (2002).

within an African context, or indeed any other cultural context that does not share similar features to the central European context in which the AI4People framework was derived. We cannot simply, and without critical engagement, adopt the principles and use them to generate context-specific recommendations, at risk of resulting in ineffective processes or causing genuine moral harm. We first have to assess if the principles themselves can be recruited within the context at hand. Applying the principles of respect for autonomy, beneficence, non-maleficence and justice in an African AI context requires more examination, but our current focus is on the *new* principle of explicability. This is because there is already a rich literature within African bioethics, as well as the field of global bioethics more widely, examining the supposedly universal applicability of the standard principles of Western bioethics, whereas the principle of explicability is AI-specific and has yet to receive critical attention. So, while we could question what *form* such a principle would take in a particular cultural context—if explicability is closely related to communication and public trust as described at the end of the previous section, for instance, then different cultural norms of communication may inform what needs to be made explicable, to whom, when, and to what degree—we must first question whether the principle of explicability is relevant and applicable at all. This second level of critique, which is our focus, is crucial given the theoretical issues that warn against the uncritical assimilation of Western values into African contexts.

In the rest of this section, we critically assess whether the principle of explicability should be applied in an African context, rather than just what form it should take if it were applied. We first argue that the importance of the principle arises in part from the very nature of the technical research at hand, and in the following subsection we consider two possible reasons not to adopt it in an African research context, arguing that neither takes hold.

13.5 The Importance of the Principle of Explicability

The principle of explicability, prima facie at least, is not obviously based on strongly Western values like the individualism that underlies the principle of respect for autonomy. In fact, it is a principle that could allow us to be sensitive to cultural nuances as a matter of necessity and, as we will suggest, a principle that arises out of the nature of much of the research in question. The epistemological sense of the principle, at least, is required to address some of the computational challenges within machine learning. In this subsection, we thus illustrate how the principle of explicability ties in with some real issues and risks that computational and technical researchers are addressing, including those working in Africa, as a way of motivating for the adoption of the principle within an African research context.

The epistemological sense underpinning the principle of explicability seeks an answer to the question of 'how does it work?' There are two primary issues in which the epistemological sense of explicability is worth considering.

The first issue is that the fundamental modality of machine learning comes down to a human specifying a 'goal', or more technically an objective function, and the learning procedure is required to optimise a model, or technically the parameters of the model, for achieving this goal. This stands in stark contrast to more traditional programming paradigms where a human specifies the full set of steps (algorithm) that is to be executed by some software. Machine learning may instead, for example, require that a set of positive and negative outputs are provided to the learning system, which then infers the procedure for distinguishing between these categories itself. While this shift in attitude to problem solving has been transformative, there are at least two broad risks that arise.

The first risk is that of the human misspecifying the desired objective function. This may happen, for example, in reinforcement learning (RL), where an artificial agent is required to learn to take a sequence of decisions to achieve some long-term goal. In RL, desired states of the world are typically annotated with some positive reward, and undesirable states with some negative reward. In general, these attributions are arbitrary (both in location and magnitude), and it is trivially easy for an incorrect scaling or attribution to lead to undesired behaviours. A human, however, may not be fully cognisant of her own objectives, and as such may incorrectly imbue them into a learning system. An oft-cited example of this is the thought experiment of the paperclip maximiser: an intelligent agent tasked with running a facility to produce a maximal number of paperclips could self-improve to the extent that the result is 'a superintelligence whose top goal is the manufacturing of paperclips, with the consequence that it starts transforming first all of earth and then increasing portions of space into paperclip manufacturing facilities' (Bostrom, 2003). The scenario shows how even this simple seemingly benign goal could be sufficient to generate behaviours antithetical to human life and flourishing.

This first risk speaks directly to what is known as the value alignment problem. The value alignment problem refers to the challenge of ensuring that the goals of an artificially intelligent system do not contradict (typically inadvertently) the values of humans, or society in general. In an epistemological sense, to ensure that the values are aligned requires seeking an answer to the question: 'how does it work?' This in itself is a nontrivial question to answer, as discussed in more detail below. In a case where the goals do contradict and go against human values, we are faced with the ethical question: 'who is responsible for how it works?' For instance, who is best able to explicitly identify all the relevant values that are often implicit within ourselves and our societies, and can we hold someone accountable for failing to ensure that the goals of an AI system cohere with some set of implicit values of humans? Would explicitly identifying relevant values using quantitative methods even be sufficient for capturing the complexity and flux of human values, something that Sloane and Moss (2019) question?

This problem is exacerbated by the fact that human values differ across different societies and contexts. As a simple example, consider the 'rules of the road' which change between countries, from the side of the road on which people drive, to the rules for entering roundabouts. This is even more notable in how societal preferences change between countries in versions of the 'trolley problem', where people around the world have been surveyed on which of two random sets of people should be spared in a vehicle collision (Awad et al., 2018). One can note, for example, that there appears to be a preference for sparing the lawful and pedestrians in Japan, versus a preference for preserving humans over animals as well as high status individuals in Nigeria.[6]

The second risk is that the general form of a machine learning model may be difficult to interpret. The quintessential example of this is artificial neural networks, which are widely acknowledged to operate as 'black boxes'. This arises from the basic modelling assumptions, that the relationships between various inputs and the desired outputs are typically learned to be complex nonlinear functions, which are recursively embedded in other nonlinear functions. As the numbers of parameters that are learned in these models can easily be in the millions, interpreting these functions quickly loses feasibility. The question of 'how does it work?' thus becomes of paramount importance, with limitations for just how much detail we can give in answer. The question of 'who is responsible for how it works?' also highlights how very few humans, if any, are able to understand the processes that are followed, yet that select few still have considerably deeper understanding than the many who might be impacted by the technology.

It is interesting to note that other classes of machine learning models do not necessarily possess this same characteristic, although they seldom achieve the state-of-the-art performance that neural networks do. An example here is that of decision trees, which involve learning an ordering of features to treat as conditional rules for classifying data points. By following this sequence which is learned, one can easily trace out and validate decisions made by these models. Different models may thus generate different requirements in terms of answering the question 'how does it work?'

Another issue concerns biases that may be presented to the learning system in its training data. Examples of this have been widely seen in supervised learning, with numerous cases of racial biases being reported globally (Buolamwini & Gebru, 2018). This is particularly troublesome when confounded with the previous challenge of difficult-to-interpret models, in that it could easily become unclear that these biases have been introduced to the system. Establishing how a system is making decisions, especially when it is fed with data that we may not realise to be ethically suspect, is therefore important if we are not simply to recreate our own human inefficiencies as decision-makers and agents. When these biases reflect real-world human biases and have the potential for profound and detrimental real-world impact, we again face the ethical question of who is responsible and who should be held accountable.

The above examples illustrate some general computational issues within current research the world over, and they are issues wherever research is taking place and systems implemented, including in Africa. What becomes apparent from these examples is that we need something like the epistemological sense of the principle

[6] https://moralmachineresults.scalablecoop.org/

of explicability not just for engendering public trust and understanding and for ensuring alignment with societal values, but for actually informing research to tackle some of the computational challenges that are being faced. This is because those computational challenges themselves require alignment with societal values and needs, in turn requiring that certain values and objectives arc made explicit. We thus need to be sensitive to the values and needs of the societies where AI technologies are both developed and implemented. In the AI4People report, the authors describe the 'dual advantages' of an ethical approach to AI, which allows identifying and leveraging 'new opportunities that are socially acceptable or preferable' and 'enables organisations to anticipate and avoid or at least minimise costly mistakes' arising from 'courses of action that turn out to be socially unacceptable and hence rejected' (Floridi et al., 2018, p. 694). As we have argued, the advantages of an ethical approach go even a degree deeper than the authors originally discuss. Various challenges facing technical research are in fact 'socio-technical' in nature (Crawford, 2017). As such, applying the principle of explicability, especially in its epistemological 'how does it work?' sense, does not only have the dual advantages identified in the AI4People report, but an additional advantage in that it can help solve some of the computational problems facing AI researchers, avoiding courses of action that are ineffective in addition to but distinct from prioritising their social acceptability.

13.6 Are There Reasons Not to Apply the Principle in Africa?

While the principle of explicability is an important principle for guiding research both to achieve computational ends and to strive for societal benefits, there may nevertheless be reasons not to adopt and apply it in African research contexts. Here, we consider two such reasons and argue that they do not show that the principle itself is problematic or irrelevant. Rather the potential problems highlight at least two lessons: the principle of explicability absolutely requires contextual sensitivity in its application, and it must be balanced with other relevant principles.

A first potential problem, the trade-off problem, relates to the epistemological sense of the principle of explicability. This is the problem that we might face undesirable trade-offs in demanding explicability. One of the recommendations put forward by AI4People is that, in a European context at least, a framework that enhances the explicability of AI systems that make socially significant decisions is developed, where 'central to this framework is the ability for individuals to obtain factual, direct, and clear explanation of the decision-making process' (Floridi et al., 2018, p. 702). One way to meet this demand is by requiring that systems produce explanations of their own behaviour (see, for instance, Selbst & Powles, 2017; Doshi-Velez & Kim, 2017; Winfield & Jirotka, 2018). Yet, requiring explanations in this manner for a system to meet explicability requirements could hypothetically mean that the capabilities of that system are severely handicapped (Wachter et al., 2017). In a similar fashion, London (2019) has recently argued that a demand for explicability or for making something interpretable is typically a demand for an explanation of causal relations. Domains such as AI and even medical decision-making, however, typically involve associations that are not necessarily causal. As London argues, in a domain where we lack causal knowledge but where predictive and diagnostic accuracy are nevertheless important, a demand for explicability can needlessly detract from accuracy and reliability.

So, if a system would lose accuracy or reliability in diagnosing some life-threatening disease by some percentage, how should we view this trade-off? This is a challenge that all societies need to address, but it is particularly pertinent in many African contexts where other solutions, such as medical professionals and state-of-the-art laboratories, are not easily at hand. As a representative example, consider Tanzania: as high as 71% of the population lives in rural, difficult-to-access areas with poor infrastructure, a fact that informs the Tanzanian government's current 5-year health sector strategic plan for increasing access to healthcare services (United Republic of Tanzania, 2015) and a fact that explains the welcoming of the use of drones to provide basic medical supplies (Landhuis, 2017). This challenge is significant in the health sector, as a result of a number of factors such as different disease profiles around the world. Malaria, for example, poses a much greater risk in Africa than it does in Europe, and this coupled with a shortage of experts necessitates automated solutions (Brown et al., 2019).

Challenges also exist in the social sphere. Africa is home to an estimated 2000 languages, and addressing communication barriers is an important step towards advancing these societies. The sheer scale of this problem again calls for AI-based solutions in automated translation (Abbott & Martinus, 2019).

Part of the attraction of the development and implementation of AI solutions in Africa is that doing so can address challenges like these and others faced by African societies that arise from social, historical and geographical inequities that make solutions available elsewhere in the world untenable. This is something that the Microsoft white paper discussed earlier does indeed highlight, by focussing on the way AI could be used to improve various sectors, such as agriculture, healthcare, public services and finance (Microsoft, 2019). In this context, the stakes for demanding explicability at the expense of accuracy or reliability can be particularly high.

This problem, however, does not show that the principle is itself problematic or irrelevant in an African context. For one thing, there are two senses of explicability contained within the principle, the epistemological and the ethical. In the epistemological sense, we might seek alternative and less demanding ways to account for how a system works. We have argued, for instance, that solving some of the computational problems facing machine learning requires making objectives and goals explicit. As such, we could plausibly achieve explicability in the epistemological sense by specifying a system's design goals more carefully. Indeed, Kroll (2018) has proposed such an approach for intelligibility, one that shifts from a focus on understanding technical tools to understanding the overall system, which includes people. Such a tactic need not require an explanation in terms of causal relations, as per

London's (2019) worry. In fact, making an overall system intelligible, including the people that are part of it, may require non-causal explanations, such as functional or hermeneutical explanations and those found more widely in the social sciences. In this way, the machine learning-based decision-making system can be made intelligible, in terms of its goals and objectives, and accountability can be demanded of the entire system, which includes the people specifying those goals and objectives.

Alternatively, perhaps in a situation like the trade-off described above, we should step back from the epistemological sense and focus instead on the ethical sense of explicability, establishing a clear line of accountability, such as holding those who are specifying the goals and objectives accountable. But more generally, the principle is not intended as a standalone principle. It would still need to be balanced with other acceptable principles, such as the principle of beneficence—how can we best capitalise on AI technologies to ensure the well-being of people?—or, even, the principle of justice, concerning the fair distribution of goods or what constitutes fair compromises to ensure that, say, access to health services is available to all. This allows variability in what is demanded of a particular system with particular goals and within a particular context.

A second problem, a problem of compromise, focuses more on the ethical sense of the principle of explicability, and the concomitant demand for accountability. This is the problem that a demand for accountability could plausibly limit progress in a field where African nations and research institutions could be firmly entrenched among world leaders. The development of AI and related technologies promises to tackle African-specific problems that can aid in social and economic development, can create jobs, and is an arena where African researchers are already increasingly active. Indeed, the growth and appetite for events such as those of the Deep Learning Indaba, Data Science Africa and Data Science Nigeria shows that there is interest in upskilling in this direction. Imposing lines of accountability could result in onerous regulatory constraints on an industry we want to encourage, with parties becoming less willing to pursue potentially fruitful but risky research or implementation.

This problem is speculative and overlooks that the principle of explicability does not state what the accountability requirements are, just that we establish lines of accountability. Like the previous problem, this allows contextual sensitivity in devising recommendations from the principle, where that contextual sensitivity may consider different cultural norms regarding what needs to be explained, to whom, when and to what degree, but also must consider the cost–benefit ratio of potential regulations. Further, and as discussed with the previous problem, devising recommendations from the principle of explicability would work in tandem with other principles. For instance, justice might require differential treatment for how research is conducted in Africa, to target economic and historical imbalances between African nations and centres in the developed world. The principle itself is not obviously problematic but we have to take care with how it is applied.

Further, if Africa is to capitalise on the progress it is making with growing AI research across the continent, we do still need to ensure that it does so in a way compatible with the values and needs of those living there. In order to actually do the computational research, we will often have to address requirements that are closely related to those put forward by the principle of explicability, such as by tackling the value alignment problem. Tackling the value alignment problem requires that we identify our own objectives; that is, we must go some way towards answering the question 'how does it work?' in order to make it, the system, work for what it is designed for. If this is the case, the research and technology that we want to flourish and advance will often depend on addressing questions that the principle of explicability raises, such as demanding intelligibility. In also requiring accountability for the systems, we would be requiring accountability for something that would have to be done, at least to some extent, in order to advance the research itself.

These two problems, as we have seen, can be dealt with by highlighting that the principle of explicability would, ideally, be applied in tandem with other principles and applying it requires contextual sensitivity, not just to ensure that values are aligned with a society's values, but also to ensure that computational challenges are themselves addressed. These problems do not show that the principle of explicability itself is problematic or irrelevant.

13.7 Closing Thoughts on Who Is Accountable for How a Decision-Making System Works

We have proposed that the principle of explicability, when applied in the epistemological sense to typical areas of machine learning research, requires identifying objectives and goals for a system that cohere with those of a given society in which the system will operate. But what implications does this have for the ethical sense of the principle and the question of who, exactly, should be held accountable for how such a decision-making system works? A third potential problem could arise here, to do with demandingness: the principle of explicability as we have developed it may be too demanding on researchers in a developing field in Africa who are frequently dependent on international input. Holding those researchers to account would be unfair. To address this problem, we tentatively propose that the demands of explicability require a division of labour, and as a result accountability could in fact be diffuse.

Suppose that the machine learning researchers based in Africa and developing a system to be implemented in an African context are to be held accountable for how the system works. As part of the demand for explicability, in the epistemological sense, we have argued that objectives and goals of the system need to be identified. But who should identify these objectives and goals?

Identifying the goals, objectives and underlying values of a society is not a straightforward matter and not something one can simply consult a rulebook for. In South Africa, for instance, it is officially required that vehicles yield right of way to pedestrians crossing at a pedestrian crossing (Department of Transport, 2012). In practice, however, this seldom happens and stopping at a pedestrian crossing can surprise other vehicles on the road. Simply consulting the rulebook would not prepare anyone, person or machine, for actual driving.

The machine learning researchers, however, are technical experts, not necessarily experts in identifying the goals, objectives and underlying values of a society with which their system's goals and objectives need to be aligned. Further, they may be contributing to global work or be part of an international research team, such as by working at one of IBM's research labs in South Africa or Kenya, or Google's research lab in Ghana, or be funded by international bodies like Google and Facebook, who fund students pursuing the African Masters in Machine Intelligence in Kigali, Rwanda. Yet, demanding that they make goals and values explicit and then holding the African-based researchers accountable for a system that is not entirely in their hands would be placing an onerous and unfair burden on them.

Identifying the goals, objectives and underlying values of a society, as those working on the ethical design of technology already emphasise (see, for instance, Crawford & Calo, 2016; Crawford, 2017; Friedman et al., 2017; Sloane & Moss, 2019), needs to draw on a wider body of stakeholders, which includes those who are experts on the values and goals of a given society, such as researchers in the social sciences and humanities, and even members of society themselves. This would obviously have to be within reason, as not just any lay person will be knowledgeable, nor should they be held accountable for something over which they have no knowledge or control. However, even with bringing in the expertise of a range of people, technical researchers may still shoulder a higher degree of burden because of the fact that these researchers must acknowledge that other players need to be involved and consulted, not as a matter of courtesy or annoyance, but as central to advancing the actual research. Alternatively, organisations driving research should be required to engage a diversity of relevant experts to ensure that the epistemological sense of explicability is met, and be held accountable if they fail to do so. It is those involved in or driving the actual research who are in a position to ensure that a range of interests and values are acknowledged and, ideally, addressed in both local and international research, or that international research is not uncritically implemented across a range of differing contexts.

Ensuring that relevant experts from a range of backgrounds are engaged speaks in favour of promoting interdisciplinary research and societal engagement as a matter of necessity, not simply for ethical considerations but for advancing the research itself. Luckily, the value of interdisciplinary and multi-stakeholder engagement is already recognised in the various centres and initiatives being set up in Africa, such as the Centre for Artificial Intelligence Research (CAIR) and the South African Affiliate Centre of the C4IR. Applying a principle of explicability in an African context that recognises the necessary involvement of a range of actors, a kind of division of labour for addressing the epistemological sense of explicability, could thus generate diffuse patterns of accountability when addressing the ethical sense of explicability. What exactly this would entail in terms of recommendations, and whether accommodating a diffuse notion of accountability is feasible on the ground, however, is beyond the scope of this chapter. Nevertheless, adopting and applying a principle of explicability in an African research context should aim to address these complexities.

In closing, then, we have argued that existing principles and frameworks for the development of Good AI should not be adopted uncritically into an African research context. We thus took initial steps for critically assessing one such framework, that of the AI4People report, by addressing whether the AI-specific principle of explicability should be applied in an African context. We argued that, when designing a decision-making system making use of some form of machine learning, an approach that requires adhering to a principle of explicability in both an epistemological sense (of 'how does it work?') and an ethical sense (of 'who is responsible for how it works?') not only contributes to the responsible and thoughtful development of AI that is sensitive to African interests and needs but can also advance tackling some of the computational challenges in machine learning research. The principle thus should be adopted in an African context. Adopting the principle, however, requires that African researchers and societies, as well as organisations driving research, ensure that values are aligned, and doing so requires the involvement of a range of knowledgeable stakeholders.

Acknowledgements We would like to thank participants at the Third CAIR Symposium on AI Research and Society held at the University of Johannesburg in March 2019, for feedback and discussion on an earlier version of the paper. We would also like to thank the two reviewers and editors for the journal *Ethics and Information Technology* for their comments.

Compliance with Ethical Standards **Conflict of Interests:** Benjamin Rosman is one of the founders and organisers of the Deep Learning Indaba that we mention as an example of the growth of machine learning across Africa.

References

Abbott, J., & Martinus, L. (2019). Benchmarking neural machine translation for southern African languages. In *Proceedings of the 2019 workshop on widening NLP.*

Andoh, C. (2011). Bioethics and the challenges to its growth in Africa. *Open Journal of Philosophy, 1*(2), 67–75.

Asilomar AI Principles. (2017). Retrieved May 29, 2019 from https://futureoflife.org/ai-principles

Awad, E., Dsouza, S., Kim, R., Schulz, J., Henrich, J., Shariff, A., et al. (2018). The moral machine experiment. *Nature, 563*(7729), 59.

Barugahare, J. (2018). African bioethics: Methodological doubts and insights. *BMC Medical Ethics*. https://doi.org/10.1186/s12910-018-0338-6

Beauchamp, T. L., & Childress, J. F. (2012). *Principles of biomedical ethics* (7th ed.). Oxford University Press.

Behrens, K. (2013). Towards an indigenous African bioethics. *The South African Journal of Bioethics and Law, 6*(1), 32–35.

Biko, S. (2002). *I write what I like: Selected writings*. University of Chicago Press.

Bostrom, N. (2003). Ethical issues in advanced artificial intelligence. In I. Smit et al. (Eds.), *Cognitive, emotive and ethical aspects of decision making in humans and in artificial intelligence* (2nd ed., pp. 12–17). International Institute of Advanced Studies in Systems Research and Cybernetics.

Brown, B. J., Przybylski, A. A., Manescu, P., Caccioli, F., Oyinloye, G., Elmi, M., Shaw, M. J., et al. (2019). Data-driven malaria prevalence prediction in large densely-populated urban holoendemic sub-Saharan West Africa: Harnessing machine learning approaches and 22-years of prospectively collected data. *arXiv preprint arXiv:1906.07502*.
Buolamwini, J., & Gebru, T. (2018). Gender shades: Intersectional accuracy disparities in commercial gender classification. In *Proceedings of the 1st conference on fairness, accountability and transparency, PMLR*, 81, pp. 77–91.
Chukwuneke, F. N., Umeora, O. U. J., Maduabuchi, J. U., & Egbunike, N. (2014). Global bioethics and culture in a pluralistic world: How does culture influence bioethics in Africa? *Annals of Medical and Health Sciences Research, 4*(5), 672–675.
Crawford, K. (2017). The trouble with bias. *NIPS 2017 Keynote Address*. Retrieved August 19, 2019 from https://www.youtube.com/watch?v=fMym_BKWQzk
Crawford, K., & Calo, R. (2016). There is a blind spot in AI research. *Nature, 538*, 311–313.
Deep Learning Indaba. (2019). *Together we build African AI: Outcomes of the 2nd annual Deep Learning Indaba*. Retrieved March 1, 2020 from https://www.deeplearningindaba.com/uploads/1/0/2/6/102657286/annualindaba2018report-v1.pdf
Department of Transport. (2012). *SA learner driver manual: Rules of the road*. SA Department of Transport.
Doshi-Velez, F., & Kim, B. (2017). *Towards a rigorous science of interpretable machine learning*. Retrieved May 29, 2019 from https://arxiv.org/abs/1702.08608
European Group on Ethics in Science and New Technologies. (2018). *Statement on artificial intelligence, robotics and 'autonomous systems'*. European Commission. Retrieved May 29, 2019 from https://ec.europa.eu/research/ege/pdf/ege_ai_statement_2018.pdf
Floridi, L., Cowls, J., Beltrametti, M., Chatila, R., Chazerand, P., Dignum, V., et al. (2018). AI4People: An ethical framework for a Good AI Society: Opportunities, risks, principles, and recommendations. *Minds and Machines, 28*, 689–707.
Friedman, B., Hendry, D., & Borning, A. (2017). A survey of value sensitive design methods. *Foundations and Trends in Human Computer Interaction, 11*(23), 63–125.
Gbadegesin, S. (1991). *African philosophy: Traditional Yoruba philosophy and contemporary African realities*. Peter Lang.
Gyekye, K. (1987). *An essay on African philosophical thought: The Akan conceptual scheme*. Cambridge University Press.
Hellsten, S. (2006). Global bioethics: Utopia or reality? *Developing World Bioethics, 8*(2), 70–81.
House of Lords Artificial Intelligence Committee. (2018). *AI in the UK: Ready, willing and able?* UK Parliament. Retrieved May 29, 2019 from https://publications.parliament.uk/pa/ld201719/ldselect/ldai/100/100.pdf
IEEE Global Initiative on Ethics of Autonomous and Intelligent Systems. (2019). *Ethically aligned design: A vision for prioritising human well-being with autonomous and intelligent systems* (1st ed.). Retrieved May 29, 2019 from https://ethicsinaction.ieee.org
Kroll, J. A. (2018). The fallacy of inscrutability. *Philosophical Transactions A, 276*, 20180084.
Landhuis, E. (2017). Tanzania gears up to become a nation of medical drones. *npr.org*. Retrieved February 28, 2020 from https://www.npr.org/sections/goatsandsoda/2017/08/24/545589328/tanzaniagears-up-to-become-a-nation-of-medical-drones
London, A. (2019). Artificial intelligence and black-box medical decisions: Accuracy versus explainability. *Hastings Center Report, 49*(1), 15–21.
Mbembe, A. (2001). *On the postcolony*. University of California Press.
Mbiti, J. (1990). *African religions and philosophy* (2nd ed.). Heinemann.
Microsoft. (2019). *Artificial Intelligence for Africa: An opportunity for growth, development and democratisation*. Retrieved May 29, 2019 from https://info.microsoft.com/ME-DIGTRNS-WBNRFY19-11Nov-02-AIinAfrica-MGC0003244_01RegistrationForminBody.html
Montreal Declaration for a Responsible Development of Artificial Intelligence. (2017). Retrieved May 29, 2019 from https://www.montrealdeclaration-responsibleai.com/the-declaration

Moodley, K. (2007). Microbicide research in developing countries: Have we given the ethical concerns due consideration? *BMC Medical Ethics*. https://doi.org/10.1186/1472-6939-8-10

Murove, M. F. (2005). African bioethics: An explanatory discourse. *Journal for the Study of Religion, 18*(1), 16–36.

Partnership on AI. (2018). *Tenets*. Retrieved May 29, 2019 from https://www.partnershiponai.org/tenets

Rakotsoane, F., & Van Niekerk, A. (2017). Human life invaluableness: An emerging African bioethical principle. *South African Journal of Philosophy, 36*(2), 252–262.

Ramose, M. (2005). *African philosophy through Ubuntu* (Revised ed.). Mond Books Publishers.

Selbst, A. D., & Powles, J. (2017). Meaningful information and the right to explanation. *International Data Privacy Law, 7*(4), 233–242.

Senghor, L. (1988). *Ce Que Je Crois*. Grasset.

Sloane, M., & Moss, E. (2019). AI's social sciences deficit. *Nature Machine Intelligence, 1*, 330–331.

Steyn, L. (2018). Watch your job, the bots are coming. *Mail & Guardian*, December 8. Retrieved May 29, 2019 from https://mg.co.za/article/2017-12-08-00-watch-your-job-the-bots-are-coming

United Republic of Tanzania Ministry of Health and Social Welfare. (2015). *Health sector strategic plan July 2015–June 2020*. Retrieved February 28, 2020 from https://www.moh.go.tz/en/strategic-plans

Wa'Thiongo, N. (1986). *Decolonising the mind*. James Curry.

Wachter, S., Mittelstadt, B., & Floridi, L. (2017). Transparent, explainable, and accountable AI for robotics. *Science Robotics*. https://doi.org/10.1126/scirobotics.aan6080

Winfield, A. F. T., & Jirotka, M. (2018). Ethical governance is essential to building trust in robotics and artificial intelligence systems. *Philosophical Transactions A, 376*, 20180085.

World Health Organisation (WHO). (2020). Guidelines on reproductive health research and partners' agreement. *Sexual and Reproductive Health*. Retrieved February 21, 2020 from https://www.who.int/reproductivehealth/topics/ethics/partners_guide_serg/en/